POPE
AND HIS CONTEMPORARIES

POPE

AND HIS CONTEMPORARIES

Essays presented to

GEORGE SHERBURN

Edited by
JAMES L. CLIFFORD
and
LOUIS A. LANDA

OCTAGON BOOKS

A DIVISION OF FARRAR, STRAUS AND GIROUX

New York   1978

First Published in 1949 by the Clarendon Press, Oxford

Reprinted 1978
by special arrangement with Oxford University Press

OCTAGON BOOKS
A DIVISION OF FARRAR, STRAUS & GIROUX, INC.
19 Union Square West
New York, N.Y. 10003

Library of Congress Cataloging in Publication Data

Clifford, James Lowry, 1901-   ed.
  Pope and his contemporaries.

  Reprint of the 1949 ed., Oxford University Press, New York.
  Bibliography: p.
  1. English literature—18th century—History and criticism. 2.
  Sherburn, George Wiley, 1884- I. Sherburn, George Wiley, 1884-
  II. Landa, Louis A., 1902- III. Title.
PR442.C6   1978   820′.9′005   78-17494
ISBN 0-374-91700-0

Printed in USA by
Thomson-Shore, Inc.
Dexter, Michigan

PREFACE

'WE have left off beating the eighteenth century.' As the bicentenary of Pope's birth drew near, Augustine Birrell made this premature pronouncement—far too confidently. But if it were repeated to-day, there would be few to challenge its validity, for the classical period in English literature has at last come into its own. Witness in recent years the steady stream of sympathetic biographies of both major and minor authors, accurate editions of their works, and investigations of the ideas and assumptions of the age. With infectious excitement research scholars and the critics have united in rediscovering the Augustans. The many biases and misconceptions of the nineteenth century, so long accepted as dogma, are finally fading into historical perspective.

Professor George Sherburn has been one of the scholars most responsible for bringing about this change in attitude. No one has contributed more to making possible an enlightened appreciation of Alexander Pope and his circle. As biographer of the youthful Pope and as literary historian of the age, he is everywhere known as a staunch adherent of the eighteenth century. His *Early Career of Alexander Pope* set a standard of careful, patient, biographical research, and presented us with Pope as a credible personality, free from the traditional half-truths, suspicions, and animosities which in the past obscured both the poet and the man. His recently published literary history, 1660 to 1800, is the most extensive study of the period approaching it in terms of its own principles and assumptions—a work in which critical perception and broad scholarship combine to reinterpret and revitalize the age.

His influence, moreover, has not been confined to his published works. With never-failing generosity he has for years given personal aid and encouragement to scores of scholars on both sides of the Atlantic. Not only to his students at Northwestern, Chicago, Columbia, and more recently at Harvard, has he been 'guide, philosopher, and friend'; his warm, sympathetic help has been freely extended to anyone genuinely interested in the eighteenth century. If there is anywhere a serious student of this period who does not owe some debt of gratitude to George Sherburn, he is indeed rare. Certainly it is fitting that a collection of essays devoted to Pope and Pope's contemporaries be gathered in his honour.

Only a few of the many who would wish to honour George Sherburn are represented in this volume. Since limitation was necessary, essays were accepted from scholars in America and Britain whose research and special interests closely parallel his own. This procedure has resulted, it is hoped, in a unified volume instead of a collection of unrelated studies. Some are chiefly critical; some stress the historical approach. There are new estimates of major authors, studies in the background of Augustan thought, reinterpretations of well-known poems, and the first printing of newly discovered documents of lasting significance. Despite this diversity of approach, it is nevertheless Alexander Pope, his friends and contemporaries, who have remained the central theme of the volume.

It is the hope of the contributors that these essays will please George Sherburn, to whom in gratitude and affection they are herewith presented.

J. L. C.
L. A. L.

CONTENTS

CONTENTS

THE GLOOM OF THE TORY SATIRISTS

LOUIS I. BREDVOLD

GLOOM, in all its varieties, is distasteful, and we are always pleased to have remedies for it, and even excuses for avoiding it. Dr. Johnson, who wrestled manfully with his own painful melancholia, once counselled Lucy Porter that it is useless and foolish, and perhaps sinful, to be gloomy. This is the language of good sense. But Dr. Johnson would have been the first to admit that this good sense is a standard of but limited application to great literature, certainly to the gloom of satire. It is hardly the final word on the great denunciations of mankind by Hamlet and King Lear. But it has too often been accepted as the final word on the satire of Pope and Swift. They have been charged with the sin of excessive gloom, of bitterness so extreme that it becomes unwholesome malignancy. Readers who will respond whole-heartedly to other satire hesitate before the work of these men, on guard against the moral perversity they are sure they will find there. That a dark, almost impervious gloom enveloped them is undeniable. But it may be well to inquire into the question whether it is so un-wholesome. Gloom may have a variety of causes and take a variety of forms, and some of them are certainly free from the spiritual darkness which could be called sin.

Our judgement of Swift and Pope, and our insight into them as well, depend not a little on our preserving proportion, on our recognition of their normal human qualities, and on our restraint in playing up sensational elements. The charitable-ness of both men, for instance, has been acknowledged with more perplexity than sympathetic understanding.[1] Even Leslie Stephen, as he was trying to present Pope sympathetically, could write: 'There is no particular merit in loving a mother' (a painful remark, not to be matched elsewhere in biography; it could have appeared only in a life of Pope), 'but few bio-graphies give a more striking proof that the loving discharge of a common duty may give a charm to a whole character. It is

---

[1] The need for correction in Swift's case is thoroughly shown by Louis A. Landa in an article on 'Jonathan Swift and Charity', in the *Journal of English and Germanic Philology*, xliv (1945), 337–50.

melancholy to add that we often have to appeal to this part of his story, to assure ourselves that Pope was really deserving of some affection.'[1] Such an admission that some human qualities, at once heavily discounted, may be discovered in a venomous creature lays bare the whole mental process of denigration in a passage which its author probably did not intend to be harsh.

It would seem, too, that too much has been made of the impairing influence on Swift and Pope of their 'crazy constitutions', as if their satire were a phase of their medical history. There has grown up around them a kind of cult of the satiric genius as a tortured mind inhabiting a tortured body. Pope's deformity and weakness seem to add an appropriate grotesqueness to a sinister character. Swift's final insanity, which, so far as modern medical authorities can determine, was most likely the last stage of a life-long disease of the inner ear and which was therefore unrelated to his satire either as cause or effect, is raised to a more than medical significance as the fitting conclusion of the career of a bitter satirist, the awful disintegration of a great mad genius in self-devouring rage. And his remark that he would die like the tree, first at the top, is repeated with all the solemnity of an oracular doom in Greek tragedy, whereas common sense tells us that, within the limits of Swift's medical knowledge, it could only have been the apprehension of a sufferer from chronic headaches. Had Swift not lived beyond the scriptural age of three score and ten, his biographies would not have been overcharged with these dramatic themes of premonition and fate. We should still have had the 'mad parson', but we might have had fewer intimations that his satire verges on madness, in quite another sense.

As for the diseases of the mind, the heaviest charge against Pope and Swift is a negativeness of spirit which depresses the worth and dignity of human life. But pessimism is a concept so vague and broad that it often leads to erroneous inferences and interpretations. The Tory satirists, the group gathered about Pope and Swift, did not suffer from philosophical or religious pessimism, or from anything that can be called *Weltschmerz*. There is no spiritual *malaise* in them; their gloom is not an enervating apathy. They seem generally to have had firm faith in the ultimate right order of things, and we must avoid carrying back to them such more recent philosophies of despair as are

<hr>

[1] *Alexander Pope* (1908), p. 100.

familiar in our post-Schopenhauer era. We do not even find in
them that melancholy brooding over the destiny of man which
in their century oppressed Johnson and Gray. The Christian
resignation of Johnson to a world in which there is little to be
enjoyed and much to be endured would have fitted well with
their satire—as it did with Johnson's—but it is not an attitude
characteristic of Swift or Pope. Nor were they steeped, as Gray
was, in the melancholy wisdom of the Greeks, which in its
sobriety and humility was so nearly allied to the sadness of
Johnson. Gray's *Ode on a Distant Prospect of Eton College* with its
motto from Menander, and his *Hymn to Adversity* with a similar
motto from Aeschylus, all admonish us that an enduring heart
is the gift the gods have fittingly bestowed on the sons of men.

Such views of human fate touch issues above and beyond the
reach of satire, and it was not any such cosmic gloom which
hung over the Tory satirists, but a mundane darkness conjured
up by human folly and knavery. The satirists were much more
attentive to the problems of the world of men than to ultimate
questions of philosophy and religion. Even Pope's *Essay on Man*
(radiating optimism, not gloom), which seems to have come as
a surprise to Swift ('I confess I did never imagine you were so
deep in morals'),[1] and Bolingbroke's philosophical excursions,
were speculations of a kind not common among them, and
certainly did not constitute any bond of union. Prior rebuked
the system-building pretensions of the human reason in both
Alma and *Solomon*. Swift habitually ridiculed those philosophers
who deal in cosmic explanations, and in *A Tale of a Tub* (Section ix) attributed their 'innovations' to madness. The learning
of the Brobdingnagians 'is very defective', reports Gulliver,
'consisting only in morality, history, poetry, and mathematics,
wherein they must be allowed to excel. But the last of these is
wholly applied to what may be useful in life, to the improvement of agriculture, and all mechanical arts; so that among us
it would be little esteemed. And as to ideas, entities, abstractions, and transcendentals, I could never drive the least conception into their heads.' Stella, indeed, 'understood the Platonic
and Epicurean philosophy, and judged very well of the defects
of the latter', as Swift recorded in his memoir of her, and her
programme of studies, we may be sure, reflected the intellectual
character of her friend and tutor, who never in his writings

[1] Swift to Pope, 1 Nov. 1734.

alluded to Socrates or Plato except with respect. But we know
that Swift valued the Socratic dialogues, not for any 'abstractions and transcendentals', but for their ethical and political
wisdom. Gulliver's master among the Houyhnhnms laughed
'that a creature pretending to reason should value itself upon
the knowledge of other people's conjectures, and in things where
that knowledge, if it were certain, could be of no use. Wherein
he agreed entirely with the sentiments of Socrates, as Plato delivers them; which I mention as the highest honour I can do that
prince of philosophers.' Moral and political wisdom occupies
a level a little lower than metaphysics, and doubtless a little
lower also than the greatest poetry. But Swift's genius moved in
this middle flight, and here his massive common sense and his
satiric gift had their full opportunity. The moment we try to
read more into Swift than he read in Socrates, we misinterpret
him. In one of his greatest passages he praised credulity as 'a
more peaceful possession of the mind than curiosity', and laid
down the proposition 'that wisdom, which converses about the
surface', is therefore preferable 'to that pretended philosophy,
which enters into the depth of things, and then comes gravely
back with information and discoveries, that in the inside they
are good for nothing'.[1] Anyone who has had experience in
reading this passage with modern young people can testify that
it is more often than not taken as the language of philosophical
nihilism. But Swift was not thinking in metaphysical terms
about appearance and reality. He was letting his irony play
over the repugnance some people feel for satire, for 'the art of
exposing weak sides, and publishing infirmities'. It was in
'most corporeal beings', that is, human beings, such as the
flayed woman and the stripped carcass of the beau, that 'the
outside hath been infinitely preferable to the in'. The 'serene,
peaceful state, of being a fool among knaves' is a moral condition which we may choose, but for which we must ourselves
accept the responsibility.

In this exposure of the insides of human nature, in stripping
the human carcass, the satirists were united, but again only
on the level of practical common sense; they were observers,
not spinners of theory. They naturally ignored the cynical
materialistic psychology of Hobbes and Mandeville, which was
completely alien to their spirit. But it is significant that they

[1] *A Tale of A Tub*, section lx.

could not agree even on the system of La Rochefoucauld. When Pope wrote Swift in October 1725 that he was busy with 'a set of maxims in opposition to all Rochefoucauld's principles', he drew from Swift the celebrated confession that La Rochefoucauld 'is my favourite, because I found my whole character in him. However I will read him again, because it is possible I may have since undergone some alterations.'[1] Bolingbroke promptly dissociated himself from 'the founder of your sect, that noble original whom you think it so great an honour to resemble'.[2] From Gay and Arbuthnot we have no comment on the matter. Swift therefore stands alone among these men as a professed disciple of the author of the *Maxims*.

But we must not take this profession too literally, as Professor Quintana has already warned us.[3] The famous system of reducing every virtue to a form of disguised selfishness, though far from being the whole of the *Maxims*, is nevertheless their conspicuous and distinguishing feature. With a finesse far beyond the capacity of either Hobbes or Mandeville, whose systems at some points paralleled his, La Rochefoucauld exposed certain kinds of deception which human nature practises on itself. He applied his method with brilliant virtuosity, but it must be admitted that his commentary on human nature is rather specialized and iterative. One can learn and practise the trick of it. To turn from the *Maxims* to the works of Swift is like passing from a narrow room into the great world. Swift also probed the deceitfulness of the human heart, but his *art de connaître les hommes* is not reducible to rule or system. In both originality of thought and fertility of wit Swift was the greater man, and the philosophy of the *Maxims* could have filled only one corner of his capacious mind. When Swift remarks that 'complainers never succeed at Court, though railers do',[4] we note his characteristic qualities in the brief pronouncement; the startling, amusingly cynical paradox mellows, as we linger over it, into an utterance of shrewdness and practical wisdom.

Swift habitually wrote with the purpose of imparting wisdom, and his satire is therefore quite different in tone and temper from that of La Rochefoucauld. The latter composed his observations in the period after his retirement from active life,

---

[1] Swift to Pope, 26 Nov. 1725.   [2] Bolingbroke to Swift, 14 Dec. 1725.
[3] *The Mind and Art of Jonathan Swift* (1936), pp. 159–62 and 301–2.
[4] Swift to Pope, 29 Sept. 1725.

when he could assume the vantage of a seigniorial detachment; he played the roles of spectator, psychologist, and stylist. For the author of the *Maxims* a fault in mankind was something to be disdainfully indicated and wittily exposed; but for Swift it was also something to be judged, castigated, and corrected. Swift wrote, not from a position of detachment, but in the stream of events. Aside from his *bagatelles*, he was normally a publicist, a man of action, by every instinct a manager of affairs. From his retreat at Letcombe in the fateful month of July 1714 he truly described himself to Arbuthnot: 'I could never let people run mad without telling and warning them sufficiently.' His whole biography is a continuous record of his attempts to patch up differences, guide the choice of policies, abolish abuses, manage the presentation of new political and ecclesiastical measures, and in general serve as counsellor to anyone and everyone with whom business or friendship brought him into contact. His interest in history, which Professor Nichol Smith has noted,[1] is another aspect of his eminently practical cast of mind. His satire is so largely occasional and journalistic because of this innate urge for action, and it can be fully understood only as a part of the history of his time.

As these practical urges of Swift's nature differentiate his satire on the one hand from the amused detachment of La Rochefoucauld, so on the other they distinguish it from the depressive melancholy that feeds on stagnant brooding. The satire of Swift, even at its bitterest, never depends for its intensity on any sense of frustration; it has the force of intellectual statement—often mock-scientific in tone—and has the effect of arousing in the reader, by means of the *vis comica* and indignation, a will to action which is sympathetic with Swift's own character. Even the darkest page of Swift leaves us with this feeling of soundness at the core, with a firm conviction of our moral competence and responsibility. It is the expression of a bitter but not a sick mind, and has the invigorating power of a call to action.

This firm grip on actualities is characteristic also of the satire of the other members of Swift's brotherhood, Arbuthnot, Gay, and Pope. They were as ready as Swift, whose genius towered among them, to aline themselves in political struggles, even though political parties were still thought undesirable in prin-

---

[1] *Letters of Swift to Ford* (1935), Introduction, pp. xxxi ff.

ciple. A political party—that is, the party one was opposed to —was a faction seeking to disrupt the national unity. To give up one's neutrality and become a party man, even with the right party, was in a sense a sacrifice of moral position and justifiable only because the nation was in danger. In an age when each party maintained that it was the voice of the nation and the other was a faction, it was natural that imputations of political and moral turpitude should be freely exchanged in the controversy on the real issues. Friendships across the political line were chilled by suspicion and could be maintained only by cautious and magnanimous demeanour on both sides. Hence the peculiarly bitter asperities of both Whig and Tory satirists and their tendency to resort to the lampoon, the popular weapon of all parties in all the controversies of the age, literary as well as political. Hence also the practical intent of so much of the Tory satire. For better as well as for worse, the Tory satirists were in the mêlée, not above it, and they wrote with the conviction that they were dealing battle-blows to save from extinction the virtue and glory of England.

Wit and politics drew them together before the end of Queen Anne's reign into a literary collaboration symbolized by the Scriblerus Club, which diverted itself by ridiculing pedantry rather than political iniquity. But the inclusion in this brotherhood of Oxford and Bolingbroke indicates that the Tory complexion of the group was as openly professed as the Whiggism of Button's Coffee House. Arbuthnot, the universally beloved physician to the Queen, had already ventured into Tory journalism and thus discovered that vein of satire which 'lay like a Mine in the Earth, which the Owner for a long time never knew of'.[1] In a companionship so intimate and so congenial it is difficult to divine what each individual contributed to the other; but in the free give and take many a suggestion thrown out by one man in a convivial hour was later developed by another into a major literary work. Henceforth the members of the Scriblerus Club constituted a defensive and offensive alliance; they freely exchanged confidences; they distrusted the same men and the same measures; above all they were agreed on the unreliability of the nature of that animal called man.

The sincerity of their professions was immediately put to the severest test by the disintegration of the ministry of Oxford and

[1] Swift to Arbuthnot, 25 July 1714.

Bolingbroke. In the sequence of events leading up to the final catastrophe they had an opportunity to observe how precariously the welfare of the whole nation, present and future, depended on traits of human character. In bitterness they had to admit to themselves and to one another that England was, from their point of view, being betrayed by their own friends, Oxford and Bolingbroke, not to mention the indecisive poor sick queen. Swift indicated publicly his own forecast of the disaster that was coming by withdrawing early in the summer to Letcombe, whence he refused angrily all solicitations to return to the scene where the drama was playing itself out. He was 'weary to death of Courts and Ministers and business and politics. . . . I shall say no more but that I care not to live in storms when I can no longer do service in the ship and am able to get out of it.'[1] He was, however, busy writing something that he thought would 'vex' the great ministers; it was the pamphlet, *Some Free Thoughts upon the Present State of Affairs*, in which he set forth how, with other policies, and more wisdom, and less foolish dissension among the ministers, the 'present state of affairs' might have been far different. 'It may serve for a great lesson of humiliation to mankind', Swift was writing in the rectory at Letcombe, 'to behold the habits and passions of men otherwise highly accomplished, triumphing over interest, friendship, honour, and their own personal safety, as well as that of their country, and probably of a most gracious princess, who hath entrusted it to them.'[2] Such were the reflections Swift intended to publish to the nation as the crisis was approaching. The pamphlet was a castigating sermon to his friends, the Tory ministers, who had been measured by the moral test and found wanting. They had also failed by the test of common sense, from first to last so important in the eyes of Swift; their 'mystical manner of proceeding' baffled and galled him:

I have been frequently assured by great ministers, that politics were nothing but common sense; which, as it was the only thing they spoke, so it was the only thing they could have wished I should not believe. God hath given the bulk of mankind a capacity to understand reason when it is fairly offered; and by reason they would easily be governed, if it were left to their choice. Those

---

[1] Swift to Archdeacon Walls, 11 June 1714.
[2] Swift, *Prose Works*, ed. Temple Scott, v. 405.

princes in all ages who were most distinguished for their mysterious skill in government, found by the event, that they had ill consulted their own quiet, or the ease and happiness of their people.[1]

Swift's bitter anger at Oxford and Bolingbroke in 1714 reappeared years later as the contempt of the King of Brobdingnag for 'all *mystery*, *refinement*, and *intrigue*, either in a prince or a minister'. The lovable Arbuthnot was, if anything, more severe even than Swift:

I have an opportunity calmly and philosophically to consider that treasure of vileness and baseness, that I always believed to be in the heart of man; and to behold them exert their insolence and baseness; every new instance, instead of surprising and grieving me, as it does some of my friends, really diverts me, and in a manner improves my theory.[2]

That is a satirist's view of human nature, but Swift and Arbuthnot were not at this time engaging in satire; they were assessing in all seriousness the moral meaning of the Tory collapse. Their intellectual honesty and resolute clear-sightedness in this episode vouches for their integrity when they turn to satire.

In spite of these strains the personal friendships between wits and ministers held fast, not least perhaps because of the candour and sincerity in which Swift set an example. 'In your public capacity', Swift told Oxford, 'you have often angered me to the heart, but, as a private man, never.'[3] The threats of danger which for a time hung over Oxford, Bolingbroke, Ormond, and Prior naturally only strengthened the loyalties of the whole group. However, defeated and dispersed as they were, they hardly ventured into politics for a dozen years. Swift won a heartening victory in the early twenties with his *Drapier's Letters*, but it was only towards 1726, when Swift first dared to return to London, carrying with him the completed manuscript of *Gulliver's Travels*, that the survivors of the Scriblerus Club (Oxford and Parnell and Prior had died) resumed their old intimacy and gathered their forces for their great campaign. Bolingbroke had returned from France and rejoined Pope. Letters to and from Swift became more frequent and in 1725 contained suggestions that he might risk a visit to England.

[1] Ibid. 396.
[2] Arbuthnot to Swift, 12 Aug. 1714.
[3] Swift to Oxford, 3 July 1714. Swift was equally frank to Bolingbroke in his letter of 7 Aug.

On 15 October Pope expressed a hope that 'you are coming towards us, and that you incline more and more to your old friends in proportion as you draw nearer to them; in short that you are getting into our vortex'. Two days later Arbuthnot added his plea: 'I cannot help imagining some of our old club met together like mariners after a storm.' It was as mariners after a storm that they met again the following summer.

But new storms had been brewing, and, with their sense of solidarity renewed, they were soon to be engaged in a prolonged satirical crusade against the degeneracy of the times. Even their ridicule of pedantry, dullness, and bad taste now assumed a larger social significance, as related to their general attack on moral and political corruption. Dr. Johnson, whose misfortune it was never to understand Swift, thought they were all guilty of self-righteousness:

From the letters that pass between him [Swift] and Pope it might be inferred that they, with Arbuthnot and Gay, had engrossed all the understanding and virtue of mankind, that their merits filled the world; or that there was no hope of more. They shew the age involved in darkness, and shade the picture with sullen emulation.[1]

The satirist is perforce a judge, and he is nothing unless he can speak with the voice of righteousness. The darkness of his gloom is the measure of the depth of his indignation, and a sense of isolation is inevitable in his calling. Johnson had himself in his younger days joined forces with the Tories against the corruption of the Walpole era, and his satire in *London* is as gloomy and scornful as any. The warm friendship and mutual confidence which Pope and Swift and their friends so constantly reaffirmed in their letters was the obverse of their common bitterness over the decay of the nation. It is possible to agree in substance with the somewhat sentimental comment of Richter, with which Birkbeck Hill annotated the passage just quoted from Johnson:

Have not many others felt themselves, like me, warmed and encouraged by the touching quiet love of these manly hearts, which, though cold, cutting, and sharp to the outer world, yet laboured and throbbed in their common inner world warmly and tenderly for one another?[2]

Good satire may be withering, it may be dark anger, it may be painfully bitter; but it cannot be great satire without having at

[1] *Lives of the Poets*, ed. Birkbeck Hill, iii. 61.   [2] Ibid. 62, note 1.

its core a moral idealism expressing itself in righteous indignation. The *saeva indignatio* which Swift suffered from is radically
different in quality from a morbid *Schadenfreude*. Once that
distinction is admitted we have the essential justification for our
pleasure in satire, as well as an understanding of the fellow
feeling with which the satirists sustained one another.

In the declining moral tone of England under Walpole they
now professed to see the extinction of the best elements of English life. Under the circumstances it was inevitable that they
should turn their satire on the political situation. The leaders
of the Opposition to Walpole and the Court were mostly
veteran Tories, old friends of Swift and Pope, and there was
Bolingbroke operating without much disguise in the background.
The satirists had a score to settle with the Whigs in general, but
Walpole provided them with special opportunities for the exercise of their talent, which they were not backward to improve.
John Gay was able, by adding some political touches to his
ballad operas, to raise an ominous political storm, accompanied
by a minor social disturbance at Court; the inoffensive Gay, as
Arbuthnot wrote Swift, became 'one of the obstructions to the
peace of Europe', and 'if he should travel about the country he
would have hecatombs of roasted oxen sacrificed to him'. Swift,
from Dublin, congratulated Gay on 'the felicity of thriving by
the displeasure of Courts and Ministers'.[1] The political strains
and tensions of the time became increasingly apparent in
the life and work of Pope, now entering upon the period of
his greatest poetic achievement. It was therefore only to be
expected that, in spite of his professed resolution to avoid party,
he should find that his satire involved him in attacks on the
corruption emanating from high places. In the final *Dunciad*
the celebration of the Greater Mysteries of the Goddess of
Dullness is opened by a wizard who represents the Court
influence and who is therefore assumed to stand for Walpole
himself:

> With that, a Wizard old his Cup extends;
> Which whoso tastes, forgets his former friends,
> Sire, Ancestors, Himself. One casts his eyes
> Up to a Star, and like Endymion dies:
> A Feather, shooting from another's head,
> Extracts his brain; and Principle is fled;

[1] Swift to Gay, 20 Nov. 1729.

> Lost is his God, his Country, every thing:
> And nothing left but Homage to a King!
> The vulgar herd turn off to roll with Hogs,
> To run with Horses, or to hunt with Dogs;
> But, sad example! never to escape
> Their Infamy, still keep the human shape.[1]

The Mysteries which are thus happily initiated under the highest auspices lead directly to the final triumph of Chaos and Universal Darkness in those concluding lines which Dr. Johnson always praised as noble, and which bring to a climax and conclusion the satirical career of Pope in all its aspects. After that pronouncement of doom there was nothing more to be said.

But Pope and his friends, apostles of disenchantment, were by no means alone in their apprehensions for England. Walpole enjoys a bad pre-eminence among English statesmen for drawing upon himself the hostility of writers of all parties and shades of party, men representing the best elements in the nation. Poets and satirists alike show the age involved in darkness. The old Tories associated amicably with the younger Whigs, the Boy Patriots. By 1735 Pope was on the friendliest terms with the future Earl of Chatham, whose letters and speeches at this time abounded with such expressions as 'this gloomy scene' and 'this disgraced country'. This was the age that we know from Hogarth's pictures, from Fielding's political farces and *Jonathan Wild*. The literature of protest was copious, and Warton's list of some of the notable contributions will indicate its great variety of source and nature:

About this time a great spirit of liberty was prevalent. All the men of wit and genius joined in increasing it. Glover wrote his *Leonidas*; Nugent his *Odes to Mankind* and *to Mr. Pulteney*; King his *Miltonis Epistola* and *Templum Libertatis*; Thomson his *Britannia*, his *Liberty*, and his *Agamemnon*; Mallet his *Mustapha*; Brooke his *Gustavus Vasa*; Pope his *Imitations* and these two *Dialogues* [the *Epilogue to the Satires*]; and Johnson his *London*.[2]

In his poem Johnson described the metropolis of those 'degenerate days' in these terms:

> Here let those reign, whom pensions can incite
> To vote a patriot black, a courtier white;

---

[1] *Dunciad*, iv. 517–28.
[2] Quoted by Birkbeck Hill in Johnson's *Lives of the Poets*, iii. 179, note 6.

Explain their country's dear-bought rights away,
And plead for pirates in the face of day;
With slavish tenets taint our poison'd youth,
And lend a lie the confidence of truth.[1]

This gloomy theme of the decadence of England continued to occupy English writers as long as English politics remained in the doldrums, even after Walpole was gone. The sentimentalists echoed its phrases, especially in their eulogies of the life of primitive man; Joseph Warton, in *The Enthusiast* (1744), wished to escape to a life among the simple Indian swains of the New World, 'since Virtue leaves our wretched land'. John Brown summed up the whole case thoroughly and elaborately when he published in 1757 his famous *Estimate of the Manners and Principles of the Times*. The 'ruling character' of the times he asserted to be 'a vain, luxurious, and selfish effeminacy'. He laid the blame impartially at the door of every portion of the public; but the political significance of his indictment is evident from his characterization of Walpole 'in these few words, that while he seemed to *strengthen* the *Superstructure*, he *weakened* the *Foundations* of our Constitution'.[2]

But Brown's sensational book, after being the town talk for a season, lapsed thereafter into an obscurity from which even modern scholars have been reluctant to rescue it. It happened to come out in the very year when Pitt began the great administration which was to win England glorious victories abroad and restore her morale at home. The grim predictions of Brown were made to seem spectral and unreal by the splendours of Pitt's leadership, and therefore, as Lecky long ago pointed out, it is difficult even for us to do full justice to the *Estimate*.[3] The Tory satirists of course suffered a similar loss of credit. When Dr. Johnson in his old age was writing the *Lives of the Poets* he had only words of disparagement for the 'long course of opposition to Sir Robert Walpole', the opposition to which he had in 1739 contributed *Marmor Norfolciense*, but which he now said 'had filled the nation with clamours for liberty, of which no man felt the want, and with care for liberty, which was not in danger'.[4] About the same time Joseph Warton expressed a

---

[1] *London*, 51–6.
[2] *Estimate* (1757), p. 115.
[3] Lecky, *History of England in the Eighteenth Century* (1892), ii. 91.
[4] *Lives of the Poets*, ed. Hill, iii. 289.

similar judgement in his commentary on Pope's two *Dialogues* of 1738:

The satire in these pieces is of the strongest kind; sometimes, direct and declamatory, at others, ironical and oblique. It must be owned to be carried to excess. Our country is represented as totally ruined, and overwhelmed with dissipation, depravity, and corruption. Yet this very country, so emasculated and debased by every species of folly and wickedness, in about twenty years afterwards, carried its triumphs over all its enemies, through all the quarters of the world, and astonished the most distant nations with a display of uncommon efforts, abilities, and virtues. So vain and groundless are the prognostications of poets, as well as politicians.[1]

It was the fate of all the literature of the Opposition to Walpole to appear excessive as it receded into the past. All the Cassandra prophecies of doom, the bitter diatribes of the satirists, the patriotic appeals of the poets, even the jeremiads of Pitt himself, faded into historical documents. Henceforth, to recapture their original appeal, and even to understand what they contributed to the regenerative forces aroused by Pitt, has required the exercise of the historical imagination.

On the whole, these historical considerations seem favourable to the satirists and a justification of their indignation. Literal accuracy is not, of course, to be expected in satire, which, like caricature, presents a truth by means of a distortion. In satire, as in any art which aims to imitate nature under ideal conditions, the general ideas and qualities of mind of the artist command our real attention and determine our response. The mass of contemporaneous references in the work of the Tory satirists, with the subsidiary question of their faithfulness to fact, must not be allowed to obscure the permanent values enveloped in the tissue of particulars. The satire of this group, taken as a whole, reflects the general views of life held by all its members. They were not content with attacking moral and political corruption merely on the superficial level of fashions or manners or passing social conditions. They would not 'sodder and patch up the flaws and imperfections of nature'. Basically, they were opposed to the sect, to be met with in all ages, which holds that the evil in the world is not in men, but between them. They probed for its origin in the recesses of human nature; they cut

---

[1] *Essay on Pope* (1782), ii. 357. Warton adds a note: 'We cannot ascribe these successes, as M. de Voltaire does, to the effects of *Brown's Estimate*.'

into the flesh. All their allusions to particular individuals provide so many case-histories of the baseness of man. Their work
remains for all ages a painful discipline in self-examination and
humiliation.

In this disillusionment, as in their politics, the satirists were
old-fashioned. When they are viewed against the setting of the
history of literature and thought of the whole eighteenth century, they appear as survivors of a dying era. Even as they were
at work, they were challenged by what seemed a more modern
spirit, a more sympathetic and comforting way of looking at
human nature. The 'softness of the heart', Steele intimated in
his preface to *The Conscious Lovers* (1723), is a greater merit than
the 'hardness of the head'. In the early years of the century this
spirit flourished in Whig literary circles, very obvious in Steele,
more subtly pervasive in Addison. As the century progressed
it gradually prevailed everywhere; in spite of the declared
opposition of Fielding and Johnson and Burke, the 'new sensibility' dominated in poetry, drama, and fiction. The same
change was going on in France and the rest of Europe. La
Rochefoucauld was replaced by Vauvenargues; Rousseau
attacked Molière and drenched Europe in sentiment. Towards
the end of the century the doctrine of the essential goodness
of man became the basic tenet of the French revolutionary
philosophers, and of William Godwin, who believed that nature
never made a dunce. In our own time it serves as the indispensable assumption of those schools of political thought which
attribute the evils of our human condition exclusively to environment, absolve human nature from all fault, and, as a
logical consequence, outlaw genetics as an 'anti-social science'.
In the present day the Tory satirists appear as old-fashioned,
and to young readers as novel, as the doctrine of original sin.

The new literature of sentiment in the eighteenth century
had, of course, its merits, especially as an influence in the
reformation of manners, and Addison's work was highly praised
for this reason by both Gay and Pope.[1] But ever since the
eighteenth century the custom has obtained of pointing the
praise of these merits by adding some disparagement of Pope
and Swift. Joseph Warton quoted with approval James Harris,
nephew and disciple of Shaftesbury: 'Whoever has been reading

---

[1] Gay, *The Present State of Wit* (1711), quoted in Lewis Melville, *Life and Letters
of John Gay* (1921), pp. 11–14; Pope, *Epistle to Augustus*, 215–20.

this unnatural Filth', Harris wrote, referring to the fourth book of *Gulliver's Travels*, 'let him turn for a moment to a *Spectator* of Addison, and observe the Philanthropy of that Classical writer.'[1] As no one writer is adequate to all the needs of literature or life, it may be equally appropriate to recommend the satirists as a complement and correction to the literature of philanthropy.

Mandeville, a tavern character whose malice sharpened his wit, was especially qualified to expose the weaknesses of what he disliked. He disliked the *Characteristics* of the third Earl of Shaftesbury, which presented a system of ethics not only contrary to his own, but, he maintained, contrary to the teachings of 'the generality of moralists and philosophers' up to that time. Shaftesbury, he said,

imagines that men without any trouble or violence upon themselves may be naturally virtuous. He seems to require and expect goodness in his species, as we do a sweet taste in grapes and China oranges, of which, if any of them are sour, we boldly pronounce that they are not come to that perfection their nature is capable of. . . . His notions I confess are generous and refined; they are a high compliment to human-kind, and capable by the help of a little enthusiasm of inspiring us with the most noble sentiments concerning the dignity of our exalted nature. What a pity it is that they are not true![2]

Mandeville likewise turned his sarcasm on Steele:

When the incomparable Sir Richard Steele, in the usual elegance of his easy style, dwells on the praises of his sublime species, and with all the embellishments of rhetoric sets forth the excellency of human nature, it is impossible not to be charmed with his happy turns of thought, and the politeness of his expresions. But tho' I have been often moved by the force of his eloquence, and ready to swallow the ingenious sophistry with pleasure, yet I could never be so serious, but reflecting on his artful encomiums I thought on the tricks made use of by the women that would teach children to be mannerly.[3]

These criticisms of Shaftesbury and Steele stem from Mandeville's materialistic system, but they have a value of their own as shrewd observations. Dr. Johnson, who of course abhorred any materialistic system, could say late in his life: 'I read Mandeville forty, or, I believe, fifty years ago. He did not puzzle me; he opened my eyes into real life very much.'

---

[1] Warton, *Essay on Pope* (1782), ii. 344–5.
[2] *Fable of the Bees*, ed. F. B. Kaye (1924), i. 323.
[3] Ibid. i. 52–3.

All readers have, like Mandeville, been charmed by the gentleness and easy indulgence which grace the *Tatler* and the *Spectator*, even in their satiric moods. But complacency is an extremely vulnerable attitude. At the end of a paper recommending the art of dancing as 'a great improvement, as well as embellishment to the theatre', Steele observes, with perhaps a touch of humour, that 'delicacy in pleasure is the first step people of condition take in reformation from vice'.[1] A jolly way of doing the best one can with people of condition, but on second thought a most incautious remark on the part of one who professed to abhor cynicism, and most undiscriminating coming from a moral reformer. Burke, in a famous passage, said that 'vice itself lost half its evil, by losing all its grossness'; but he avoided saying that vice in this way lost its viciousness and changed into virtue. Addison charmed his friends, but he was apparently not a laughing man. He agreed with Hobbes that laughter 'is nothing else but sudden Glory arising from some sudden Conception of some Eminency in our selves, by Comparison with the Infirmity of others, or with our own formerly'; that is, laughter arises from the passion of derision and is reprehensible.[2] It is therefore not surprising that Addison 'always preferred Chearfulness to Mirth'.

The latter I consider as an act, the former as a Habit of the Mind. Mirth is short and transient, Chearfulness fix'd and permanent. Those are often raised into the greatest Transports of Mirth, who are subject to the greatest Depressions of Melancholy: On the contrary, Chearfulness, tho' it does not give the Mind such an exquisite Gladness, prevents us from falling into any depths of Sorrow.[3]

In unperturbable serenity Addison concluded that 'there are but two things which, in my Opinion, can reasonably deprive us of this Chearfulness of Heart', namely, Guilt and Atheism. Admitting that Addison does himself some injustice in this paper, granting that a perverse generation, perhaps of Tory fox-hunters, might really drive him at times to what Mark Twain called a state of mind bordering on impatience, the reader cannot but remark how perfectly this celebration of cheerfulness betrays Addison's limitations, his complacency, his lack of penetration. This is, indeed, the 'serene, peaceful state, of being a fool among knaves'. There is an abysmal division

---

[1] *Spectator*, 370.   [2] Ibid., 47.   [3] Ibid., 381.

between men of this cast of mind and the satirists. When Thomas Tickell, Addison's friend and biographer, had newly arrived in Dublin as under-secretary and had established himself on a friendly footing with Swift, he ventured to inquire regarding the manuscript of an 'imaginary treatise' of which he had heard. But Swift declined to favour him, saying that *Gulliver's Travels* would not please Tickell, 'chiefly because they wholly disagree with your notions of persons and things'.[1]

Through all the ages there has been this opposition of the tough-minded and the tender-minded—William James's classification of philosophies and philosophers. In the eighteenth century it was the tender-minded who were gaining in popularity and were controlling the new literary modes. They were the party of the moderns, and until recently they have prescribed the tone of most of the criticism of the satirists. But the tough-minded also, in their way, have a claim to the title of friend of man. They warn against the illusions which not only end in bitterness but corrupt the heart in the process. They provide a discipline in looking steadily at the stark truth. In September 1725, shortly before Swift penned the famous letter to Pope about the philosophy of *Gulliver's Travels*, he was busy assisting and advising the mercurial Thomas Sheridan, who was in trouble over a politically imprudent sermon and had been removed from the Viceroy's list of chaplains. Swift interceded with Tickell, to whom he explained that Sheridan, 'as he is a creature without cunning, so he hath not overmuch advertency'. To the naïve Sheridan himself he gave this advice: 'You should think and deal with every man as a villain, without calling him so, or flying from him, or valuing him less. This is an old true lesson.'[2] There appears the paradox of Swift's misanthropy, and perhaps it is the paradox also of Pope's portrait of Atticus, where, to use the words of Wotton, 'grief is forced to laugh against her will'. For all his perspicacity into the nature of 'that animal called man', Swift heartily loved individuals, and did not value them less because he had to speak to them with candour.

The tough-minded have always produced realistic literature, sometimes certainly very unpleasant. The Tory satirists shared the temper and ideals of the great French classical

[1] Swift to Tickell, 7 July 1726.
[2] Swift to Sheridan, 11 Sept. 1725.

writers of the age of Louis XIV, who also aimed to anatomize man with complete honesty, to portray man in his true colours and lineaments. 'Rien n'est beau que le vrai', said Boileau, their literary dictator. This very general dictum meant, among other things, that all extravagance and sentimentality, all credulous softening of the harsh truth, were to be shunned as offensive weakness. This is what the French call *le naturalisme classique*. The same spirit pervades the work of the Tory satirists— the pastorals, fables, and ballad operas of Gay, the poems, histories, and polemics of Swift, the political satires of Arbuthnot, the ethic and satiric poems of Pope. The gloom of these men is not an indulgence in lyrical melancholia, but the astringent and penetrating observation of the realist. That is why the tough-minded literature they left behind has recommended itself to generations of English-speaking readers. The popular appropriation of the figure of John Bull as representative of the English character is a tribute, not only to the genius of Arbuthnot, but in a larger way also to the spirit of the *naturalisme classique* of the whole group. If the Tory satirists are rightly called pessimists, their pessimism is of a variety both tonic and exhilarating.

'WIT AND POETRY AND POPE':
SOME OBSERVATIONS ON HIS IMAGERY

MAYNARD MACK

I

THE point of departure of this essay is the current and useful description of Pope's kind of poetry as a poetry of statement.[1] One advantage of this description is that it is general enough to apply to other poetry as well. It asks us to bear in mind—what the temper of our present sensibility often disposes us to forget—that all poetry is in some sense poetry of statement; that without statement neither the Metaphysical kind of poem, witty, intellectual, and definitive, nor the Romantic kind, fluid and as it were infinitive (to mention only two) could be articulated at all; and accordingly, that the project of discrimination we are engaged on here is one of degree and not of kind.

Still, the real merit of the phrase is that it can apply specifically to Pope: it can set the problem. On the one hand, Pope writes a poetry with striking prose affinities. It has the Augustan virtues of perspicuity and ease which, whatever their status in poetry, are among the distinguishing attributes of prose discourse. It utilizes the denotative emphasis of Augustan diction, its precision and conciseness; the logical emphasis inherent in couplet rhetoric, its parallelism and antithesis. And it honours a whole body of reticences, reserves, restraints, exemplified perhaps best in the term 'correctness', which tend to subdue and generalize its feeling and its wit. On the other hand, every reader of Pope is conscious of a host of qualities that look the other way. There is the kind of thing that Mr. Eliot is apparently glancing at when he says of Dryden's poetry that it states 'immensely'.[2] Or Mr. Tillotson, when he remarks in Pope a 'composite activity', 'a combination of simultaneous effects'.[3] Or what Mr. Leavis and Mr. Wimsatt have pointed to in saying

---

[1] The phrase probably owes its present currency to Mr. Mark Van Doren's use of it in his study of *The Poetry of John Dryden* (1920; republished in 1931 and 1946).

[2] T. S. Eliot, 'John Dryden', 1922 (*Selected Essays*, 1932, p. 273).

[3] G. Tillotson, *On the Poetry of Pope* (1938), pp. 156, 141. Cf. also his *Essays in Criticism* (1942), p. 103.

that Pope reconciles correctness with a subtle complexity, offsets and complicates the abstract logical patterns of his verse with counter-patterns which are alogical, poetic.[1]

Facing this duality in its leading poet, the eighteenth century (if I may over-simplify to make the point) was usually able to read the terms as 'poetry is statement' and dismiss the problem: 'If Pope be not a poet, where is poetry to be found?'[2] The nineteenth century tended to re-aline the terms in an antithesis, 'poetry or statement', and rested its case by denying Pope a poet's name: 'Dryden and Pope are not classics of our poetry, they are classics of our prose.'[3] Our own present rephrasing, in which the antithesis becomes a paradox, seems to me an improvement. It enables us to take account of both extremes; to see that if Johnson was right in his evaluation of Pope's success, Arnold was right in his perception of some of the conditions out of which the success was made. By the same token, it enables us to situate the distinctive character of Pope's achievement—and hence of the critical problem he presents—in a very special kind of reconciliation between qualities of poetry and prose, a reconciliation managed even after the maximum concessions have been made to prose.

In this essay I want to discuss some of the aspects of this reconciliation that affect Pope's imagery. We regard imagery to-day, especially metaphor, as the most essential of the means by which language achieves poetic character, whether we choose to designate this character in its totality as 'iconic', 'alogical', 'opaque', 'complex', or by any other of our present set of honorific terms. If we are right in this assumption about metaphor, it implies that a poetry of statement will be signalized not by the absence of metaphorical effects but by their use in such a way that they do not disturb a logical surface of statement. And this, I think, is true in the case of Pope. In response to the sensibility of his time (and doubtless his own sensibility, too), Pope seems to me to have evolved an amazing variety of ways of obtaining the interest, richness, or tensions of metaphor while preserving, at any rate in appearance, those prose-like

---

[1] F. R. Leavis, *Revaluation* (1936), p. 71; W. K. Wimsatt, 'Rhetoric and Poems: The Example of Pope' (an essay to be included in *English Institute Essays, 1948*, published by the Columbia University Press, 1949).

[2] Johnson, 'Life of Pope' (*Lives of the Poets*, ed. G. B. Hill, iii. 251).

[3] Arnold, 'The Study of Poetry', *Essays in Criticism, Second Series* (*Wks.*, 1903, iv. 31).

simplicities without which (as he probably agreed with Swift) 'no human Performance can arrive to any great Perfection'.[1] My purpose here is therefore to indicate some of the general principles that govern the effect of metaphor in Pope's poetry and then proceed to several of his characteristic methods of obtaining the benefits of metaphor without being, in any of the ordinary senses, strikingly metaphoric.

II

Probably the best place to begin an examination of this kind is with a passage from Pope's *Elegy on the Death of an Unfortunate Lady*, which has often been cited as evidence of his belonging to the Metaphysical 'line of wit':

> Most souls, 'tis true, but peep out once an age,
> Dull sullen pris'ners in the body's cage:
> Dim lights of life that burn a length of years,
> Useless, unseen, as lamps in sepulchres;
> Like Eastern kings a lazy state they keep,
> And close confin'd to their own palace sleep.[2]

The general affinities of these lines with Metaphysical poetry certainly need no emphasis, and the opening metaphor, at least, can be traced back through Dryden's

> imprison'd in so sweet a cage
> A soul might well be pleas'd to pass an age[3]

to Donne's

> She, whose faire body no such prison was
> But that a Soule might well be pleas'd to passe
> An age in her.[4]

Since we are looking for differences, however, we must not fail to notice that Pope rarely uses these extensive collocations of witty and ingenious images, and that when he does, it is almost always to establish something that his poems intend to disvalue—here a death-in-life theme, contrasting with a life-in-death theme built up around the lady. In consequence, only certain areas in Pope's poetry show the type of imagery that

---

[1] *A Letter to a Young Clergyman*, 1721 (*Wks.*, ed. Herbert Davis, ix. 68).
[2] Ll. 17–22. This passage is cited for its metaphysical character by Middleton Murry, *Countries of the Mind* (1922), p. 86, and F. R. Leavis, op. cit., pp. 70 ff.
[3] *To the Duchess of Ormond*, ll. 118–19.
[4] *The Second Anniversary*, ll. 221–3.

most Metaphysical poems tend to show throughout, with the result that the centre of gravity in his poetry often passes to other kinds of complication. It passes, for example, to such powerful counterpointings of tone and meaning as are obtained in the *Unfortunate Lady* by modulating from lines like those quoted to those beginning 'Yet shall thy grave with rising flow'rs be drest'.[1] The contrast in theme and feeling that these lines offer to those above is one that Donne would have elected to obtain through a conjunction of brilliant images. Pope obtains it—not only here, but habitually in his poems—through a conjunction of styles. The implied comparison usually possesses the richness and suggestiveness of a metaphor but is not, in any strict sense, metaphorical.

We must notice also in the passage quoted that the images, witty and to some extent ingenious as they are, stem from comparisons that are at bottom traditional and familiar—the soul as prisoner, lamp, monarch, the body as cage, sepulchre, palace. This is Pope's normal practice. Except in comic poetry like the *Dunciad* (where, again, it is partly a matter of disvaluing) he rarely stresses heterogeneity in the objects he brings together. For this reason he has little occasion to expand or amplify his comparisons in the manner we associate with Donne. It has not been often enough remarked, I think, that the 'extended' Metaphysical image is a simple consequence of the Metaphysical discovery of 'occult resemblances in things apparently unlike'. That is to say, if one sets about comparing lovers to compasses at all, or the world to a beheaded man,[2] one is bound to specify in some detail the nature of the resemblances that make the image relevant; the value of the image is, as it were, generated in the process of constructing it. But it is also spent there. If such images seem wittier than any other kind because they display their wit at length, they also have less power in reserve. There is nothing in Donne's compass image, handsome as it is, to tempt the imagination to keep on unfolding it beyond the point at which the poet leaves it. On the other hand, Donne's gold-leaf image in the same poem has this power. It has it because it is powerfully compressed, and it can be powerfully compressed because it does not have to generate all its own potential: it is nourished at the source by normal and traditional

[1] Ll. 63 ff.
[2] For the second instance, see *The Second Anniversary*, ll. 9 ff.

associations. Pope's images, as suggested above, rely heavily
on such associations. They take the ordinary established
relationships of, say, singing and breath and soul, flesh and
oblivion and marble, sepulchre and decay, finger and flute,
parent and child, body and beauty, and with a delicate readjust-
ment, freshen and fortify their implications:

> Oft as the mounting larks their notes prepare
> They fall, and leave their little lives in air.

> Tho' cold like you, unmov'd and silent grown,
> I have not yet forgot myself to stone.

> See the sad waste of all-devouring years,
> How Rome her own sad sepulchre appears.

> Such were the notes thy once-lov'd poet sung,
> Till death untimely stopp'd his tuneful tongue.[1]

> Me, let the tender Office long engage
> To rock the Cradle of reposing Age.

> Still round and round the ghosts of beauty glide,
> And haunt the places where their honour died.[2]

Finally, we must notice that the closed couplet exercises on
images a peculiarly muting or subordinating influence. When
we look at Dryden's lines quoted earlier, we see that, though
he has taken over in large part the very words of Donne, the
image in his verse has somehow become submerged. The
reason, I think, is partly that Donne has sprawled the image
across a weak rhyme which calls no attention to itself, whereas
Dryden has suspended it within a strong rhyme which has a
meaning of its own—which suggests, in fact, a correspondence
between the soul's envelopment in body and its envelopment in
time. Partly, also, that the movement of Donne's lines (and
this is customary in his couplet poetry) exists simply to carry
the image on its back; its pattern, in so far as it has any, is
determined by and coextensive with the image. Dryden's

---

[1] This example illustrates particularly well the way in which an unbroken
logical surface can cushion and absorb a powerful or even violent image. If we
were to paraphrase the image, we should have to say something like: 'Death took
up the instrument of Parnell's music, and fingering (stopping) it in his own
(untimely) tempo, brought the music to a premature (untimely) stop.' Yet the
effect of the normal logical meaning of 'stopp'd' is to carry us smoothly across the
opposites that are being yoked here.

[2] The quotations are from *Windsor Forest*, ll. 133–4; *Eloisa to Abelard*, ll. 23–4; *To
Mr. Addison*, ll. 1–2; *To Robert, Earl of Oxford*, ll. 1–2; *Epistle to Dr. Arbuthnot*,
ll. 408–9; and *Moral Essays*, ii. 241–2.

couplet, on the other hand, being closed, has an assertive pattern of its own. The coiling and uncoiling rhythmical effect that comes from alternation of inverted with normal word order works with the movement of meaning to emphasize the logical stages of the soul's acceptance ('so sweet a cage'; 'might well be pleas'd'; 'pleas'd to pass an age') and the climactic stage is affirmed by rhyme. The closed couplet, in other words, tends to subdue images by putting them into competition with other forms of complication.

This point can be illustrated equally well from Pope. In the lines from the *Unfortunate Lady*, certainly the wittiest and boldest image is that in the third couplet. Yet here again the interest of the comparison has to compete with other interests—the strong rhyme, the parallelism, the humorously inverted syntax in both lines, which by withholding the completion of the sense units as long as possible keeps rather a lazy state itself.[1] Or take a passage in which Pope is developing one of Donne's images. This is Donne:

> Now,
> The ladies come; As Pirates, which doe know
> That there came weak ships fraught with Cutchannel
> The men board them.[2]

This is Pope:

> Painted for sight, and essenc'd for the smell,
> Like Frigates fraught with Spice and Cochine'l,
> Sail in the Ladies: How each Pyrate eyes
> So weak a Vessel, and so rich a Prize!
> Top-gallant he, and she in all her Trim,
> He boarding her, she striking sail to him.[3]

Donne is not at his best in this case, and Pope has the advantage of maturing Donne's idea at length—about as much at length as he was ever inclined to go. Still, leaving all that aside, one can see, I think, that Pope's figure, in spite of its richer elaborations, is not the primary and exclusive focus of attention that Donne's is. Donne's, as in our earlier instance, is the sole occupant of the verse rhetoric which presents it; Pope's is jostled for *Lebensraum* by many other contenders. There is, first, the

---

[1] This effect is easily verified by rearranging the words in normal order.
[2] *Satyre IV*, ll. 187–90.
[3] *The Fourth Satire of Dr. John Donne, Versifyed*, ll. 226–31.

drama of the ladies' arrival, which the verse itself is at some pains to enact in the first two and a half lines. Then there is the confrontation of forces in line 3, and the double assessment of the booty in line 4, both again rhetorically enacted. Finally, in line 5 comes a brilliant chiastic *rapprochement* of male and female in their bedizenment, to be followed in line 6 by an extension and also a qualification of this *rapprochement* with respect to sex (both parties are interested in the amorous duel, but their functions differ), the former carried by the metrical parallel, the latter by the antithesis in the sense. All these effects grow out of the potentialities of couplet rhetoric, not out of the image; and though they may co-operate with imagery, as here, they have a life of their own which tends to mute it.[1]

III

So far we have been discussing orthodox kinds of imagery in Pope's poetry, together with some of the modifications to which this imagery is subjected. It is time to turn now to some of his more reticent modes of imaging, which achieve metaphorical effect without using what it is customary to regard as metaphor. The first of these may be studied in his proper names.

Pope's names warrant an essay in themselves. With the possible exception of Milton, no poet has woven so many so happily into verse. And this is not simply because, as Pope said of himself,

> Whoe'er offends, at some unlucky Time,
> Slides into Verse, and hitches in a Rhyme,[2]

but because Pope saw, like Milton, the qualitative elements (including in Pope's case the humorous qualities) that could be extracted from proper names. For an effect of romance, sonority, and exoticism akin to Milton's, though much mitigated by the couplet, any passage of his translation of Homer's catalogue of ships will do:

> The Paphlagonians Pylaemenes rules,
> Where rich Henetia breeds her savage Mules,
> Where Erythinus' rising Clifts are seen,
> Thy Groves of Box, Cytorus! ever green;

---

[1] See also on this point, with respect to Dryden, M. W. Prior, *The Language of Tragedy* (1947), p. 169.

[2] *Imit. of Hor., Sat. II*, i, ll. 77–8.

And where Aegyalus and Cromna lie,
And lofty Sesamus invades the Sky;
And where Parthenius, roll'd thro' Banks of Flow'rs,
Reflects her bord'ring Palaces and Bow'rs.[1]

For a combination of romance and humour, this passage:

First he relates, how sinking to the chin,
Smit with his mien, the Mud-nymphs suck'd him in:
How young Lutetia, softer than the down,
Nigrina black, and Merdamante brown,
Vy'd for his love in jetty bow'rs below,
As Hylas fair was ravish'd long ago.[2]

And for pure humour:

'Twas chatt'ring, grinning, mouthing, jabb'ring all,
And Noise and Norton, Brangling and Breval,
Dennis and Dissonance, and captious Art,
And Snip-snap short, and Interruption smart,
And Demonstration thin, and Theses thick,
And Major, Minor, and Conclusion quick.[3]

It will be observed in all these passages that as the names slide into verse they tend to take on a metaphorical colouring. Those in the first and third passages are of real places and persons, but the poetry does not require, any more than Milton's, that we identify them closely. Instead they become vehicles of an aura of associations clinging to epic warriors before Troy, or else of the vulgarity of a disputatious literature, which swallows up writers as Noise, Brangling, Dissonance swallow up Norton, Breval, and Dennis. Pope is a master of this metaphorical play with names. Sometimes the names he uses are quasi-metaphorical to begin with, like those he has invented in the Lutetia passage above. Or like those which allude—Adonis, Atossa, Shylock, Balaam, Timon, Sporus. Or those which have an allegorical cast—Uxorio, Worldly, Sir Morgan, Sir Visto, Patritio, Papillia, Hippia. Or those which personify—Avarice, Profusion, Billingsgate, Sophistry, Mathesis. Pope's habit with these classes of names is to interlayer them among his real objects and real persons, so that there results an additional and peculiarly suggestive kind of metaphorical play between concrete and abstract: allegorical Sir Morgan astride his cheese;[4] allusive

[1] *Iliad*, ii. 1034 ff.
[3] Ibid. 237–42.
[2] *Dunciad* (1743), ii. 331–6.
[4] *Moral Essays*, iii. 61.

Adonis driving to St. James's a whole herd of swine;[1] or personi-
fied Morality, Chicane, Casuistry, and Dulness suddenly brought
into incongruous union with a judge named Page:

> Morality, by her false Guardians drawn,
> Chicane in Furs, and Casuistry in Lawn,
> Gasps, as they straiten at each end the cord,
> And dies, when Dulness gives her Page the word.[2]

Unquestionably, however, Pope's best metaphorical effects
with names were obtained from specific ones, as in the lines on
Dennis and Dissonance above. Did a certain duchess show an
indiscriminate appetite for men? How better image it than
with a nice derangement of proper names, opened with a particularly felicitous 'what':

> What has not fired her bosom or her brain?
> Caesar and Tall-boy, Charles, and Charlemagne.[3]

Did the vein of poetry in contemporary versifiers hardly weigh
up to a gramme? Then doubtless it was an age when

> nine such Poets made a Tate.[4]

Why was philosophy at Oxford so backward, so ponderous?
Because the Oxford logicians came riding whip and spur,
through thin and thick,

> On German Crousaz and Dutch Burgersdyck.[5]

Or, since the current drama was slavishly derivative, why not
let the patchwork image be projected partly with syntax and
partly with names—a roll-call of stately ones, a tumbling
huddle of risible ones:

> A past, vamp'd, future, old reviv'd, new piece,
> Twixt Plautus, Fletcher, Shakespeare, and Corneille
> Can make a Cibber, Tibbald, or Ozell.[6]

A second restrained mode of imaging in Pope's poetry is the
allusion. Not simply the kind of descriptive allusion to persons,
places, events, and characters that all poets make continual use
of, and of which I shall say nothing here, but a kind that is
specifically evaluative, constructing its image by setting beside
some present object or situation not so much another object or
situation as another dimension, a different sphere—frequently

---

[1] *Moral Essays*, iii., 73–4.
[2] *Dunciad* (1743), iv. 27–30.
[3] *Moral Essays*, ii. 77–8.
[4] *Epistle to Dr. Arbuthnot*, l. 190.
[5] *Dunciad* (1743), iv. 198.
[6] Ibid. i. 284–6.

for the purpose of diminishing what is present, but often, too, for the purpose of enlarging or elevating it. Familiar examples of the first use are the correspondence of Sporus to Satan in one of his more degrading disguises—'at the Ear of *Eve*, familiar Toad';[1] or (more humorously) of Cibber to Satan, on his exalted throne, at the opening of *Dunciad*, ii. A less familiar example is the witty correspondence suggested in *Dunciad*, iv between the dunces irresistibly drawn into the gravitational field of Dulness—

> by sure Attraction led
> And strong impulsive gravity of Head[2]—

and the feeling Sin has in Milton's poem, after the Fall, of being pulled toward earth by 'sympathy, or some connatural force',

> Powerful at greatest distance to unite
> With secret amity things of like kind. . . .
> Nor can I miss the way, so strongly drawn
> By this new-felt attraction and instinct.[3]

As for the second use, the *Essay on Man* begins with a particularly fine example, in the 'garden tempting with forbidden fruit';[4] while *Windsor Forest* both begins and ends with one; the groves of Eden, which establish the central symbol of the poem; and the dove of Noah, also described as the dove of grace and peace, which throws around Pope's vision of England as she comes out of her continental wars all the seventeenth-century religious associations of covenant, happy rescue, and divine mission.[5]

This evaluative kind of metaphor in Pope, whether diminishing or enlarging, is usually religious, and often very powerfully so. Here are some instances in the lighter hues (I limit myself to instances that I think have not been recorded by Pope's editors):

> And Heav'n is won by violence of Song.[6]

> And Zeal for that great House which eats him up.[7]

> Blest be the *Great*! for those they take away.[8]

> And instant, fancy feels th' imputed sense.[9]

[1] *Epistle to Dr. Arbuthnot*, l. 319.   [2] Ll. 75–6.   [3] Bk. x, ll. 244 ff.
[4] Ep. i. 8.   [5] Ll. 8 and 429–30.
[6] *Imit. of Hor.*, *Ep. II*. i, l. 240. Cf. Matt. xi. 12.
[7] *Moral Essays*, iii. 208. Cf. Ps. lxix. 9.
[8] *Epistle to Dr. Arbuthnot*, l. 225. Cf. Job i. 21.
[9] *Dunciad*, ii. 200. Cf. the theological sense of 'imputed'.

These colours are darker:

> Each does but hate his neighbour as himself.[1]
> What Lady's Face is not a whited Wall?[2]

And this, though light in tone, carries a scathing indictment of
the perversion of religious values in a money culture. Since it
admirably illustrates the way allusion can construct a cogent
metaphor without intruding on a casual surface and is, in fact,
one of the most scarifying passages Pope ever wrote, I quote it
in full:

> On some, a *Priest* succinct in Amice white,
> Attends; *all flesh is nothing in his Sight*!
> Beeves, at his touch, at once to jelly *turn*,
> And the huge Boar is shrunk into an *Urn*:
> The board with specious *miracles* he loads,
> *Turns* Hares to Larks, and Pigeons into Toads.
> Another (for in all what one can shine?)
> Explains the Seve and Verdeur of the *Vine*.
> What cannot copious *Sacrifice attone*?
> Thy Treufles, Perigord! thy Hams, Bayonne!
> With French *Libation*, and Italian Strain
> *Wash* Bladen *white*, and *expiate* Hays's stain.
> Knight lifts the head, for what are crowds undone
> To *three essential* Partridges *in one*?[3]

There are two other modes of imagery of which Pope is fond,
modes that the concision of the closed couplet encourages and
almost insists on, though no other writer of the couplet has
perfected them to a like extent. These are pun and juxtaposition.
Juxtaposition operates in Pope's poetry in several ways. One
of them, as has lately been pointed out,[4] is through zeugma,
which the economy of this verse form often calls for and which
can itself be modulated either into metaphor—'Or stain her
Honour, or her new Brocade', or into pun—'And sometimes
Counsel take—and sometimes *Tea*.'[5] (In either case, the effect
is ultimately metaphorical, a correspondence being suggested

---

[1] *Moral Essays*, iii. 108. Cf. Matt. xxii. 39. I have noticed this allusion elsewhere
(*College English* (1946), vii. 269).

[2] *The Fourth Satire of Dr. John Donne, Versifyed*, l. 151. Cf. Matt. xxiii. 27. (The
allusion is Pope's addition.)

[3] *Dunciad* (1743), iv. 549–62. (Italics mine.)

[4] In Mr. Wimsatt's essay cited above, p. 21, n. 1. Cf. also Austin Warren, 'The
Mask of Pope' (*Rage for Order*, 1948, p. 45).

[5] *Rape of the Lock*, ii. 107, iii. 8.

between Belinda's attitudes to chastity and brocade, or between
Queen Anne's, and her society's, to politics and tea.)

My own concern, however, is not with zeugma, but with the
metaphorical effects that can arise from simple juxtaposition.
For example, from a list of items *seriatim*, with one inharmonious
term:

> Puffs, Powders, Patches, Bibles, Billet-doux.[1]

Or from a simple parallel inside the line:

> Dried Butterflies, and Tomes of Casuistry.[2]

Or from a similar parallel inside the couplet:

> Now Lapdogs give themselves the rowzing Shake,
> And sleepless Lovers, just at Twelve, awake.[3]

This is a very versatile device. In the *Rape of the Lock*, from
which the above examples are taken, Pope uses it to mirror in
his lines and couplets the disarray of values in the society he
describes, the confounding of antithetical objects like lapdogs
and lovers, bibles and *billets-doux*. On the other hand, in the
Essay on Man, this same device, redirected by the context, can
be made to mirror the 'equalizing' view of antithetical objects
taken by the eye of God or by the god-like magnanimous man:

> A hero perish, or a sparrow fall.[4]

> As toys and empires, for a god-like mind.[5]

It is also a very sensitive device. The potential metaphor that
every juxtaposition tends to carry in suspension requires only
the slightest jostling to precipitate it out. Sometimes a well-
placed alliteration will do it:

> The Mind, in Metaphysics at a Loss,
> May wander in a wilderness of Moss.[6]

Sometimes an inter-animation of words, as here between the
'smooth' eunuch and the 'eas'd' sea:

> Where, eas'd of Fleets, the Adriatic main
> Wafts the smooth Eunuch and enamour'd Swain.[7]

---

[1] Ibid. i. 138.

[2] Ibid. v. 122. A particularly graceful comparison in its suggestion of a common
animation, brilliance, delicacy of movement, and perishableness in the worlds of
ethics and Lepidoptera.

[3] Ibid. i. 15–16.   [4] Ep. i. 88.   [5] Ep. iv. 180.

[6] *Dunciad* (1743), iv. 449–50.   [7] Ibid. 309–10.

And sometimes a set of puns, as in this example, fusing the biologist with the object of his study:

> The most recluse, discreetly open'd, find
> Congenial matter in the Cockle-kind.[1]

Pun, of course, brings before us Pope's most prolific source of imagery in his comic and satiric poetry—which is to say, in the bulk of his work. His puns in other poems—*Windsor Forest*, *Eloisa*, the *Essay on Man*, the *Essay on Criticism*—are deeply buried and always reticent. But in the satires and the *Dunciad*, particularly the latter, he spends them openly and recklessly, with superb effect. They cease to be in these poems ordinary puns, like those we find in Metaphysical poetry, where, because of the conceit, pun has a lesser job to do; they become instead Metaphysical conceits themselves, yoking together violently, as Mr. Leavis has noticed,[2] the most heterogeneous ideas. Moreover, when they are used together with ordinary images, the real metaphorical power is likely to be lodged in them. Thus the following figures are not especially bold themselves, but the puns inside them open out like peacocks' tails:

> Ye tinsel Insects! whom a Court maintains,
> That counts your Beauties only by your *Stains*.

> On others Int'rest her gay liv'ry flings,
> Int'rest that waves on *Party-colour'd* wings.

> At length Corruption, like a gen'ral flood,
> (So long by watchful ministers withstood)
> Shall deluge all; and Av'rice, creeping on,
> Spread like a *low-born* mist, and blot the sun.[3]

Here, then, are four classes of metaphorical effect in Pope's poetry, all of them obtained outside the normal channels of overt simile and metaphor. One of them, juxtaposition (its collateral descendant, zeugma, would make a second), stems from the structure of the closed couplet itself. Two more, allusion and pun, are encouraged to a large extent by its fixed and narrow room. And none of them, it is important to notice, calls attention to itself as metaphorical. Between them, nevertheless, without violating at all the prose conventions of the Augustan mode, they do a good deal of the work that we to-day associate with the extended metaphor and conceit.

---

[1] *Dunciad* (1743), iv. 447–8.   [2] Op. cit., p. 99.
[3] From *Epil. to the Sats.*, Dial. ii. 220–1; *Dunciad* (1743), iv. 537–8; and *Moral Essays*, iii. 135–8. (Italics mine.)

IV

The devices of complication touched on in the preceding sections pertain primarily to local texture: the line and couplet. I want to add to these, in conclusion, three patterns that are more pervasive; that help supply the kind of unity in Pope's poems which he is popularly not supposed to have. Actually, there is a wide variety of such patterns. There are the characteristics of the dramatic speaker of every poem, who shifts his style, manner, and quality of feeling considerably from poem to poem, as anyone will see who will compare carefully the *Essay on Criticism* with the *Essay on Man*, or the *Epistle to Dr. Arbuthnot* with that to Augustus. There is the character of the interlocutor in the poems that have dialogue, by no means a man of straw. There is the implicit theme, usually announced in a word or phrase toward the outset of the poem, and while seldom developed in recurrent imagery, as in Shakespeare, almost always developed in recurrent references and situations. There is also, often, a kind of pattern of words that reticulates through a poem, enmeshing a larger and larger field of associations—for instance, words meaning light in the *Essay on Criticism*, or the word 'head' (and, of course, all terms for darkness) in the *Dunciad*. And there are a great many more such unifying agents.

The three that I shall examine briefly here are irony, the portrait, and mock-heroic. Pope's irony, fully analysed, would require a book. The point about it that is most relevant to our present topic is that it is a mode of complication closely resembling metaphor. At its most refined, in fact, as in Swift's *Modest Proposal* or Pope's praise of George II in the *Epistle to Augustus*, it asks us to lay together not two, but three, different perspectives on reality. First, the surface, and second, the intended meanings, these two corresponding roughly to vehicle and tenor in a metaphor; and then, third—to use again the Pope and Swift examples—the kind of propositions that English projectors were *usually* making about Ireland, or the poets about George II. Pervasive irony of this type—of which there is a good deal in Pope—tends to resist the presence of bold imagery, for two reasons. In the first place, because it consists already in a mutual translation, to and fro, between one kind of complex whole with all its particularities clinging to it (what is said), and a different complex whole with all its revised particularities (what is meant); a translation that profuse or striking imagery only clutters and impedes. And in the second place, because the success of the medium depends on adopting the attitudes, motives, and so far as possible even the terms of a very conventional point of view. If one is going to write an ironic love song 'in the modern taste', one almost has to refer to 'Cupid's purple pinions'[1]; or if a panegyric on George II, to the usual terms for kingly prowess:

> Your Country, chief, in Arms abroad defend.[2]

To find a more striking phrase would destroy the subtlety of the ironic comment (i.e. its resemblance to what a Cibber might have said); and would, of course, too, destroy the mutual translation between the arms of battle and those of Madame Walmoden.

To all this, in the *Epistle to Augustus*, is added the further layer of metaphor that results from Pope's imitation of what Horace had written about *his* Caesar. Nor is this layer confined alone to the poems which are imitations. The Roman background, it has been well observed, is a kind of universal Augustan metaphor or 'myth'.[3] It lies behind Pope's work, and much of Swift's and Fielding's, like a charged magnetic field, a reservoir of attitudes whose energy can be released into their own creations at a touch. Not through the Horatian or Virgilian or Ovidian tags; these are only its minor aspect; but through the imposed standard of a mighty and civilized tradition in arts, morals, government. At the same time, conveniently, it is a standard that can be used two ways: for a paradigm of the great and good now lost in the corruptions of the present, as in the comparison of George II with Augustus Caesar; or for the headwaters of a stream down which still flow the stable and continuing classic values:

> You show us Rome was glorious, not profuse.
>
> The world's just wonder, and ev'n thine, O Rome!
>
> Who would not weep, if Atticus were he![4]

This last example brings us to Pope's portraits. These, again, have the complicating characteristics of metaphors, without

---

[1] Cf. Swift's *A Love Song, in the Modern Taste*, st. 1.

[2] *Imit. of Hor., Ep. II*, i, l. 3.

[3] Cf. J. C. Maxwell, 'Demigods and Pickpockets', *Scrutiny*, xi (1942–3), 34 ff.

[4] From *Moral Essays*, iv. 23; *Essay on Criticism*, l. 248; *Epistle to Dr. Arbuthnot*, l. 214.

drawing attention to themselves as such. They are often erroneously called 'illustrations', as if their content were exhausted in being identified with some abstraction implied or stated by the poem. But what abstractions will exhaust the characters of Atticus, Sporus, Atossa, Balaam, and a score of others? To instance from one of the simplest portraits, so that it may be quoted entire, here is Narcissa:

> 'Odious! in woollen! 'twould a saint provoke!'
> (Were the last words that poor Narcissa spoke):
> 'No, let a charming chintz, and Brussels lace
> Wrap my cold limbs, and shade my lifeless face:
> One would not, sure, look frightful when one's dead:
> And—Betty—give this cheek a little red.'[1]

This, to the extent that it illustrates anything, illustrates the poem's prose argument that our ruling passion continues to our last breath. But as a metaphor it explores, not without considerable profundity, through the character of one type of woman, the character of the human predicament itself. Here we have, as her name implies, the foolish self-lover; but also— in a wider, more inevitable, and uncensorable sense—the self-lover who inhabits each of us by virtue of our mortal situation, the very principle of identity refusing to be erased. Here, too, we have the foolish concern for appearances, vastly magnified by the incongruity of its occasion; but also the fundamental human clutching at the familiar and the known. And embracing it all is the central paradox of human feelings about death and life. Cold limbs don't need wrapping (the conjunction of terms itself suggests that death can be apprehended but not comprehended), nor dead faces shading; and yet, as our own death rituals show, somehow they do. The levels of feeling and experience startled into activity in this short passage can hardly be more than pointed at in the clumsiness of paraphrase. The irony of words like 'saint', the ambiguities of 'charming' and 'shade', the tremendous compression in 'frightful' of 'the anguish of the marrow, The ague of the skeleton', accumulate as one contemplates them.

All of Pope's portraits have at least the complexity of this one, and all are equally metaphorical in effect. If they do not call attention to themselves as metaphors, it is probably because in them the vehicle has largely absorbed the tenor; for metaphors

[1] *Moral Essays*, i. 246–51.

in general seem to take on prominence according as both the tenor and the vehicle (viz. lovers as well as compasses) are insisted on at once. In any case, they behave like metaphors in Pope's poems, usually assuming, in addition to their functions locally, an important unifying role. Sometimes they define the entire structure of a poem, as in *Moral Essays*, ii, where they develop the easy-going aphorism of the opening—'Most women have no characters at all'—into a mature interpretation of what personality is. Sometimes they supply the central symbols, as with Timon in *Moral Essays*, iv, 'Vice' in Dialogue ii of the *Epilogue to the Satires*, or the Man of Ross and Balaam in *Moral Essays*, iii. Likewise, in *Arbuthnot*, Atticus and Sporus appear at just the crucial phases in the argument and knit up, as it were, the two essential ganglia in the sinews of the drama that the poem acts out between the poet and his adversaries. They give us, successively, the poet analytical and judicial, who can recognize the virtues of his opponents ('Blest with each Talent and each Art to please'), whose deliberation is such that he can even mirror in his language—its subjunctives, its antitheses, the way it hangs the portrait over an individual without identifying it with him—the tentative, insinuating, never-wholly-committed hollow man who is Atticus; and then the poet roused and righteous, no longer judicial but executive, touching with Ithuriel's spear the invader in the garden, spitting from his mouth (with a concentration of sibilants and labials) the withered apple-seed. Both portraits are essential to the drama that unifies the poem.

The great pervasive metaphor of Augustan literature, however, including Pope's poetry, is the metaphor of tone: the mock-heroic. It is very closely allied, of course, to the classical or Roman myth touched on earlier and is, like that, a reservoir of strength. By its means, without the use of overt imagery at all, opposite and discordant qualities may be locked together in 'a balance or reconcilement of sameness with difference, of the general with the concrete, the idea with the image, the individual with the representative, the sense of novelty and freshness with old and familiar objects'—the mock-heroic seems made on purpose to fit this definition of Coleridge's of the power of imagination. For a literature of decorums like the Augustan, it was a metaphor with every sort of value. It could be used in the large, as in *Joseph Andrews*, *Tom Jones*, *The*

Beggar's Opera, The Rape of the Lock, The Dunciad, or in the small—the passage, the line. It could be set in motion by a passing allusion, not necessarily to the classics:

> Calm Temperance, whose blessings those partake,
> Who hunger, and who thirst, for scribling sake;

by a word:

> Glad chains, warm furs, broad banners, and broad faces;

even by a cadence:

> And the fresh vomit run for ever green.[1]

Moreover, it was a way of getting the local, the ephemeral, the pressure of life as it was lived, into poetry, and yet distancing it in amber:

> That live-long wig, which Gorgon's self might own,
> Eternal buckle takes in Parian stone.[2]

It was also a way of qualifying an attitude, of genuinely 'heroicizing' a Man of Ross, a parson Adams, a School-mistress, yet undercutting them with a more inclusive attitude:

> Rise, *honest* Muse! and sing the Man of Ross.[3]

Above all—and this, I think, was its supreme advantage for Pope—it was a metaphor that could be made to look two ways. If the heroic genre and the heroic episodes lurking behind *The Rape of the Lock* diminish many of the values of this society, they also partially throw their weight behind some others. Clarissa's speech is an excellent case in point.[4] Her words represent a sad shrinkage from the epic views of Glaucus which reverberate behind them, views involving real heroism and (to adapt Mr. Eliot's phrase) the awful daring of a real surrender. Still, the effect of the contrast is not wholly minimizing. Clarissa's vision of life, worldly as it is when seen against the heroic standard, surpasses the others in the poem and points, even if obliquely, to the tragic conflict between the human lot and the human will that is common to life at every level.

This flexibility of the mock-heroic metaphor is seen in its greatest perfection in the *Dunciad.* There are, indeed, three thicknesses of metaphor in this poem: an overall metaphor, in

---

[1] From *Dunciad* (1743), i. 49–50, 88; ii. 156.
[2] *Moral Essays,* iii. 294–5.
[3] Ibid. 250. (Italics mine.) The blend of irony and praise is carefully maintained throughout the passage.   [4] Canto v, ll. 9 ff.

which the poem as a whole serves as vehicle for a tenor which is the decline of literary and human values generally; a network of local metaphor, in which this poem is especially prolific; and in between, the specifically mock-heroic metaphor which springs from holding the tone and often the circumstances of heroic poetry against the triviality of the dunces and their activities. But what is striking about this metaphor in the *Dunciad*, and indicative of its flexibility, is that it is applied quite differently from the way it is applied in the *Rape of the Lock*. There, the epic mode as vehicle either depresses the values of the actors, as with Belinda, or somewhat supports them, as with Clarissa. Here, on the contrary, one of the two lines of development (the comic) grows from allowing the actors to depress and degrade the heroic mode, its dignity and beauty. Again and again Pope builds up in the poem effects of striking epic richness, only to let them be broken down, disfigured, stained—as the word 'vomit' stains the lovely movement and suggestion of the epic line quoted above. Thus the diving and other games in Book II disfigure the idea of noble emulation and suggest the befoulment of heroic values through the befoulment of the words and activities in which these values are recorded. Thus the fop's Grand Tour in IV mutilates a classical and Renaissance ideal (cf. also Virgil's Aeneas, to whose destined wanderings toward Rome the fop's are likened) of wisdom ripened by commerce with men and cities. Indeed, the lines of the whole passage are balanced between the ideal and the fop's perversions of it:

> A dauntless infant! never scar'd with God.
> Europe he saw, and Europe saw him too.
> Judicious drank, and greatly daring dined;

or between related ideals and what has happened to them:

> To happy Convents, bosomed deep in Vines,
> Where slumber Abbots, purple as their Wines.

or between epic resonances, the epic names, and the sorry facts:

> To where the Seine, obsequious as she runs,
> Pours at great Bourbon's feet her silken sons.[1]

This is one line of development in the *Dunciad*. The other is its converse: the epic vehicle is gradually made throughout the poem to enlarge and give a status of serious menace to all this

---

[1] *Dunciad* (1743), iv. 284 ff.

ludicrous activity. Here the epic circumstance of a presiding goddess proved invaluable. Partly ludicrous herself, she could also become the locus of inexhaustible negation behind the movements of her trivial puppets; her force could be associated humorously, but also seriously, with the powerful names of Chaos, Night, Anti-Christ, and with perversions of favourite order symbols like the sun, monarchy, and gravitation. Here, too, the epic backgrounds as supplied by Milton could be drawn in. Mr. C. S. Lewis has remarked of *Paradise Lost* that 'only those will fully understand it who see that it might have been a comic poem'.[1] The *Dunciad* is one realization of that might-have-been. Over and above the flow of Miltonic echoes and allusions, or the structural resemblances like Cibber's (or Theobald's) Pisgah-vision based on Adam's, or the clustered names of dunces like those of Milton's devils, thick as the leaves that strew bad books in Grubstreet—the *Dunciad* is a version of Milton's theme in being the story of an uncreating Logos. As the poem progresses, our sense of this increases through the calling in of more and more powerful associations by the epic vehicle. The activities of the dunces and of Dulness are more and more equated with religious anti-values, culminating in the passage on the Eucharist quoted earlier. The metaphor of the coronation of the king-dunce moves always closer to and then flows into the metaphor of the Day of the Lord, the descent of the anti-Messiah, the uncreating Word. Meantime, symbols which have formerly been ludicrous—insects, for instance, or sleep—are given by this expansion in the epic vehicle a more sombre cast. The dunces thicken and become less individual, more anonymous, expressive of blind inertia—bees in swarm, or locusts blackening the land. Sleep becomes tied up with its baser physical manifestations, with drunkenness, with deception, with ignorance, with neglect of obligation, and finally with death. This is the sleep which *is* death, we realize, a *Narren-dämmerung*, the twilight of the moral will. And yet, because of the ambivalence of the mock-heroic metaphor, Pope can keep to the end the tension between all these creatures as comic and ridiculous, and their destructive potentiality in being so. Certainly two of the finest puns in any poetry are those with which he continues to exploit this tension at the very end of the poem, when Dulness finally *yawns* and Nature *nods*.

[1] *A Preface to Paradise Lost* (1942), p. 93.

V

The purpose of this essay has been to supply a few, a very few, of the materials that are requisite for giving the phrase 'poetry of statement' specific content. I have tried to suggest that Pope is poetic, but not in the way that the Metaphysicals are poetic, even where he is most like them; that if the prominent metaphor is the distinctive item in their practice, this has been replaced in Pope's poetry partly by devices of greater compression, like allusion and pun, partly by devices that are more distributive, like irony and mock-heroic, and of course by a multitude of other elements—the net effect of all these being to submerge the multiplicities of poetic language just beneath the singleness of prose. Twenty-five years ago it would have been equally important to say that Pope is not poetic as the Romantics are poetic, for in this century there has always been a tendency to subsume him as far as possible under the reigning orthodoxy. It is true that in certain areas Pope's poetry faintly resembles that of the Romantics; in certain others, that of the line of wit. But the task of criticism for the future, when we are likely to be paying more and more attention to Pope as our own poetry moves in the direction suggested by Mr. Auden, and by Mr. Eliot in his *Quartets*, is not with Pope as a pre-Romantic or a post-Metaphysical, but as an Augustan poet whose peculiar accomplishment, however we may choose to rate it on the ultimate scale of values, was the successful fusion of some of the most antithetical features of verse and prose.

'A MASTER KEY TO POPERY'

JOHN BUTT

WHEN Pope's friend, the Earl of Burlington, died in 1753 he left his possessions to his daughter and sole heir, Charlotte Baroness Clifford, who was married to the fourth Duke of Devonshire. That is why the library at Chatsworth contains several letters from Pope to Lord and Lady Burlington. With these letters is the manuscript of a prose pamphlet, neatly transcribed in Lady Burlington's hand, entitled 'A Master Key to Popery', which I am permitted by the kindness of the Duke of Devonshire to print for the first time.

The manuscript bears no statement of authorship, nor is there any mention of this pamphlet in the Burlington papers. But Pope and the Burlingtons refer on several occasions to Lady Burlington transcribing Pope's compositions, and I have little doubt that this is one that she copied for him. It is very much in his manner.

There is only one other writer to whom the 'Master Key' could be attributed, and that is William Cleland, a friend of Pope, whose name is found in the *Dunciad Variorum* at the foot of 'A Letter to the Publisher', and who is credited by Pope with writing a letter 'to *J. G.* Esq;' in defence of the *Epistle to Burlington*, printed first in the *Daily Post-Boy* of 22 December 1731, reprinted in the *Daily Journal* the following day, and subsequently included by Pope in the collected edition of his *Letters* (1735). Except for this letter, Pope acknowledged the authorship of every other defence of his poem; and it seems probable that if he did not himself write this letter for Cleland's signature, he supplied Cleland, as he had already supplied him for the 'Letter to the Publisher' of the *Dunciad*, with the information to be used, and approved the defensive policy to be adopted. Similarly, if Cleland was the author of 'A Master Key to Popery', Pope must have told him who had attacked the poem in speech and in print and what they had said, and he must have directed the line of defence. He must have informed Cleland of the letter he had had from the Duke of Chandos[1]

---

[1] This letter was published by Professor Sherburn in ' "Timon's Villa" and Cannons' (*Huntington Library Bulletin*, no. 8, Oct. 1935, pp. 131–52), an article

saying that he did not take the character of Timon to himself (p. 55); and Cleland must have learned from Pope of Pope's friendship with the Vicar of Chiswick (p. 50), of his visits to Lord Burlington's neighbour at Chiswick (p. 49), and of his never having seen Walpole's place at Houghton (p. 55). In directing the defence, Pope must have ordered special attention to those points in the description of Timon's villa which did not correspond with what could be found at Canons, and he must have emphasized that Chandos's pictures were by Bellucci and Zeman and not by Verrio and Laguerre, a point which Pope himself made in a letter to Aaron Hill dated 5 February 1731/2. The distinction between composition and such detailed oversight is so slight that I feel justified in dropping the intermediary. I think that Pope wrote the 'Master Key' himself, and I feel the more confident in the attribution when I notice Pope anticipating the first use of his favourite *soubriquet* for Lord Hervey on page 46.

The *Epistle to Burlington* had appeared in print on or about 13 December 1731—it was advertised in the *Daily Post* as published that day. The earliest known attack in print appeared in Henley's *Hyp-Doctor* on 21 December; but although that was a mere eight days after the publication of the poem, other critics had already made enough noise to reach Pope's ears. On 21 December Pope wrote to Burlington from Twickenham saying that he had been confined at home for ten days by his mother's dangerous illness, and consequently he had 'never heard till two days since of a most Extravagant Censure wch they say ye whole Town passes upon ye Epistle I honourd myself in addressing to your L^{d}ship, as if it were intended to expose the D. of Chandos. Either the whole Town then, or I, have lost our Senses; for nothing is so evident . . . as that Character of Timon is collected from twenty different Absurditys & Improprietys: & was never ye Picture of any one Human Creature'. The following day Pope wrote to Hill in similar terms, denying that Timon was Chandos, and saying that it was but two days since he had heard of 'the uproar on this head'. 'Two days', if interpreted literally, would be enough

which covers some of the same ground as this article, and to which I am much indebted. I also wish to record my gratitude to Mr. Francis Thompson, the Duke of Devonshire's librarian, and to Dr. R. Wittkower, who have most generously advised me on a number of difficult points, and to Mr. Norman Ault and Mr. F. W. Bateson, who have made many useful suggestions.

for writing, or for briefing Cleland to write, the letter which appeared in the *Daily Post-Boy* on 22 December, but the interpretation would have to be more generous if that letter was written on 16 December, as stated in the *Daily Journal* the following day.

Who had made these attacks? Professor Sherburn suspected that 'the first outcry . . . must have been oral rather than printed, and it may have been voiced by persons of importance'. 'A Master Key', which he had not seen, amply supports his conjecture. Pope mentions that complaints had been raised by such 'honourable Persons as Lord Fanny [Hervey], Mr Dorimant [Dodington], the Lady De-la-Wit, the Countess of Methusalem, and others' as well as by Colley Cibber, 'Sr William Sweet-Lips' [Yonge], 'the Lady Knaves-acre', Moore, Concanen, Welsted, Mrs. Haywood, Henry K[else]y, Theobald, and Goode. Before the discovery of 'A Master Key', only Welsted had been certainly known to have attacked the *Epistle*,[1] though it has been suspected that Concanen was responsible for *A Miscellany of Taste*, published on 20 January 1731/2. The newspapers during that month advertised three other attacks, all of them anonymous: *Of Good Nature. An Epistle humbly inscrib'd to his G—ce the D—ke of C—s*, 'occasion'd by Mr P—'s impudent satire', and published on 22 January;[2] *Malice Defeated. A Pastoral Essay. Occasioned by Mr Pope's Character of Lord Timon, in his Epistle to the Earl of Burlington*, published on 27 January; and *A Letter to a Noble Lord, on the Conduct of Mr. Pope, in first defaming a Great Man, and next in abusing the Town for their Resentment of the Libel*, advertised for publication in the last week of January. I have not seen these attacks, but I suppose Pope had read them, as well as the attack in the *Whitehall Evening Post* (4 January), of which an extract appears in the *Gentleman's Magazine* (1732, ii. 555), and that he either knew or suspected the authors.

Pope does not state that all who had complained about his *Epistle* had written against it. Indeed he implies that several had only voiced their complaints—Welsted's 'considerable writings' seem to be distinguished from Kelsey's 'Discourses' on the subject (p. 47), Cibber had 'affirmed with Oaths' that Timon

---

[1] In *Of Dullness and Scandal*, addressed to the Duke of Chandos, and published on 3 Jan., and *Of False Fame*, published on 10 Feb.

[2] It is attributed to the Rev. John Cowper.

was Chandos (p. 52)—and in general looks upon himself as the printer of opinions 'propagated in all Conversations' and as 'but the Collector of . . . dispers'd Remarks'. 'A Master Key', in fact, was designed as a reply to gossip as well as to printed abuse. We know that many of those he mentions had attacked him before—there is no surprise in finding such gentlemen of the *Dunciad* mentioned as Moore, Concanen, Theobald, Welsted, and Goode—but the appearance of Hervey, Dodington, and Yonge in their company calls for some comment. I have attempted elsewhere to account for the prominence these men achieved in Pope's satire, but that account needs rewriting in the light of the 'Master Key'. It is now clear that rightly or wrongly Pope associated them with gossip about Timon. Their offences were amply revenged in the *Imitations of Horace*, the *Epistle to Dr. Arbuthnot*, and the *Epilogue to the Satires*.

When was 'A Master Key' written? Hill pointed out to Pope in a letter dated 23 December that the dissociation of Timon and Chandos in the *Daily Post-Boy* and the *Daily Journal* was not altogether convincing. The dissociation was not specific enough. When Pope replied to Hill on 5 February he produced a few more details to show how unlike Chandos Timon was, and the passage in his letter reads like a summary of the arguments used in the 'Master Key' (p. 53). If the 'Master Key' was written by 5 February 1731/2, it had only just been finished, for the references to Welsted's 'writings' suggests that Pope had heard about *Of False Fame*, advertised on 3 February, as well as the earlier *Of Dullness and Scandal*. It is unlikely that 'A Master Key' was written later than February 1731/2, since public interest in the subject was then no longer fresh.[1] The newspapers continued to advertise Welsted's attacks throughout February, but no fresh ones are mentioned. Perhaps Pope recognized that the clamour had died down, that the disclaimer he had printed with the third edition of his poem[2] was enough, and that the most favourable opportunity for publishing 'A Master Key' was already past.

[1] Mr. Ault has drawn my attention to two further attacks, *Mr. Taste, The Poetical Fop: or, the Modes of the Court. A Comedy* (advertised 8 April 1732) and *Ingratitude* (advertised 25 May 1733). These, however, provide no arguments for dating 'A Master Key' any later in the year. By the time *Ingratitude* was written, Tyers's plans for restoring Vauxhall Gardens (see p. 51) must have been widely known: clearly they were not known when 'A Master Key' was written.

[2] Published on 15 Jan. according to the *London Evening Post*.

A Master Key to Popery

or

A True and Perfect Key to Pope's Epistle to the Earl of Burlington

I have undertaken at the Request of Several Persons of Quality, the Explanation of a piece very loudly and justly complain'd of; or more properly a Dissection of the Bad Heart of the Author. It cannot be displeasing to any Man of Honour, to see the same Fair Opinions and good Reasons in *Print* which he has vented & pro- 5 pagated in all Conversations: It must be pleasing, to see here the *Proofs* of many Charges against him, which have hitherto been advanc'd without full demonstration: And it must be an additional Satisfaction to find him guilty of many *others*, which I shall prove, upon the *Same Principles*. 10

The Poet's Design is two-fold, to *affront* all the *Nobility* & *Gentry*, and to *Starve* all the *Artisans* & *Workmen* of this Kingdom. Under pretence of destroying the *Vanity* of the former, he aims to ruin the *Support* of the latter; and by rend'ring the Patrons discontented with all such works, put a Stop to the Arts, & obstruct the Circulation of 15 Money, in this Nation, to Send a begging the Industrious Mechanicks we have at home, & introduce Italians, Frenchmen, Papists & Foreigners, in their Stead.

I appeal to all my Superiors, if any thing can be more insolent than thus to Break (as I may say) into their Houses & Gardens, Not, 20 as the Noble Owners might expect, to *Admire*, but to *laugh* at them? or if any thing can be more Grating and vexatious, to a Great Peer or an Opulent Citizen, than to see a Work, of the expence of twenty or thirty thousand pounds, which he thought an Ornament to the Nation, appear only a Monument of his own Folly? Insolent 25 Scribler! that being unable to tax Men of their Rank & Worth with any Vice or Fault beside, is reduced to fall upon their *Taste* in those polite Expences & elegant Structures which are the Envy of all other Nations, and the Delight of our own! God forbid, it should hinder any of those Magnificent Persons, from enjoying their Noble 30 Fancies, & delighting in their own Works! May every Man *Sit peaceably Under his own Vine*, in his own Garden; May every *Man's House be his Castle*, not only against Thieves, but against *Ill Eyes* & Envious Observers; and may those who have succeeded the worst, meet with a better fate than to be at once *Ill-lodg'd* & 35 Ridiculed.

To avoid the imputation of any Envy against this Poet, I shall first confess that I think he has some Genius, and that it is *Only his Morals* that I attack.

But what seems very unaccountable is, that A Man of any *Genius* (which one wou'd think has its foundation in *Common Sense*) shou'd be the *Greatest Fool* in his age, & constantly choose for the Objects of 5 his Satire, the Best Friends he has? All the Noblemen whom we shall prove him to abuse in this Epistle are such, whose Esteem and Distinction he seem'd most to Court, & to possess; or whose Power and Influence cou'd best protect or credit him: Nay all the Criticks who have been most provok'd at it, are such, as either had been his 10 Friends or call'd themselves so, or had made some pretence to his Acquaintance or Correspondence.

It it [*sic*] to *some* of *these* that I am beholden for many In-lets into his *Meaning* & *Thoughts*: For a man's meanings & Thoughts lye too remote from any such, as cou'd make the discovery from *Private* 15 *Conversation*, or some degree of *Confidence*, or *Familiarity*. The Honour & Veracity of such I will not doubt: especially of so honourable Persons as Lord Fanny, Mr Dorimant, the Lady De-la-Wit, the Countess of Methusalem, & others.

I confess further, that I am in many instances, but the Collector 20 of the dispers'd Remarks of his Majesty's Poet Laureat, his Illustrious Associate Sr William Sweet-Lips, the Lady Knaves-acre & Mrs Haywood (those ornaments of their Sex) and Capt. Breval, and

1–2. *Only his Morals*] Pope was specially sensitive to attacks upon his morals. He told Hill (26 Jan. 1730–1) that he 'never thought any great matters of my poetical capacity; I only thought it a little better, comparatively, than that of some very mean writers, who are too proud. But, I do know certainly, my moral life is superior to that of most of the wits of these days.'

18. *Lord Fanny*] Pope's earliest use hitherto of this *soubriquet* for Lord Hervey ('Sporus') was *Imit. of Hor., Sat. II. i* (1733), l. 6.

Mr Dorimant] Probably George Bubb Dodington, see p. 54, ll. 10 ff. Pope mentions Dorimant again in *Imit. of Hor., Ep. I. i* (1738), l. 88. For Pope's subsequent use of Dodington as a type-figure, see *Imitations of Horace*, ed. J. Butt, 1939, pp. 112–14.

Lady De-la-Wit] The choice lies between Lady Mary Wortley Montagu, 'that dang'rous thing, a female wit' (manuscript variant of *Ep. to Arbuthnot*, l. 369), and Lady Delorain; see *Imitations of Horace*, ed. cit., p 365.

19. *The Countess of Methusalem*] I do not know which elderly peeress is meant.

21. *his Majesty's Poet Laureat*] Colley Cibber had been appointed to succeed Eusden fourteen months before this was written. Pope's grievances against him are dealt with by Professor Sutherland in his edition of the *Dunciad* (1943, p. 433), and by Mr. Ault in his *New Light on Pope*.

22. *Sr William Sweet-Lips*] Sir W. Yonge, a valued political supporter of Walpole. Pope derided his oratory in the *Epilogue to the Satires*, i. 68, but Dr. Johnson thought him the best speaker in the House of Commons (Boswell, *Life*, ed. Hill-Powell, ii. 161).   *the Lady Knaves-acre*] I do not know who is meant.

22–3. *Mrs Haywood*] Novelist, dramatist, and writer of scandalous memoirs. See *Dunciad*, ed. cit., p. 443.

23. *Capt. Breval*] One of the 'dunces'. See ibid., p. 430.

James Moore Esqr: and Mr Concanen, & Mr Welsted, and Henry
K—y Esqr of the two last of whom I ought in Justice to say, we owe
to the one the most *considerable writings*, & to the other the *Longest
Discourses* on this Subject.

My First Position is, that this Poet is a man of so *Bad a Heart*, as
to stand an Exception to the Rule of Macchiavel, who says 'No
Man, in any Nation, was ever Absolutely Wicked, *for nothing*.' Now
this Poet being so, it is fair to Suppose, that of *two* or *more* persons
whom he may be thought to abuse, we are always to understand it
of the Man he is *most oblig'd to*: but in such cases where his obligations
seem *equal*, we impartially suppose the Reflection on *both*. Secondly,
when so malevolent a man draws any character consisting of *many
Circumstances*, it must be apply'd, not to the person with whom *most*
but with whom *fewest* of those Circumstances agree: And this for
a plain reason, because it is a stronger mark of that Artifice &
Cowardice on the one hand, and of that Injustice & Malice on the
other, with which such a Writer abounds.

I am nevertheless so reasonable as not to insist as some Criticks
on this occasion have done, that when a Circumstance will not suit
with a Father, it shou'd be apply'd to a Son or Grandson, but I must
insist on my two former Positions, upon which depends all which
others have said, & which I shall say on this subject.

To begin with his Title, It was first, of *Taste*, Now 'tis of *false
Taste*, to the Earl of Burlington. Is this alteration made to impute
False Taste to that Earl? or out of unwillingness to allow that there
is any True Taste in the Kingdom?

Nothing is more certain, than that the Person first & principally
abus'd is the said Earl of Burlington. He cou'd not well abuse him
for *Want* of *Taste*, since the allowing it to him was the only Channel

1. *James Moore Esqr.*] Moore Smythe. His offence had been that he had refused
to remove some of Pope's verses from his play, *The Rival Modes* (1727), after Pope
had withdrawn permission to use them. See *Imitations of Horace*, ed. cit., p. 383, and
Dunciad, ed. cit., p. 455.

Concanen] Another 'dunce'. See ibid., p. 434.

Welsted] A poet and critic of some ability. Pope summarized the history of their
quarrel in a note to *Epistle to Arbuthnot*, l. 375.

2. *K—y*] Kelsey's reputation as a talker is recorded in the *Dunciad*, ed. cit., p. 147 f.
Nothing else is known of him; but since the *Dunciad* manuscript reads 'Kelsall' for
'Kelsey', he may be identical with Henry Kelsall, who was a Clerk to the Treasury.
See *Dunciad*, loc. cit.

23–4. *Of False Taste* was the title given, at Aaron Hill's suggestion, to the second
edition of the *Epistle to Burlington*. The poem, with that title, was advertised as
published 'this day' in the *London Evening Post* on 4–6 Jan. 1731–2.

27–8. *the Person . . . principally abus'd*] Cf. Pope to Burlington, 21 Dec. 1731: 'I hope
you are not abused too, because I meant just ye contrary; I can't tell, but I fancy
your L^dship is not so easy to be persuaded contrary to y^r senses, even tho ye whole
Town & Court too should require it.'

to convey his Malignity to others: But he abuses him for a *worse want*, the want of *Charity* (one from which his Lordship is as free as any man alive). This he tells him directly, without disguise, and in the second person,

> —What thy hard heart denies,   5
> Thy charitable Vanity supplies.

So much for Malice; now for ill-nature,

> Another age shall see the golden Ear
> Imbrown *thy* Slope, and nod on *thy* Parterre,
> Deep Harvest bury all *thy Pride* has plann'd,   10
> And laughing Ceres re-assume the Land.

That is, 'My Lord, your Gardens shall soon be Plow'd up, & turned into Corn-fields.'

How he indulges himself in drawing this picture? and with what joy does he afterwards expatiate upon the mortifying Consideration, 15 how all his Lordships labours in Architecture shall be lost, and his Models misapply'd by imitating Fools?

> —Reverse your Ornaments & hang them all
> On some patch'd Dog-hole &c

This is his Element! this his Pleasure! when he comes at last, with 20 much ado, to comend the Noble Lord, how spareing, how short, is he! The whole is but two lines,

> In you, my Lord, Taste Sanctifies Expence,
> For Splendour borrows all her rays from *Sense*.

which amounts just to this, 'My Lord, you are no Fool.' but this we 25 shall see by what follows, he thinks a great distinction for a Lord in these days.

> Oft' have you hinted to your Brother Peer—
> Something there is—'Tis Sense.—Good Sense.

A Hint does he call it? 'tis a very broad one, that there is a Want 30 of Sense in his Brother Peers, that is to say, in the whole House of Lords. Mr Concanen & Mr Theobald (both Lawyers) are of opinion, this may be prosecuted as Scandalum Magnatum on the whole Collective Body. From what we have observ'd of his Prophecy of the Destruction of Chiswick Gardens, it shou'd seem as if this 35 wretch alluded to his Lordships want of a *Male Heir*. If he had one, he had been probably treated like another of his *Friends*, the Lord

32. *both Lawyers*] Perhaps an allusion to Concanen's appointment, 30 Jan. 1731–2, as attorney-general of Jamaica. Theobald had been an attorney before abandoning the law for literature.

37–49. l, 1. *Lord Bathurst*] The friend whom Pope helped to lay out his grounds at Cirencester, and to whom he addressed *Of the Use of Riches* (the third *Moral Essay*).

Bathurst: whose noble Plantations at Cirencester he prophecy's with
like Malignity shall be destroy'd & lay'd levell by his Lordships *Son*;
for which no doubt, that ingenious and sober young Gentleman is
much oblig'd to him.

> Thro' his young Woods how pleas'd Sabinus stray'd,　　　　5
> Or sate delighted in the thick'ning Shade,
> With annual joy the red'ning shoots to greet,
> And see the stretching branches long to meet.
> His Son's fine Taste an op'ner Vista loves,
> Foe to the Dryads of his Fathers Groves;　　　　　　　10
> The thriving Plants ignoble Broomsticks made
> Now sweep those Allyes they were born to shade.

I wonder this piece of Malice has escap'd all the Criticks; and I
suspect it was to screen this Author, that his gentle Friend Lord
Fanny apply'd to this Nobleman the Character of Villario　　　15

> His bloomy Beds a waving Glow display,
> Blushing in bright Diversities of Day,
> With silver-quiv'ring Rills mæander'd o'er,
> —Enjoy them you! Villario can no more:
> Tir'd with the Scene Parterre & Fountains yield,　　　20
> He finds at last he better likes a Field.

For first, my Lord Bathurst is known to be of the most constant
temper in the world in all his Pleasures: Secondly, he never was a
Florist, is so much an Enemy to *nice Parterres*, that he never mows,
but grazes them, & thirdly, has no water at Cirencester to squander 25
away in Mæanders. I should rather think we are still at Chiswick,
abusing all my Ld Burlington's Friends & Neighbours. I know such
a Garden, which has an Out-let too into the *Fields*, where this
Nobleman sometimes takes the Air, the name of Villario shews him
to live near the Town; where Flowers & Parterres are most in 30
Vogue; & (which is more with me than all other circumstances)
where this very Author has been often receiv'd in a manner far
superiour to his deserts.

The Houses of these two Lords have escaped Abuse, for a plain
reason; neither of them wou'd be hurt by it—and the latter has by 35
good fortune some Works at present under the direction of the Earl
of Burlington.

23–4. *a Florist*] For Pope's contempt for florists, see *Dunciad*, iv. 403 ff.
27–8. *such a Garden*] Possibly the estate adjoining the Burlington estate at Chiswick.
It was bought in 1682 by Sir Stephen Fox, who built a house there on the site of the
present great conservatory of Chiswick House. Pope's acquaintance, Lord Wil-
mington, lived there from 1728 till 1743. See D. Lysons, *Environs of London* (1795),
ii. 209; W. Draper, *Chiswick* (1923), p. 87; *Imitations of Horace*, ed. cit., pp. 352 ff.
36. *some Works*] One of Burlington's drawings, dated 1732, for alterations in Wil-
mington's hall, was published by R. Wittkower in the *Archaeological Journal* (1947).

We have now done with Chiswick, a Soyl so fruitfull of Satyr for
the Poet, that I tremble for the *Reverend Vicar* of the *Parish*! not only
as he is his *Friend*, but as his eminent Learning, & particularly in the
Greek, must have made him sorely obnoxious to him.

Being arrived in Town, where should he begin but with the *Best,* 5
Good Man of the City, even the Father of the City, Sir Gilbert!

What brought Sr Shylocks ill-got wealth to waste!

There could not be invented a falser Slander, or one that would
more hurt this eminent Citizen, than to insinuate that he had *wasted
his wealth*. 'Tis true, I think as well as Sir Gilbert, that *every Expence is* 10
Some Waste: yet surely so small a sum, as ten pounds eleven shillings,
for Iron Rails to secure his Court-yard, ought never to have been thus
pointed out & insulted? But what means he by wealth ill-got?
neither Sir G nor I know of any such thing. This is as errant
nonsense as what follows— A *Wealthy Fool*. How can that be? 15
Wealth is the proof of Wisdom, & to say that Sir G—'s wealth is
wasted, is to say that his Parts are decay'd.

See Sportive Fate—Bids Babo build—

Here the Criticks differ. Some read, for Babo, Bubo. Others fix
this on a Peer who I confess is noble enough for our Authors abuse; 20
but (what I always take for a cause to doubt it) one to whom he has no
sort of Obligation. Tis certain Sh—d is this Nobleman's Builder,
but why should he satyrize Sh—d? Sh—d is none of his *Friends*. I am
persuaded that by Sh—d he means *Gibs* with whom he is acquainted.

The next we shall take notice of is the only Person he seems 25

2. *Vicar*] The Vicar of Chiswick at this time was Thomas Wood (1681–1732).
An epigram written in a copy of Evelyn's *Numismata*, given by Wood to Kent,
and attributed to Pope, appeared in the *Gentleman's Magazine* (1735). A slightly
different version was published in *Notes and Queries* (13 March 1851) and included
by Carruthers in his edition of Pope's poems:

> Tom Wood of Chiswick, deep divine,
> To painter Kent gave all this coin.
> 'Tis the first coin, I'm bold to say,
> That ever churchman gave to lay.

7. *Sr Shylock*] Later changed to 'Sir Visto'. Sir Gilbert was Sir Gilbert Heath-
cote, Lord Mayor of London, and one of the founders of the Bank of England.
Though reputed to be the richest commoner in England, he had a reputation for
parsimony. Pope mentions him again in *Moral Essays*, iii. 101, and *Imit. of Hor.*,
Ep. II, ii, l. 240.

20. *a Peer*] In *A Miscellany of Taste* Babo is identified with 'Lord C—d—n', i.e.,
presumably, Charles, second Baron Cadogan (1691–1776). I have not been able
to discover whether Cadogan employed Edward Shepherd [Sh—d] as a builder.
Shepherd, who died in 1747, built a house for the Duke of Chandos on the north
side of Cavendish Square about 1720. He had also been at work on the north side
of Grosvenor Square. See J. Summerson, *Georgian London* (1945), pp. 87, 92.

24. *Gibs*] James Gibbs (1682–1754), the architect of St. Martin's-in-the-Fields,
London, and the Radcliffe Camera, Oxford. Two letters from him to Pope survive.

willing to praise, & perhaps loves (if he loves anybody) the Lord
Cobham. Yet when he speaks of his Gardens or some other of his
L^dships personal performances (for I am not clear of which) what
a filthy stroke of smut has he bestowed upon him?

> Parts answ'ring Parts, shall slide into a *whole*   5

As if his L^dsps fine Gardens were to be just such another Scene of
Lewdness as Cupids Gardens or Faux-hall.—I ought not to suppress,
that I owe this Remark to a Right Honourable Lady.

Here we have a fling at honest Bridgeman. I don't wonder to see
his name at length, for he is his particular Acquaintance. What a 10
Malicious Representation of one who lives by his profession, as
taking pleasure to destroy and overflow Gentlemens fine Gardens!

> The vast Parterres a thous^d hands shall make
> Lo Bridgeman comes, & floats them with a Lake.

As if he should have the Impudence, when a Gentleman has done 15
a wrong thing at a great Expence, to come & pretend to make it a
right one? Is it not his business to please Gentlemen? to execute
Gentlemen's will and Pleasure, not his own? is he to set up his own
Conceits & Inventions against Gentlemen's fine Taste & Superiour
Genius? Yet is this what the Poet suggests, with intent (doubtless) to 20
take the Bread out of his mouth, & ruin his Wife & Family.

We come now to the Character (or rather Description) of Timon:
and it is in this I shall principally labour, as it has chiefly employ'd
the pains of all the Criticks. I shall enumerate the several opinions
of all others, & shew the Malice & Personal Reflection to extend 25
much farther than has hitherto been imagin'd by any. It is shewing
the Author great & undeserv'd Indulgence to confine it to any One,

1–2. *Lord Cobham*] The friend to whom Pope addressed the *Characters of Men* (the
first *Moral Essay*). His gardens at Stowe were laid out by Bridgeman in a manner
of which Pope highly approved.

7. *Cupids Gardens*] Cuper's Gardens, Lambeth. Cunningham and Wheatley,
Dictionary of London Topography, quote from the prologue to Mrs. Centlivre's *Busy
Body*:

> The Fleet Street sempstress, toast of Temple sparks,
> That runs spruce neckcloths for attorney's clerks,
> At Cupid's gardens will her hours regale,
> Sing 'fair Dorinda', and drink bottled ale.

The gardens were suppressed in 1753.

Faux-hall] An allusion to the New Spring Gardens, which had ceased to be a
resort of persons of quality. They were to enter a new period of splendour, as
Vauxhall Gardens, less than six months after 'A Master Key' was written, when
they were reopened under the management of Jonathan Tyers with a magnificent
ridotto, at which the Prince of Wales was present.

9. *Bridgeman*] The famous gardener who laid out the gardens at Stowe and the
royal gardens at Richmond and at Kensington Palace. He knew Pope and more than
once sought his advice.

tho' that one were the Best Man in the world: There are so many
By-peeps & squinting Glances, besides the main View, that instead
of twenty things being aim'd at one, every one Circumstance is
aim'd at twenty.

I must first take notice of the greatest Authorities which seem 5
against me, and great ones they are indeed, Sir William Sweet-lips
and Mʳ Dorimant. Equal Genius's! Equal Judges! every way equal
Ornaments to their Country! the Mecænas, & the Phoebus of our
Age! and to both of whom our Poet has been indebted for as great
Commendation & Praise as was consistent with their own Superio- 10
rity. In order to give due Weight to their several arguments, I must
take a View of Timon's character in all its Circumstances.

A Proud, haughty Man, with no other Idea of Greatness but
Bulk and Size, but himself a little contemptible Creature. His
House consists of Unequal Parts, heap'd one upon another like a 15
Quarry of Stones. His Gardens are choak'd up with Walls, every
where in sight, which destroy all Appearance of Natural Beauty.
The Form of his Plantation is stiffly regular, & the same repeated.
A vast Lake-fall to the North: an immense Parterre with two Small
Cupids in it: Trees cut into human figures, & statues as close as 20
Trees: his Fountains without Water: a Terras of Steep Slopes with
a Study opening upon it, where he receives his guests with the utmost
Affectation: his Books chosen for their Printers or Binders, no good
Modern Books, & (to make them perfectly a Show) the upper Shelves
only Wooden and painted ones. He has a Chappel, with Musick & 25
Painting in it, but the Musick consists of Jigs and loose Airs, and
the painting of indecent or naked figures. He gives Entertainments
attended by an hundred Servants, in a Hall paved with Marble;
his Bufet is ornamented with Serpents & Tritons; his Dinner is a
solemn, formal, troublesome thing, with perpetual rounds of Salvers 30
& Sweet wine, & upon the whole with so much Pride & affected
State, as to make every man Sick both of his Dinner & of Him.

This is the Character, which Mʳ Dorimant, Mʳ K—y, the Lord
Fanny, have imputed to the D. of C. This is what has been affirmed
with Oaths by Mʳ C—r and very publickly by Mʳ Theobalds, Mʳ 35
Goode, Mʳ James Moore, the whole Herd of Criticks, & all the
honourable Gentlemen of the Dunciad.

8. Yonge's claim to be the Phoebus of the age rests partly on some trifles in
verse and partly on some songs in the comic opera, *The Jovial Crew*, which had
recently been produced at Drury Lane. Dodington's pose as the Maecenas of the
age was assisted by Edward Young, amongst other writers, who dedicated his third
satire to him in 1726, and by Thomson, who dedicated *Summer* to him in 1727.

36. Barnham Goode (1674–1739), a master at Eton College and one of Walpole's
writers in the *Daily Courant*. Pope believed that 'sneering Goode, half malice and
half whim', had written a libel on him called *The Mock Æsop*. See *Dunciad*, ed. cit.,
p. 441.

I have the greatest temptation imaginable to wish this could be proved. Nothing would be so high an instance of this Man's Wickedness as to fix the worst-natured Satire on the best-natured Man; to tax with Pride the most Affable, with Vanity the most Charitable, with the worst Choice of Books one of the most Learned 5 of our Nobility, with the Pride of Prayer one of the sincerest Worshippers of God, and with ill-judged Extravagance one of the most hospitable and hearty Lovers of his Neighbour.

This would have been such a Pleasure to me, that I thought no pains too great to procure it; and therefore (out of my great Love 10 to Truth, & for the same reason that Pythagoras and Plato travel'd into Ægypt) I took a Journey to C—n—ns. I may venture to say, few Criticks have been at the trouble: & yet it is impossible to judge exactly of this Authors Spite & Malice, without being at the pains, both of knowing the place, & of reading the Poem. 15

I went first to the Chappel: I ask'd after the *Musick*; they told me there had been none for several years. I ask'd for the *Dean*, there was no such Man. I enquir'd for the *hundred servants*, there had been no such number. There was no *Silver Bell*; no Paintings of Verrio or La guerre, but of Bellucci or Zeman; no Study opening on a Terras, 20 but up one pair of stairs; no Books dated on the back or painted, and as many Modern as Ancient ones. In the Garden, no Walls crossing the eye, no large Parterre at all, no little Cupids, no Lake to the North, no cut Trees, no such Statues, no such Terras; in a word, no one Particular resembling: only what is common to all great 25 Men, there was a large House, a Garden, a Chappel, a Hall, and a Dinner.

I must declare Not One of these Circumstances to be True, which *so many Gentlemen have affirm'd upon their own Knowledge*. I am sensible of the Consequence of giving *Gentlemen* the LYE, but it is 30 ever held fair among *Criticks*, practis'd by the *most Learned* and both given & taken reputably by the best Authors.

Yet far be it from me to say, but in spite of the disagreement of All the Particulars, there may yet be Excellent Reasons for fixing the whole on the Duke. However it is but fair to report the Arguments 35 on all sides. Timon (says one) was a Man-Hater, ergo it is not the

2. Pope was not personally acquainted with the Duke of Chandos; but since Arbuthnot knew him well, Pope had ample opportunity of learning what sort of a man Chandos was and of acquiring the details about Canons which follow.

20. *Bellucci or Zeman*] Antonio Bellucci (1654–1726) was 'employed on the chapel of Canons', according to Horace Walpole (*Anecdotes of Painting*, ed. R. N. Wornum, London, 1888, ii. 283). Enoch Zeeman (d. 1744) was a portrait-painter. Cf. Pope to Hill, 5 Feb. 1731/2: '. . . many circumstances you have heard, as resemblances to the picture of Timon, are utterly inventions of liars; the number of servants never was a hundred, the paintings not of Verrio or Laguerre, but Bellucci and Zeeman; no such buffet, manner of reception at the study, terrace, &c.'

Duke. But Mr Moore replys very wittily, Timon lov'd Mankind *before* he hated them, he did not hate men till they had *abus'd* him, and the Duke may now with some cause, for he has been *very much abused*. Timon was famous for Extravagancies, the Duke for well-judg'd Bounties; but Peter W—rs Esq. argues thus. 'He that is 5 'bountifull: is not so rich as if he had never been bountifull: what-'ever a man parts with, he is so much the poorer for; & he that has 'but a hundred pounds less than he had, is in some decline of Fortune.' This he thinks a plain reason for any body to disesteem, or abuse a Man. And Mr Dorimant also thinks nothing so natural, as to 10 *Desert* or *fall upon* a *Great Man* on the *first suspicion* of his *Decline* of *Fortune*. But certainly every Man of Honour who is what another-guess Author than this, in another-guess Epistle than this, describes himself,

In Power a Servant, out of Power a Friend,   15

must feel the highest Indignation at such a practise. Indeed our Poets Enemies (and to such only I give Credit) have often severely lash'd him in sharp Satyrs & lively Ballads for the Contrary practise: for his adhering to some Folks in their Exile, to some in their disgrace, & others in their Imprisonment. And I do think there is 20 one good reason why he should rather attack a Man in Power, because it were a greater Object of his Envy, and a greater Proof of his Impudence.

Let us then hear Sir William (who thinks in this against the Majority, as he never sides with it, but on cogent reasons.) Why 25 (says he) for God's sake may not this be Sir Robert? are not his works as great as any man's? Who has more Groves nodding at Groves of his own plantation? I cannot say much as to his Chappel; but who has rival'd his Dinners? especially at the Time this Poem was publish'd, when he was splendidly entertaining the Duke of 30 Lorain? Has he not a Large Bufet? Has he not a hundred, nay near five hundred, Servants? (In power, your Servants) and who oftener drinks the King's Health? How convincing are all these

---

5. *Peter W—rs*] Peter Walter or Waters (1664?–1746), a moneylender, and a favourite butt in Pope's satire. See Pope's note to *Moral Essays*, iii. 20, and *Imitations of Horace*, ed. cit., p. 390.

15. *In Power a Servant*] From Dodington's *Epistle to . . . Sir Robert Walpole* (1726). Pope quotes it again in *Epistle to Satires*, ii. 161.

19. Pope had adhered to Atterbury in exile, to Bolingbroke in disgrace, and to Oxford in imprisonment. Cf. also *Imit. Hor., Sat. II. i*, l. 125 f.; *Epistle to Satires*, ii. 74 ff.; and the 'Epistle to Robert Earl of Oxford', prefixed to Parnell's poems.

26. *Sir Robert*] Walpole.

30–. Francis, Duke of Lorraine, later Emperor Francis I (1708–65) and husband of Maria Theresa, paid a much-publicized visit to England in the autumn of 1731. On Monday, 15 Nov., the *Daily Journal* reported that His Serene Highness had come to Town 'last Saturday' from Sir Robert Walpole's seat in Norfolk.

circumstances! I defy the Partizans of the other opinion to match them. And yet there is one which convinces me more than all; the Author never Saw Houghton: and how marvellously does it suit with his Impudence, to abuse the Things he never Saw?

But what principally inclines Sir William to this opinion is, that unless Sir Robert be abus'd here, he is not abus'd in the whole Poem, a thing which he thinks altogether Incredible. And I may add another reason which persuaded Mr Welsted (and doubtless will many others) that the Duke does not take this to himself, therefore it can do the Poet no hurt; unless we can fix it on another.

Furthermore, if (as some have suggested) this Malevolent Writer hates any man for Munificence to his Brethren, certainly Sir Robert of all Mankind must be the Man he hates. Tis true he never endeavour'd to obstruct that Munificence to any of them, but that is to be imputed to his Malice, as he thought those Distinctions would be no Credit to that great Minister.

Be it as it will, this Poet is equally happy when he can abuse either side. To shew his wicked Impartiality, at the same time he is squinting at Sir R. he has not spared his old Friend the Lord Bolingbroke.

A gaping Triton spews to wash y^r face,

is the exact Description of the bufet at Dawley. Nothing sure can equal the Impudence of such a Guest, except the Indifference of that stupid Lord, who they say is not provok'd at it. I doubt not the Honourable Mr Pulteney wou'd have had his share, but that he, poor Gentleman! has no Villa to abuse.

I return to my first Position. The Extent of this mans malice is beyond being confin'd to any One. Every Thrust of his Satyr, like the Sword of a Giant tranfixes four or five, and serves up spitted Lords and Gentlemen with less ceremony than Skew'r'd Larks at their own Tables.

I am very sure that all he says of the Chappel, its Painting & its Musick, is to be apply'd to his Grace the Duke of R—tl—d's at Be—ir-Castle. Why not to several other Lords who have Musick in their Chappels, unless Organs be no Musick?

I am as certain that what follows was to ridicule the Dignity & the Dinners, the Solemnity and the Salvers, the numerous attendants

9. The Duke of Chandos had admitted as much to Pope in a letter dated 27 Dec. 1731.

13. *Munificence*] Alluding, no doubt, to 'All men have their price', the notorious perversion of a remark of Walpole.

26. For Pope's relations with William Pulteney, see *Imitations of Horace*, ed. cit., p. 378.

& gaudy Sideboard, of a Nobleman (who to inhance the Ill-nature of the Satyr) has lay'd all his Vanities in the Grave. I mean the Companion in arms & Friend of the great Duke of Marleborough.

I know that the Building describ'd to be so huge, so like a Quarry, such a Heap, &c. is the Immortal Castle of Blenheim (to which the 5 Spite of a Papist may well be imagin'd) and I know my Lord F—th will be of my opinion. And possibly had not the Duke of Shrewsbury been once a Papist, he wou'd never have call'd it a *Quarry of Stone above-ground*: That well known saying of his fixes this to Blenheim.

Were it to be apply'd to a House and not a Castle, I should fancy 10 it must be to one in Dorsetshire of the same Architect; It would be like this Poets Injustice, to reflect on a Gentleman's Taste for a thing which he was oblig'd to build on another Man's scheme—But this Gentleman's Taste is since fully vindicated, by what has been built on his own Directions, that most Genteel Pile in Pall-Mall, which is 15 the Admiration of all Beholders.

No, the Greater the Object, the Stronger is his malice. Greatness itself is his Aversion; nay he hates Pride for being only the Shadow of Greatness. From National Works he would proceed to Royal, if he durst. Who but must have observ'd in this light that monstrous 20 Couplet?

—Proud Versailles! thy Glory falls,
And Nero's Terrasses desert their walls.

What an Impudent Reflection on the memory of Lewis the Fourteenth of France, and another Great Prince!　　　　25

I hope the Zeal which has been shewn hitherto only in general against this Poet, may soon operate farther when the Three Estates are assembled, and Proper Pains and Penalties be found to repress such Insolence.

1. *a Nobleman*] William, Earl of Cadogan (1672–1726), Marlborough's quarter-master-general in the war of the Spanish Succession. He had earned Pope's resentment for saying of Atterbury, imprisoned in the Tower, 'Fling him to the lions' (Spence, *Anecdotes*, ed. Singer, 1820, p. 156). Cadogan's vanity had been amply demonstrated at Marlborough's funeral (J. R. Sutherland, *Background to Queen Anne* (1939), p. 226 f.).

6. *Lord F—th*] Hugh Boscawen, Viscount Falmouth (1680?–1734), who had married Marlborough's niece.

8. *a Papist*] The Duke of Shrewsbury had been brought up a Roman Catholic, but had transferred his allegiance to the Church of England in 1679. For Pope's relations with him, see *Imitations of Horace*, ed. cit., p. 386.

11. *one in Dorsetshire*] Sir John Vanbrugh, the architect of Blenheim, had been employed by Dodington's uncle to rebuild the great house at Eastbury in 1718, and had been retained by Dodington when he inherited the estate in 1720. The work was not completed till 1738 (J. Hutchins, *Hist. Antiq. County of Dorset* (1868), iii. 456 f.).

15. *that most Genteel Pile in Pall-Mall*] 'Dodington's house in Pall Mall stood close to the garden the Prince [of Wales] had bought there of Lord Chesterfield' (Hervey, *Memoirs*, ed. Sedgwick (1931), p. 388).

After all, it would seem unfair not to own, there is something at the end of his Epistle which looks like a Complement to the King: But sure 'tis a very strange one! just to single out the Only Good & great things which his Majesty has *Not* done for his Subjects. His Majesty may do them yet; but so much as I wish the Publick Good, 5 I can hardly desire it should be just at the Time, when an Impertinent Poet prescribes it. No—may those Usefull and popular Works be first advised by such whose Office and Dignity it better agrees with, by Men less warp'd by Interest than he, less led by Party than he, less affected by Passion than he; in whom, the same suggestions, 10 wch in him are doubtless Dis-affection & Malice, may be look'd upon as Affection & Loyalty: And who (tho' the Things propos'd be the same) may yet be better heard, & therefore may better deserve the Thanks of the Publick.

FINIS   15

POPE'S 'EPISTLE TO HARLEY':
AN INTRODUCTION AND ANALYSIS

GEOFFREY TILLOTSON

I

To be a poet is, to begin with, a matter of being; from time to time being becomes doing, and the poet writes down a poem. There is the antecedent cause, the poet's general readiness to write poetry—as when Henry Taylor remarked that Tennyson was 'full of poetry with nothing to put it in' or when Keats foresaw that in writing *Endymion* he would have to 'make 4000 Lines of one bare circumstance and fill them with "Poetry".'[1] And there is the efficient cause, the occasion, as when, at last, Tennyson found his theme. Occasions vary in their importance for the writer and the reader. On the one hand, it is clear that there must have been an occasion for Keats's 'Ode to Melancholy', a decisive moment striking into the general poeticalness of Keats's life: 'No, no, go not to Lethe . . .' seems, indeed, to record its urgency.[2] But we may suppose that Keats was scarcely aware of it. If he was, he did not require any awareness of it from his reader. On the other hand, the occasion of 'On first looking into Chapman's Homer' dictated the very title of the poem. In that title Keats dated the poem ('On *first* looking') and localized it ('looking into' a particular copy of 'Chapman's Homer'). Some poems are better left undated and unlocalized. The poetry they contain is of the kind that seems more impressive from being left floating in a general poeticalness. Not being tied to any one place, it seems more widespreading, not to any one time, more lasting. We are more impressed by Keats's melancholy when we are left to think of it vaguely as chronic: if its opening cry suggests an occasion, we accept it as prepared by many turns before this last turn of the screw. Other poems, it is equally true, need to be seen as being occasional. If Keats had agreed that poetry is emotion

[1] *Letters of John Keats*, ed. M. B. Forman (ed. 1947), p. 52.
[2] The urgency, rather, of its second moment: what is now the first stanza was originally preceded by another, now cancelled.

recollected in tranquillity, he might have left the experience on first looking into Chapman's Homer to mature unexpressed until the time came, if it ever came, when he wrote generally of the realms of gold. But we know that he could not have borne postponement any more than Wordsworth could: we know that the poem was commanded into being by the voice of Chapman, speaking out loud and bold. The occasion was sacred, as sacred as the emotion it aroused.

If a poet does mark the occasion of a poem, this means that for some reason he wants the poem kept close to the practical world. With the result that we lack his permission to treat it as the sort of poem made out of or aspiring towards what is called 'pure poetry'. 'On looking into Chapman's Homer', though it may tempt the purists, cannot be so treated. It must be kept in its place in the career of Keats. Even if that poem were not one of Keats's best, it would still be greatly valued for being a poem greatly placed in a great career. In saying this I am, of course, speaking of an organism as if it were a machine, and, worse, as if the machine had its parts loose: ultimately we cannot divide the man either from his poems or from his career. Some part of our minds is aware of Keats the man even when we are reading the 'Ode to Melancholy'. We should read it differently if it were by Browning. And if somebody were to retort that Browning could not have written it, that is another way of saying that Keats did. It seems to be according to human nature that people prefer to tie down the poems they like to time and place, or certainly to place—time is more difficult to handle: place, even if its particulars change, remains generally extant, whereas any one time becomes increasingly buried. Even though the evidence is much against Gray's having 'wrote' the *Elegy*, or any part of it, in the 'country churchyard' of Stoke Poges, people, who possess no sense of time but who do possess a sense of place, insist that he did. We cannot rule out this evidence on the ground that Stoke Poges is only honoured by readers who do not greatly care for poetry even when it is so obviously rich as that of the *Elegy*. In *Rasselas* Imlac notes that piety may be improved on a pilgrimage; and it is possible that at Canterbury, if not on the way there, the Wife of Bath improved hers as well as did the Parson. A reading of the *Elegy*—if the pilgrim qualifies for consideration by reading it at all—will probably be more vivid for a visit to a haunt of the poet. However poetical, readers of poetry cannot but remain human beings, and human beings (in the 'civilized' world, at least) have always been interested in careers, and especially in the great careers of great men. And when it comes to a poem that is declared occasional, the reader has his practical instinct already provided for. He does not need either to seek or to invent the particulars. He has his time and place fixed for him. If we are vaguely aware of Keats the man when reading the 'Ode to Melancholy', we are more particularly aware of him when reading 'On first looking into Chapman's Homer'. When a poem is declared to be occasional, we can only call ourselves readers of it if we recover as much of its occasion as we can.

II

During the eighteenth century, as everybody knows, there was too much writing-up of occasions. Innumerable 'copies of verses' 'on' this or that event printed in innumerable volumes called *Poems on Several Occasions* were firmly linked to the practical life. Human beings are so constituted that they respect the evidence of practical life whenever they meet it, but there is little to respect in most of the poems which were linked with it in the eighteenth century. We rarely condemn even trivial occasions as having been too trivial; nor do we condemn their celebration by means of verses; what we condemn is the pride that seeks the printer. When we do not condemn the printing, this means that the poems to some extent remain what Pope called 'living Lays'. And when we choose to turn back to such living occasional poems, it follows that we must attend not only to their words but to their occasion, their practical historical context. To take an instance. Dr. Delany wrote 'Verses left with a Silver Standish, on the Dean of St. Patrick's Desk, on his Birth-day', and Swift a poem in reply. Surveying Swift's achievement as a poet, Delany complimented him on his 'living Lines', and though Delany has no comparable power of vivification, his own poem is vivified a little. In 1949 it still has enough to it to interest, say, twenty readers (was not Swift always avid for statistics?). One of those twenty, a research student burrowing towards his doctorate, may read the poem because he is interested in Delany. A few others of those twenty read it because they are interested in Swift, and so in Delany, and so in every scrap of them that survives. The rest of the score read it because of an interest in English poetry of the eighteenth century, or in English poetry, or in poetry of all times and places. But if they look at the poem at all, their interest must be dubbed—of all avoided terms—'academic', unless they learn what sort of a thing a standish was, and what was its status as a gift in the mid-eighteenth century. It will not prove possible for them to achieve ocular possession of the bright particular standish that Swift found on his desk, though that for most of them would be a further help: 'the Shape you see', the poem had said, pointing at the actual thing. But Delany was practical enough, when he, or another,[1] published the poem, to be aware of this inevitable deficiency, and to see that he had made allowances for it. The twenty readers must, at any rate, have 'some' acquaintance with a standish. And I do not see that this requirement can be disputed as necessary for anyone setting up as a critic of the poem. And if this be granted, it follows that the usefulness of the historical knowledge increases in proportion as the poetry it illuminates increases in quality. After we have learned what a 1732 standish amounted to, we see more clearly what lay in these poems of Delany and Swift; but the knowledge stands us in still better stead when we read a better poem on a similar occasion, when we read Pope's 'On receiving from the Right Honourable the Lady Frances Shirley, a Standish and two Pens'.

The poem that is the subject of the present discussion is another of Pope's occasional poems. His occasion is august, and he exhibits it with a proper pride. It is fixed firmly in a context of history: of political history—Harley had been a great politician; in a context of literary history—manuals of it find a place for Parnell as well as for Pope and Swift; in a context of polite society—the poem is an epistle. If Parnell did not speak out loud and bold, the occasion and Pope did.

[1] We do not know who was responsible for the publication of both poems in the *Gentleman's Magazine* two months after presentation. Perhaps the agent was Lord Orrery, who joined Delany with a poem and gift of his own, and who, as other evidence suggests, 'took pride in [his poem]' (see *Poems of . . . Swift*, ed. H. Williams (1937), p. 609).

III

When concluding his notes to the *Iliad*, Pope thanked his assistants, one of whom had been Thomas Parnell:

I must end these Notes by discharging my Duty to two of my Friends, which is the more an indispensable piece of Justice, as the one of them is since dead: The Merit of their Kindness to me will appear infinitely the greater, as the Task they undertook was in its own nature of much more Labour, than either Pleasure or Reputation. The larger part of the Extracts from *Eustathius*, together with several excellent Observations were sent me by Mr. *Broome:* And the whole Essay upon *Homer* was written upon such Memoirs as I had collected, by the late Dr. *Parnell*, Archdeacon of *Clogher* in *Ireland:* How very much that Gentleman's Friendship prevail'd over his Genius, in detaining a Writer of his Spirit in the Drudgery of removing the Rubbish of past Pedants, will soon appear to the World, when they shall see those beautiful Pieces of Poetry the Publication[1] of which he left to my Charge, almost with his dying Breath.

This note was dated 25 March 1720, and the publication of the volume of the *Iliad* containing it followed on 12 May. Parnell had died some eighteen months earlier, in October 1718. The two poets had been close friends, and in the December of that year Pope told a friend that Parnell's death 'was . . . much in my mind', and that

to [his] memory I am erecting the best monument I can. What he gave me to publish, was but a small part of what he left behind him; but it was the best, and I will not make it worse by enlarging it.[2]

While preparing the monument Pope must have taken seriously the commission which, early in 1719, Swift conveyed to him through Charles Ford:

I think Pope should bestow a few Verses on his friend Parnels memory, especially if it is intended (as I think I have heard,) that some of Parnels scattered Things are to be published together.[3]

---

[1] Pope, as Professor Griffith has said, was the best business man among the English poets. Here he is giving his projected volume a puff of 'advance publicity'. But if he is encouraging readers, he is not deceiving them: the poems were indeed 'beautiful', and are so still.

[2] *The Works of Alexander Pope*, ed. Elwin and Courthope (1872), viii. 28.

[3] *Letters of Jonathan Swift to Charles Ford*, ed. D. Nichol Smith (1935), p. 74.

By 25 September 1721 the poem was written, though not finally. It took the form of a dedication to Robert Harley,[1] to whom on 21 October Pope sent a unique fair copy along with the body of his book.[2] The packet contained this letter:

> From my Ld Harley's in Dover Street
> Octob 21. 1721.

My Lord,

Your Lordship may be surpriz'd at the liberty I take in writing to you; tho you will allow me always to remember, that you once permitted me that honour, in conjunction with some others who better deserv'd it.[3] Yet I hope, you will not wonder I am still desirous to have you think me your gratefull & faithful Servant; but I own I have an Ambition yet farther, to have Others think me so; which is the Occasion I give your Lordship the trouble of this. Poor Parnell, before he dyed, left me the charge of publishing these few Remains of his: I have a strong Desire to make Them, their Author, and their Publisher, more considerable, by addressing & dedicating 'em All, to You. There is a pleasure in bearing Testimony to Truth; and a Vanity perhaps, which at least is as excusable as any Vanity can be. I beg you, My Lord, to allow me to gratify it, in prefixing this paper of honest Verses to the Book. I send the Book itself, which I dare say you'l receive more Satisfaction in perusing, than you can from any thing written upon the Subject of yourself. Therfore I am a good deal in doubt, whether you will care for such an addition to it? I'll only say for it, that 'tis the only Dedication I ever writ, & shall be whether you permit it or not: For I will not bow the knee to a Less Man than my Lord Oxford, & I expect to see no Greater in my Time.

After all, if your Lordship will tell my Lord Harley that I must

---

[1] For the sake of uniformity I call him throughout by his family name.

[2] Pope sent Harley the text of the volume. It was quite convenient to do this since the text was contained in a series of complete gatherings, namely, B–P^8. I assume that after receiving Harley's permission to print the dedication, that is, soon after 6 Nov., the date of his reply, Pope revised it, designed the preliminaries, and had them printed on Sheet A. The book was published on 7 Dec., though it bears the date 1722. The contents of the preliminaries are as follows: A1^r, title-page in black and red:

POEMS | ON | Several Occasions. | — | Written by | Dr. *THOMAS PARNELL,* | Late Arch-Deacon of *Clogher:* | AND | *Published by Mr.* POPE. | — | *Dignum laude Virum Musa vetat mori.* HOR. | = | *LONDON:* | Printed for B. LINTOT, at the *Cross-Keys,* between | the *Temple Gates* in *Fleet-street,* 1722.

A1^v, blank, A2^r–A3^v, Pope's dedicatory poem, signed '*Sept.* 25. 1721. *A.* POPE.', catchword 'HESIOD'; A4^r, title for the first poem of Parnell's, 'Hesiod: or, the Rise of Women.'; A4^v, blank.

[3] Pope refers to joint communications from members of the Scriblerus Club.

not do this, you may depend upon a total Suppression of these Verses (the only Copy whereof I send you). But you never shall suppress that Great, sincere, & entire, Admiration & Respect, with which I am always | My Lord, | Your most faithful, most o- | bedient, & most humble Servant, | A. Pope.

To which Harley replied:

Brampton-Castle, Nov. 6. 1721.

S.^r

I received your Packet by the Carrier, which could not but give me great Pleasure, to see you preserve an Old Friend in Memory: for it must needs be very agreable to be Remembred by those we highly Value. But then, how much Shame did it cause me! When I read your fine Verses inclos'd, my Mind reproach'd me how far short I came of what your great Friendship & delicate Pen would partially describe me. You ask my Consent to Publish it; to what Streights doth This reduce me! I look back, indeed, to those Evenings I have usefully & pleasantly spent with Mr Pope, Mr Parnel, Dean Swift, the Doctor,[1] &c. I should be glad the World knew you admitted me to your Friendship: and, since your Affection is too hard for your Judgement, I am contented to let the World see, how well Mr Pope can write upon a barren Subject. I return you an exact Copy of the Verses, that I may keep the Original, as a Testimony of the Only Error you have been guilty of. I hope very speedily to Embrace you in London, and to assure you of the particular Esteem & Friendship wherewith I am | S.^r | Your most faithful | & most humble Servant | Oxford.

I keep the Printed Paper, because I think | you have more of them.[2]

Here is the text of the dedication as Pope printed it (pp. 65–7):[3]

---

[1] Dr. Arbuthnot.

[2] I print the text of these two letters by kind permission of the Marquess of Bath. I owe my text of them to the kindness of Professor Sherburn.

[3] The text of the poem as Harley received it in manuscript is as follows (pp. 65–7):

TO THE
Right Honourable,
ROBERT,
Earl of *OXFORD*
AND
Earl MORTIMER.

SUCH were the Notes, thy once-lov'd Poet
   sung,
'Till Death untimely stop'd his tuneful Tongue.
Oh just beheld, and lost! admir'd, and mourn'd!
With softest Manners, gentlest Arts, adorn'd!
Blest in each Science, blest in ev'ry Strain!   [5]
Dear to the Muse, to HARLEY dear—in vain!
  For him, thou oft hast bid the World attend,
Fond to forget the Statesman in the Friend;
For *Swift* and him, despis'd the Farce of State,
The sober Follies of the Wise and Great;   [10]
Dextrous, the craving, fawning Crowd to quit,
And pleas'd to 'scape from Flattery to Wit.
  Absent or dead, still let a Friend be dear,
(A Sigh the Absent claims, the Dead a Tear)

To the Right Honourable,
Robert Earl of Oxford & Earl Mortimer

Such were the Notes thy once lov'd Poet sung,
When Death untimely stop'd his tuneful Tongue.
Oh just beheld, and lost! admird, and mourn'd!
With softest manners, gentlest arts adorn'd!
Blest in each Science, blest in evry Strain!   [5]
Dear to the Muse, to Harley dear—in vain!
  For him, thou oft hast bid the World attend,
Fond to forget the Statesman in the Friend;
For Swift and him, despis'd the Farce of State,
The sober Follies of the Wise and Great;   [10]
Dextrous, the craving, fawning Crowd to quit,
And pleas'd escape from Flattery to Wit.
  Absent, or dead, let either Friend be dear,
(A Sigh the Absent claims, the Dead a Tear)

Recall those Nights that clos'd thy toilsom Days,   [15]
Still hear thy *Parnell* in his living Lays:
Who careless, now, of Int'rest, Fame, or Fate,
Perhaps forgets that OXFORD e'er was Great;
Or deeming meanest what we greatest call,
Beholds thee glorious only in thy Fall.   [20]
   And sure if ought below the Seats Divine
Can touch Immortals, 'tis a Soul like thine:
A Soul supreme, in each hard Instance try'd,
Above all Pain, all Anger, and all Pride,
The Rage of Pow'r, the Blast of publick Breath,   [25]
The Lust of Lucre, and the Dread of Death.
   In vain to Desarts thy Retreat is made;
The Muse attends thee to the silent Shade:
'Tis hers, the brave Man's latest Steps to trace,
Re-judge his Acts, and dignify Disgrace.   [30]
When Int'rest calls off all her sneaking Train,
When all th' Oblig'd desert, and all the Vain;
She waits, or to the Scaffold, or the Cell,
When the last ling'ring Friend has bid farewel.
Ev'n now she shades thy Evening Walk with Bays,   [35]
(No Hireling she, no Prostitute to Praise)
Ev'n now, observant of the parting Ray,

Still think on those gay Nights of toilsome Days,   [15]
Still hear thy Parnell in his living Lays;
Who careless now of Int'rest, Fame, or Fate,
Perhaps forgets that Oxford e'er was Great;
Or deeming meanest what we greatest call,
Beholds thee glorious only in thy Fall.   [20]
   Yet sure, if ought below the Seats divine
Can touch Immortals, 'tis a Soul like thine:
A Soul supream, in each hard Instance try'd,
Above all Pain, all Anger, and all Pride,
The Rage of Pow'r, the Blast of publick Breath,   [25]
The Lust of Lucre, and the Dread of Death.
   In vain to Desarts thy Retreat is made;
Fame, and the Muse, pursue thee to the Shade.
'Tis theirs, the Brave man's latest steps to trace,
Re-judge his Acts, and dignify Disgrace,   [30]
Wait, to the Scaffold, or the silent Cell,
When the last lingring Friend has bid farewell.
Tho' In'trest calls off all her sneaking Train,
Tho' next the Servile drop thee, next the Vain,
Tho distanc't one by one th' Oblig'd desert,   [35]
And ev'n the Grateful are but last to part;
My Muse attending strews thy path with Bays,
(A Virgin Muse, not prostitute to praise),
She still with pleasure eyes thy Evening Ray,

Eyes the calm Sun-set of thy Various Day,
Thro' Fortune's Cloud One truly Great can see,
Nor fears to tell, that MORTIMER is He.   [40]

A. POPE.

Sept. 25.
1721.

The calmer Sunsett of thy Various Day;   [40]
One truly Great thro' Fortune's Cloud can see,
And dares to tell, that Mortimer is He.

A. Pope.[1]

We know from his letter what Harley thought of the poem,
even in its inferior penultimate form. We can only infer what
Swift thought. But we may infer with confidence his deep grati-
fication. He had suggested something perhaps like Dryden's
'To the Memory of Mr. Oldham', but here was a poem swelling
beyond Parnell to his circle the Scriblerus Club, and to one of
its greatest literary figures, Swift, and to its great public figure,
Swift's hero, to whom it was dedicated. The original suggestion
was overwhelmed, and with Pope's finest poetry, the only poetry
not translation which, during 1721 and longer, he seems to
have allowed himself to write.

IV

It was Pope's practice to crowd even shorter poems with as
much matter as possible, and that of different sorts. He therefore planned these shorter pieces with an Ovidian care. Such
care was particularly necessary when the poem was short: a
short poem of bits and pieces must offer those bits and pieces
neatly packed. A poet, Horace had counselled, must use art,
but art that hides itself. But from whom? The art that is
beyond the discovery of the attentive reader is the art that
is part and parcel of the 'inspired' thought, and that is the
result of a poet's mind habituated to want to produce certain
effects. There was art in the making of

eyes thy Evening Ray,
The calmer Sunsett of thy Various Day

and in the re-making of it into:

Eyes the calm Sun-set of thy Various Day.

[1] This manuscript is the property of the Marquess of Bath, with whose permission its text is here printed. Mr. Ault printed the last ten lines in his *New Light
on Pope*, 1949, p. 23.

There was art here, or, to begin with, the needs of the metre would not have been met; and better art in the revision. But we cannot explain it. The finger can touch it a little more certainly when we find that

> Above all Pain, all Anger, and all Pride

becomes, when reprinted in the *Works* of 1735 (where the Epistle is given pride of place)

> Above all Pain, all Passion, and all Pride.

But though surer, our explanation is not more than superficial. When, however, we turn from the clauses and phrases of the poem to its structure, we meet an art which is more readily tangible. An argument has a course: we may be able to discuss sequence and relationship when we cannot discuss the nature of what it is that is sequential or related. How much, then, can we say of the sequence and relationships of Pope's poem?

I have suggested that when Swift proposed that Pope should write the 'few Verses', he had in mind those few of Dryden's on the death of Oldham; and there can be no doubt that at some point, or points, Pope had. The occasion was similar: the great poet mourning the untimely loss of the smaller poet who had become his friend. Certainly Pope echoed Dryden's poem, both echoing Virgil.[1] But, as we might expect, Pope compresses Dryden's poem into 'few Verses' indeed:

> Such were the Notes,[2] thy once-lov'd Poet sung,
> 'Till Death untimely stop'd his tuneful Tongue.

[1] Cf. with Pope's
> Oh just beheld, and lost! admir'd, and mourn'd!

Dryden's
> Farewell, too little and too lately known.

Both recall Virgil's lines on Marcellus, *Æneid,* vi. 870 f.:
> Ostendent terris hunc tantum fata nec ultra
> Esse sinent. . . .

which Dryden had translated with
> This Youth (the blissful Vision of a day)
> Shall just be shown on Earth, and snatch'd away.

Dryden had also referred to Oldham as Marcellus:
> Once more, hail, and farewell! farewell, thou young,
> But ah! too short, *Marcellus* of our Tongue.

[2] 'Such . . .': Pope was publishing only a selection from the pieces Parnell left him, that made in the first place by Parnell (see p. 62 above). The rest that were in his possession Pope kept by him till his death, when Spence pleaded in vain against their destruction. Some, or all, of these poems existed in one or more other

Oh just beheld, and lost! admir'd, and mourn'd!
With softest Manners, gentlest Arts, adorn'd!
Blest in each Science,[1] blest in ev'ry Strain![2]
Dear to the Muse . . .
. . . the Dead [claim] a Tear . . .
. . . *Parnell* in his living Lays.

Parnell has to rest content with these few lines and snatches. But even of these he is not the sole tenant. Pope's poem is not an elegy (in the sense of 'a few Verses on his friend Parnels memory'): it is an epistle. Unlike an epitaph, an elegy is a poem expressing a relationship, that between the dead and the surviving friend; and usually the surviving friend is the author. But to include an elegy in an epistle is to introduce a further relationship, that between the author and the recipient.

The presence of the recipient removes Pope's poem farther from Dryden's. Moreover, Pope removes himself from his poem as much as he can. Dryden had used the 'I' boldly: Pope hides himself behind 'the Muse'. Though we *feel* that it is he who is speaking, we *see* him speaking of others. It is a nice point to his credit as a man. Of course Pope signs the poem. But that is not to be inside it. Dr. Johnson deprecated those personal poems that did not introduce the person(s) by name in the body of the poem.[3] To be named in a poem was a chance of immortality highly esteemed. Pope withdraws in favour of his three friends. And also in favour of poetry, since 'the Muse' suggests that poetry is rather the work of an impersonal agent, an agent acting from the days of Homer downwards, than the work of this or that man. Pope's withdrawal is also in favour of friendship, since it suggests that, unlike poetry, friendship is dependent on men, a thing men are proud to have achieved of themselves. The withdrawal of the author from his poem—he exists suggested as a person only in his extraneous signature—united the dead and the recipient without his agency, as it were over his head.

The relationship between Parnell and Harley is stated at

copies, and were printed later in the century (see the bibliography in G. A. Aitken's edition, 1894, p. lxviii f.). These posthumous poems did not add to Parnell's fame, which was high until well into the nineteenth century. Some of them had been printed during his lifetime.

[1] That is, 'subject' of knowledge.
[2] Pope is complimenting Parnell on the variety of metres used in his poems.
[3] *Lives of the Poets*, ed. G. B. Hill (1905), i. 35 f. and iii. 257.

once. Harley, whose name and title had been emblazoned at the head of the poem in large capitals, intrudes even into the few lines that are all that Parnell is allowed. Parnell is 'thy' poet;[1] he has been 'beheld' and 'admir'd' by Harley, and is now 'lost' and 'mourn'd' by him. But so far, at least, the relationship has been fairly level: if Harley has his capitals and his pervasiveness, Parnell has his concise, warm, bright praise. The first paragraph ends, however, with the balance tilted in favour of Harley:

> . . . to HARLEY dear—in vain!

(At the moment I am not concerned with the significance of the typography.)

The bright Parnell is already diminished, but he persists farther into the poem, even as far as into its third paragraph. In the second, however, he suffers an almost total eclipse. His relationship with Harley, which is given its concisest expression in 'him, thou', dims beside a new relationship, that between Harley and another survivor, Swift, whom Pope signalizes as greater than Parnell simply by the place he gives his name in the line and the place of the line in the paragraph:

> For him, . . .
> For *Swift* and him, . . .

(Again, I am not yet concerned with the significance of the typography.) The Parnell–Harley relationship persists into the third paragraph in 'Absent or dead', Swift being the absent friend, Parnell the dead—Swift had last seen Harley just before his fall in 1714. (The transition between these paragraphs is as firm as any in Pope: 'Absent or dead' quietly carried Swift and Parnell over the second chasm, just as the 'For him' had quietly carried over the first all that had been so far said of Parnell.) In those three words, however, the Parnell–Swift and the Swift–Harley relationships cease, survived by that between Harley and Parnell, which suddenly blazes to its height. Even Parnell, now on his last appearance, has a flash of splendour, as the author of 'Lays' which are 'living' (Pope had put on his title-page the words from Horace, 'Dignum laude virum Musa vetat

---

[1] The affixing of the possessive pronoun to the proper name indicates, expecially since the name is that of a poet, that a precious thing is being treasured against the possible attacks of barbarians. Milton had showed the power of the possessive in 'What needs my Shakespeare for his honour'd bones.'

mori'). But he never gets clear of Harley: even his immortal soul is still related to him; 'careless now' he 'Perhaps forgets'—what? Matters of concern to the practical world, and some matters perhaps still of concern to a spirit, 'Int'rest, Fame, or Fate', but also something particular about Harley, 'that OXFORD e'er was Great'. What he 'beholds' is again something particular about Harley, Harley 'glorious in thy Fall'. If Parnell persists vividly, still it is as the weaker end of a relationship. And at this point even that uneven relationship, as a thing receiving expression, ceases. The final dismissal of Parnell is done gradually in 'if ought below the Seats Divine Can touch Immortals': Parnell fades into the general shining crowd of the dead. And now Harley is free to occupy the rest of the poem, a great person followed, observed, and proclaimed by 'The Muse', who speaks with more authority than Pope of himself could, and who speaks with a startling honesty:

(No Hireling she, no Prostitute to Praise)

'Nor fears to tell' what it is she sees: 'A Soul supreme', 'One truly Great'.

Harley's greatness is even attested by means of a change in the quality of the transitions between the paragraphs of the poem. The first two were presented as coming within the poet's control, so to speak, as a discernible part of his plan, of the logic of his procedure. Their force lay in their deliberate rightness. The third is a transition that is more like a boiling-over than an arrangement. Even the transitions of arrangement had been lovingly done: 'For him . . . . Absent or dead' were transitions charged with feeling. But the feeling rises when the third transition, instead of controlling feeling, is overborne by it. The emotion of the poem by now is rising sharply. 'Such *were* the Notes, thy *once*-lov'd Poet sung': the beautiful poems were first seen as things belonging to the past. Now they are alive again, are 'hear[d]'[1] and 'living Lays', just as their dead author is still alive, though 'careless now' of worldly matters, unless—and here is the passionate transition—he still, a soul himself, remembers Harley's soul, a soul so supreme that, if anything is recalled by the careless, living dead, ''tis a Soul', anybody's if 'like thine'.

[1] Pope may be recalling a practice of reading verses aloud favoured by Harley (see *Journal to Stella*, ed. H. Williams [1948], p. 145 f.).

Between the last two paragraphs the force of the transition is quiet. It is still a transition affecting the emotions: the urgency of the 'And sure' is past, and quiet emotion simmers in its 'In vain', words heavy for Pope's first readers with the *nequiquams* of the Roman poets. But though 'made of' emotion, the transition is one of arrangement. The first two words of the last paragraph repeat the last two of the first:

> . . . in vain! . . .
> In vain . . . .

They are beautifully in place. Their quietness is also necessary to separate the preceding climax from that with which the poem closes.

V

The plan of the poem is also observable in its words taken as units, even in its typography.

Look first at its use of the word 'great'. The first appearance of this word is when Pope, not content with dubbing public affairs a 'Farce', also dubs them

> The sober Follies of the Wise and Great.

In such a context 'Great' means no more than 'highly placed'. At meetings of the Scriblerus Club, so potent was the charm of Swift's irony that statesmanship appeared temporarily as no fit work for the wise: when you did get an odd case, such as Harley's, of a man not only 'great' but wise, then his political duties seemed one of his comical weaknesses, perhaps disguised from himself, as from the public, by its soberness.[1] On its second and third appearances in the poem, the word 'great' has the same meaning: Parnell, now among the immortals,

> Perhaps forgets that OXFORD e'er was Great;
> Or deeming meanest what we greatest call,
> Beholds thee glorious only in thy Fall.

---

[1] Pope's meaning was missed by Gilbert Wakefield: 'There seems to my judgement an incongruity in this association of characters. Should [Pope] not have written,

> The sober follies of the *proud* and great?

no otherwise distinguishable from the *freaks* of *Bedlamites*, than as acted by men not literally frantic' (*The Works of Alexander Pope*, 1794, p. 285). Pope is adapting to new ends a common phrase of the time: Joseph Trapp in his poem 'To the Right Honourable Mr. Harley, On His appearing in Publick after the Wound given Him

The remainder of the poem shows Harley to be wise as well as great, shows him escaping the dangers of office, namely 'Pride', 'The Rage of Pow'r',[1] and 'The Lust of Lucre'. And the escape is possible because, for once, great place is occupied by 'One *truly* Great'. Pope's stride across the boundary between two meanings of a common word, between 'great of place' and 'great of soul', helps the poem to achieve its last climax.

There is a similar progression in the use of the word 'friend', and again with the advantage of pulling the sections of the poem more closely together. For Parnell's sake Harley is

> Fond to forget the Statesman in the Friend.

And later there is the gnomic line:

> Absent or dead, still let a Friend be dear.[2]

This straightforward use of the word implies that friendship of this quality is friendship as Harley and Pope understand and practise it. But alas, not all friends are staunch, and, at a crisis, though the fair-weather ones may survive such hangers-on as are interested, obliged, and vain, they depart at last: the Muse

> . . . waits, or to the Scaffold, or the Cell,
> When the last ling'ring Friend has bid farewel.

We should not be so sure of the irony in this last use of the word, its almost visible inverted commas, if its use earlier in the poem had not made it clear that for Pope friendship was of first importance.

Further, Pope marks the progress of the poem by means of proper names, and his manner of printing them. It was the practice of contemporary printers to distinguish proper names by a special type, by using italic (*Pope*), large caps. (POPE), small caps. (ᴘᴏᴘᴇ), a mixture of large and small (Pᴏᴘᴇ), or in the italic versions of these last three. In the printing of Pope's poem, as many as three of these methods are used, and therefore used designedly. Parnell and Swift are given italics. This

---

by *Guiscard*', had compared Harley to Julius Caesar as being 'like him Wise and Great'. In *The Drapier's Letters* Swift was to refer to Harley as 'the greatest, the wisest, and the most uncorrupt Minister, I ever conversed with' (ed. H. Davis [1935], p. 127).

[1] Johnson borrowed this Johnsonian phrase for *The Vanity of Human Wishes*, l. 33.

[2] Cf. Pope to Swift, 22 March 1740–1: 'Death has not used me worse in separating from me for ever poor Gay, Arbuthnot, &c., than disease and absence in separating you so many years' (*Works of Pope*, ed. Elwin and Courthope [1871], vii. 391).

leaves the ground clear for typography that matters. Harley is distinguished by ordinary initial caps. and small caps. ('HARLEY' and 'OXFORD') until his final appearance in large caps. as 'MORTIMER'. The typography, however, is only a second string to Pope's bow. By good fortune Pope's dedicatee had four names clustered in an 'extraordinarily worded Earldom':[1] Baron Harley of Wigmore (the ancient seat of the Mortimers, in Herefordshire, the 'Desarts' of the poem), Earl of Oxford, and Earl Mortimer. Pope makes use of three of them (to have used the fourth, Wigmore, would have been pedantic—no one used it). When he is speaking of Harley as the friend of Parnell and Swift, he uses his family name, the name representing him as a human being on a level with other human beings born with the names Parnell and Swift. When he is speaking of Harley as holding high office, he gives him the name which, after his elevation to the peerage in 1711, was in general use, the name 'Oxford'. But Harley had also the title Mortimer. He had been given it for fear that claimants to the Oxford title still survived—it had become extinct as recently as 1702. The further title had been extinct much longer. At the time Harley acquired the title Oxford, lawyers had called that name 'the noblest in the land'.[2] But the associations of 'Mortimer' were nobler still: it sounded nobler, and had nobler literary connotations. Who could forget that line of Mortimer's soliloquy in *1 Henry VI*:

Here dies the dusky torch of Mortimer,

or the two epistles passing between an earlier Mortimer and Queen Isabel in Drayton's still-popular *England's Heroical Epistles*? Moreover, the latter Mortimer was the hero of Drayton's *Barons' Wars*, entitled in its first form *Mortimeriados*. So in the last line of the poem 'OXFORD' gives place to 'MORTIMER'. This climax of Pope's must be brief, if it is to fit a poem in which so much has found a place—contrast the ending of the overture to *Ruy Blas* where Mendelssohn reiterates the tonic chord, and that the chord of C major, through fifteen bars of common time. To attain brevity Pope uses every device he has. If we had been given 'Oxford' we should have missed both the almost brandishable sonority of 'Mortimer' and its connotations of heroic greatness.

---

[1] G. E. C., *The Complete Peerage* (1945), x. 264.   [2] Op. cit., p. 262.

And, finally, among the agents binding together the remarkably varied matter of the poem, there is the diction, which works through alternations, beginning in the second paragraph, of softness and harshness. The poem opens almost as might a pastoral: its pipe is the oaten reed. And this innocency is, so to speak, the woof of the poem, the weft being harsh as hemp. A constant interchange is kept up between phrases like 'tuneful Tongue', 'softest Manners', 'silent Shade', 'calm Sun-set' and words like 'Farce', 'Blast', 'Lust', 'sneaking', 'Hireling', the harshest Saxon beloved of satirists rasping through the Sicilian. The harsh words keep the poem from languishing. Pope gives no particulars, and so cannot rely on the means of vividness that details provide readily. But the general is not necessarily feeble. Pope does not fall into the error remarked by Johnson, who complained that Sprat's life of Cowley gives 'so little detail that scarcely anything is distinctly known'.[1] Pope can give no details without writing a different sort of poem, one much longer and one necessarily less dignified. He chooses his focus and sticks to it. But though he cannot give details, he can be sharp.

VI

If Pope's poem is an occasional one, and one with an occasion of this status—a rough parallel in our own time would be to suppose that Mr. Eliot were presenting the poems of Sidney Keyes to Mr. Churchill—it follows that we cannot forget the man, Pope. If he excludes himself from his Epistle as much as he can, we grab him when he affixes his signature to it. His poem is as much a political article in a newspaper as a poem: if it is an epistle, it is also an 'open letter'. We judge it as we judge any poem, we also judge it as we judge any prose testimonial: we ask whether or not Pope's verses can meet the claim he made for them in the covering letter to Harley, the claim that they are 'honest verses'. (I do not concern myself with the further question asked by Pope's contemporaries: 'Is Pope attacking the Hanoverians and the Whigs in praising a fallen Tory statesman of the last Stuart?' Grattan was to note that to write Pope's Epistle required courage.[2])

[1] *Lives of the Poets*, ed. G. B. Hill (1905), i. 1.
[2] 'Repeated Pope's lines to Lord Oxford with great enthusiasm. They required courage in Pope.' Grattan, in Rogers' *Recollections* (1859), p. 94.

They can only seem incompletely honest to those who are blinded by the blaze of the climax praising the 'Soul like thine'. But, of course, to make that praise blind us was Pope's aim. Praise of that degree is implied as a hoped-for possibility in any dedicatory poem, as a probability in any dedicatory poem by a major poet. In trying to rise to a great occasion, a poet has to see the occasion as even greater than it is. Being a poem, it must go all out, at least at its climax. If at that point the poet vacillates, his very metre rots. But there may be a simpler explanation of the effect produced by those four lines: it may be due to Pope's describing sublime virtue in terms of its opposite. He does not tell us what Harley's soul was, but what it was 'beyond', and he therefore turns to the things in a politician that men hate, things that prompt in all but some of the saintly a vivider emotion. Pope knew that his panegyric was better poetry—better because more fiercely sensuous—for turning round from virtue and facing instead

The strong Antipathy of Good [, the] Bad.[1]

Pope, then, does blind us with his climax of praise. But though the soul of Harley as a politician is seen as perfect, Pope's vision of it is arrived at by selection rather than by fabrication. To see that this is so, we have only to consult the writings of Swift. For all his disappointment at Harley's failure to get him the post of historiographer and no nearer glory than the deanery of St. Patrick's, Swift saw to it that nothing prevented his reporting the cause of Harley aright to his own age and to posterity. The hard work he put in as historian and critic of that administration has the purposiveness of a campaign. And though Swift's praise of Harley lacks the sensuous glow of Pope's, it is not less superlative. For Swift Harley was, to choose only four of his judgements, 'the most fearless man alive',[2] 'the utter despiser of money for himself',[3] 'the humblest of men in the height of his power',[4] and 'Fear, cruelty, avarice, and pride, are wholly strangers to his nature'.[5] Swift's bequest to Pope of his miniature of Harley marks the closeness of their views on its subject.

---

1 The Epilogue to the Satires, Dialogue II, 198.
2 The Journal to Stella, ed. H. Williams (1948), p. 206.
3 Correspondence, ed. F. E. Ball (1910), i. 280.
4 Quoted by E. S. Roscoe, Robert Harley (1902), p. 198.
5 Prose Works, ed. Temple Scott (1902), x. 93 f.

Swift, however, wrote of Harley with the judiciousness of the responsible historian, and therefore with due sense of his failings. If, for him, the good in Harley heavily outweighed the bad, he paid due attention to what existed in the other scale. In a dedication, Pope cannot actually demonstrate that he is being judicious as, in his prose accounts, Swift could and did. He is judicious, nevertheless. He sees in his hero some of the failings Swift sees, and at least hints them. Pope does not, and cannot, say outright that Harley was a procrastinator, that his admired calm was sometimes that of the hopeful drifter; that, as Johnson came to put it, he was caught with

> pow'r too great to keep, or to resign.[1]

But reading his poem carefully, we see that Pope was not blind to these faults. To 'bid the World attend' is a finer compliment to Parnell's wit than to a statesman's sense of responsibility; there is some ground for political uneasiness in the word 'Fond'; no statesman should despise 'the Farce of State' lest he should come too near despising the state itself; nor can we admire the statesman who likes his private pleasures to the point of having acquired a 'dexterity' in 'escaping' to them, even if it is only from the 'craving, fawning Crowd'.[2] Harley, Pope says outright, did suffer a 'Fall'; during two years of unduly prolonged imprisonment (owing to alleged Jacobite sympathies) he faced 'the Scaffold or the Cell'. Nor does Pope blink what is least pleasant in Harley's rustication; he has made a 'Retreat' after his 'Fall', and that to the 'Desarts' on the Welsh border, where instead of buzzing with curiosity the 'Shade' is 'silent'; he is under a 'Cloud', and a 'Disgrace' that stands in need of being given its 'digni[ty]'. The climax of Pope's poem is a blaze, but the recovering eye is aware that Harley is human after all. Pope does not suffer any repercussion from that fierce line

> No Hireling she, no Prostitute to Praise.

From whatever angle we peer at the poem, we find it magnificent.

---

[1] *The Vanity of Human Wishes*, l. 134.
[2] Swift has several descriptions of the crowds at Harley's levees, e.g. 'I cald at Ld Treasr's it was his Levee day but I went up to his Bedchamber; & sd what I had to say; I came down & peept in at the Chambr where a hundred Fools were waiting, and 2 Streets were full of Coaches' (*Journal to Stella*, ed. cit., p. 499).

POPE AND THE SISTER ARTS

ROBERT J. ALLEN

POPE's interest in painting has been widely recognized by his biographers and critics, from Joseph Spence to Mr. Sherburn. They have described in some detail his relationship, as friend and pupil, with the painter Charles Jervas, and have extracted from his letters the story of his reluctant but amused abandonment of the idea that he might excel with brush and pencil. A number of critics, including Mr. Austin Warren and Miss Elizabeth Manwaring, have suggested interesting relationships between Pope's experience with painting as an art and his own literary practices as critic and poet. But even Joseph Warton, who 'beats this ample field' as thoroughly as any, has little to say about painting as a source of poetic imagery. Like the others, Warton concentrates his attention on a few of the parallels in theory which bound the two arts together, and on the effect of late Renaissance painting on Pope's pictorialism.

Although some repetition must be involved in considering Pope's use of imagery from painting, the study is revealing on a number of counts. It shows the extent to which Pope was conscious of and interested in the technique, as opposed to the critical theory, of painting; it illuminates his special habits as a practitioner in imagery; and it furnishes an interesting sidelight on the nature of Pope's conventionality and that of his time.

That the comparison between the art of the painter and the art of the poet was a commonplace during the eighteenth century hardly needs proof. Horace's *Ars Poetica* opens with such a comparison, adds another within thirty lines, and near the end contains the famous passage translated as follows by the Earl of Roscommon:

> Poems (like Pictures) are of different Sorts,
> Some better at a distance, others near,
> Some love the dark, some chuse the clearest light,
> And boldly challenge the most piercing Eye,
> Some please for once, some will for ever please.[1]

---

[1] *Horace's Art of Poetry* (1680), p. 25.

By the end of the seventeenth century Horace's classic parallel
had become accepted as fixed truth, the proper material for any
poet with wit enough to dress it to advantage. Waller, Marvell,
and a host of their imitators had written treatments of the State
and its representatives in the form of advice or instructions 'to
a painter'. Dryden had given permanence to the conception of
poetry and painting as sister arts by his highly developed use of
the figure in 'To the Pious Memory of the Accomplish'd Young
Lady, Mrs. Anne Killigrew, Excellent in the Two Sister-Arts of
Poetry and Painting' (1685) and in 'To Sir Godfrey Kneller'
(1694). Furthermore, in 'A Parallel of Poetry and Painting',
with which in 1695 Dryden prefaced his translation of Du
Fresnoy's *De Arte Graphica*, there were abundant precedents
for linking the two arts ranging in date from Philostratus to
Dryden himself. As a result of this constant association of the
two arts, poets frequently conceived of versified 'characters'
(satiric or otherwise) as portraits, descriptions as landscapes,
poetic treatments of mythological and allegorical figures as
paintings of those subjects, and heroic accounts of great events
as history-paintings. Addison's *The Campaign* (1705), to offer a
single example, ends with a passage which shows the connexion
between the two arts firmly established in his mind:

> Marlborô's exploits appear divinely bright,
> And proudly shine in their own native light;
> Rais'd of themselves, their genuine charms they boast,
> And those who paint 'em truest praise 'em most.[1]

The prevalence of such implied comparisons was not lessened
by any objections from the painters, who accepted cordially the
fraternal gestures of the poets. There is no record of how Sir
Godfrey Kneller responded to Dryden's offer of artistic brotherhood, but in view of the fact that Dryden linked Raphael with
Homer and Titian with Virgil, Sir Godfrey would have been
churlish indeed to reject Dryden's company. Pope's friend,
Jonathan Richardson, accepted the kinship heartily and
elaborated it in ways which strikingly anticipate Reynolds's
Discourses. The opening pages of Richardson's *The Theory of
Painting* (1715) treat pictures 'as another language, which com-
pletes the whole art of communicating our thoughts', and the
painter as requiring talents and learning comparable to the

---

[1] Compare the closing line of Pope's *Eloisa to Abelard*.

poet's.[1] Charles Jervas was equally happy in the relationship. Pope's epistle *To Mr. Jervas*, which is full of their artistic kinship as painter and poet, was first published in 1716. In the same year, when he joined with Gay, Arbuthnot, and Pope in writing to Thomas Parnell, Jervas attempted a witty apology for contributing to the letter in the following terms:

Though my proportion of this epistle should be but a sketch in miniature, yet I take up half of this page. . . . The poets will give you lively descriptions in their way; I shall only acquaint you with that which is directly in my province.

Then, alluding to a picture, probably of Martha and Teresa Blount, which he had just finished painting, he went on:

I have just set the last hand to a couplet, for so I may call two nymphs in one piece. . . . He [Pope] has been so unreasonable as to expect that I should have made them as beautiful upon canvas as he had done upon paper.[2]

The reference to the picture as a couplet suggests not only that Jervas was prepared to think of his art in terms of poetry, but also that drawing parallels between the two arts was so familiar a practice that it had become a game.

Since painters and poets alike had come to accept the kinship of the sister arts, it is not surprising to find Pope making extensive use of painting in his imagery. Indeed, he was inclined to enlarge the conception of the sister arts, as Jonathan Richardson was, to include sculpture, architecture, and music. Describing 'Leo's golden days', near the end of *An Essay on Criticism*, he wrote:

> The sculpture and her sister-arts revive;
> Stones leaped to form, and rocks began to live;
> With sweeter notes each rising temple rung;
> A Raphael painted, and a Vida sung.

A considerable number of images derived from these arts are scattered through his poems,[3] and gardening and the decorative arts are also frequent sources of imagery, the latter usually with suggestions of pretty triviality. He even used, in the *Dunciad*,[4] one fairly elaborate comparison drawn from the art of tapestry-

---

[1] *The Works of Jonathan Richardson* (1792), pp. 6–15, *et passim*.
[2] Pope, *Works*, ed. Elwin–Courthope, vii. 458–9. Cf. ibid. viii. 5, 23.
[3] See, for example, *The First Epistle of the Second Book of Horace*, ll. 43–8, 147–54.
[4] *Poems*, Twickenham ed., v. 302.

weaving. None of these arts, however, furnished him with so
many analogies as that of the painter.

Several of his images derived from painting are of the vague,
conventional, superficial sort common in his day. When he says
in *An Essay on Criticism*, for example, that Longinus 'is himself
the great Sublime he draws', it is clear that the word 'draws'
is merely an equivalent of 'writes about', having lost all
metaphorical suggestiveness. More frequently, however, the
language of painting invites the reader to think of accepted
theoretical analogies between poetry and painting. Writing to
Caryll of 'Mr. Tickell's . . . poem upon the Peace' in 1712, Pope
says:

There are also several most poetical images and fine pieces of
painting in it, particularly the lines in p. 13 of the child's emotion
at sight of the trophies at Blenheim, and the description of the fields
after the wars in p. 5 . . . .[1]

Here the subjects alluded to are of a sort appropriate to history-
painting, and the idea of painting the emotions is one that he
had found treated in detail by the theorists of painting, as a part
of the imitation of nature. Caryll was expected to make a
rather vague association between the two arts as surely as was
the reader of the *Dunciad Variorum*, when Martinus Scriblerus
informed him:

But possible it is also that on due reflection, the maker might find
it easier to paint a *Charlemagne*, a *Brute* or a *Godfry*, with just pomp
and dignity heroic, than a *Margites*, a *Codrus*, a *Flecknoe*, or a *Tibbald*.[2]

In such instances as these, where the comparison between the
two arts is undeveloped, it is hinted rather than insisted upon.
When Pope underscores the parallel it is usually in an essential
piece of poetic imagery. The most sustained example is undoubtedly the second of the *Moral Essays*, 'Of the Characters of
Women'. After a terse announcement of his theme in the first
two couplets Pope flashes before us in quick succession six
paintings of a single 'nymph', to show how differently she
appears in different costumes and settings. The first four poses
are suggested in as many lines, the last two in a couplet each.
While our minds are absorbing the ethical significance of Pope's

---

[1] *Works*, ed. Elwin–Courthope, vi. 167–8.
[2] Pope, *Poems*, Twickenham ed., v. 49.

subtle pairing of the pictures, we are aware that we are being shown through a small gallery of history-paintings, done in the manner which the theorists admired. Pope's friend Richardson had insisted that 'every historical picture is a representation of one single point of time; this then must be chosen; and that in the story that is most advantageous must be it'.[1] Pope was adopting some such idea, and the image from painting with it, to develop his views on the changeableness and inconsistencies of women's characters. He concludes our tour of the paintings with an extraordinarily economical couplet (ll. 15–16), which both reaffirms his satiric intention and shifts his role from that of docent to that of painter. Our final preparation for the double portraits which are to follow is completed in the lines:

> Come, then, the colours and the ground prepare!
> Dip in the rainbow, trick her off in air;
> Choose a firm cloud, before it fall, and in it
> Catch, ere she change, the Cynthia of the minute.

The painter's colours become a rainbow, the rainbow becomes a cloud as insubstantial as Cynthia's own character, and in the satiric sketches which follow the analogy with paintings fades, though there are suggestions of it in the line, 'See Sin in state, majestically drunk', and in the allusions to 'Lucretia's dagger, Rosamonda's bowl'. After the brilliant character of Atossa, however, Pope resumes the metaphor in the lines:

> Pictures like these, dear Madam, to design,
> Asks no firm hand, and no unerring line;
> Some wandering touches, some reflected light,
> Some flying stroke alone can hit them right:
> For how should equal colours do the knack?
> Chameleons who can paint in white and black?

The last of these lines is as good as any to illustrate Pope's control of the image and his ability to make it serve his thematic ends, reminding us as it does that Pope is in reality neither painting in colour nor drawing in black and white but (and here our minds accept an interesting ambiguity) is writing words on paper. After dealing with Chloe Pope resumes the metaphor once more to praise the virtue and beauty of the Duchess of Queensberry. Here again he depends on the practice of the painter, in choosing and dressing his model, to

[1] *Works* (1792), p. 27.

emphasize an ethical point: the inferiority of external trappings to inner virtue. The remainder of the poem is largely taken up with general advice to Martha Blount on how to grow old gracefully, but before he finally leaves the portrait section Pope makes a transition by means of one of his favourite metaphors. Explaining that men's characters are often best displayed in public, women's in private life, he writes:

> Our bolder talents in full light displayed;
> Your virtues open fairest in the shade.

Here is the old image from Horace, who had used it to show how poems may differ in tone. Pope has gone a step beyond the poetry–painting comparison and has used painting as a metaphor to give force to a generalization about human nature. This extension of the figure had appeared in his writings before, in a letter to the *Spectator*, in what purports to be a personal letter to Steele, and according to Pope's own testimony in some lines which he 'inserted into Mr. Wycherley's poem on Mixed Life'.[1] Its use in 'Of the Characters of Women' is evidence both of the liveliness with which he adapted a conventional image to his own ends and the skill with which he sustained, in this poem, a comparison on which its whole structure rests.

Much of Pope's imagery from painting comes from such connoisseurship and knowledge of its theory as he had been able to acquire, and some of the happiest results were satiric. In a *Guardian* on writers of dedications[2] is a comparison between an incompetent flatterer and 'a Dawber I have heard of, who not being able to draw Portraits after the Life, was used to paint Faces at Random, and look out afterwards for people whom he might persuade to be like them'. Many years later Pope worked out a more complex version of this parallel in the following passage of the *Dunciad*:

> Kind Self-conceit to some her glass applies,
> Which no one looks in with another's eyes:
> But as the Flatt'rer or Dependant paint,
> Beholds himself a Patriot, Chief, or Saint.[3]

In the *Epistle to Augustus* is the amusing complaint that although

---

[1] See Pope's *Prose Works*, ed. Ault, i. 42, and *Works*, ed. Elwin–Courthope, vi. 391.

[2] *Prose Works*, ed. Ault, i. 77. [3] *Poems*, Twickenham ed., v. 394–5.

Charles I and William III chose Bernini and Kneller to immor-
talize their figures in stone and on canvas, the two kings
immortalized their taste in poetry by pensioning Quarles and
knighting Blackmore. As often happens in the *Imitations of
Horace*, Pope is here using direct illustration rather than
imagery; but he goes on to the general observation, based on a
parallel between poetry and sculpture,

> Not with such Majesty, such bold relief,
> The Forms august of King, or conqu'ring Chief,
> E'er swell'd on Marble; as in Verse have shin'd
> (In polish'd Verse) the Manners and the Mind.[1]

The emphasis on the word 'polish'd', as applied to both marble
and verse, concentrates the attention directly on the two arts
being compared, and shows once more how insistently Pope
demanded a full response to such parallels.

A more subtle bit of suggestion may be found in one of the
coarsely comic passages of the *Dunciad*, where during the cere-
monial games of Book II Dulness offers prizes for the unsanitary
contest between Curll and Chetwood.[2] The consolation prize
is a jordan made of china and so becomes a sort of mock-heroic
objet d'art. The other prize is

> yon Juno of majestic size,
> With cow-like udders, and with ox-like eyes.

Even though Juno may be identified with Eliza Haywood, it is
likely that 'yon Juno' is also meant to suggest a large mythological painting, probably of the Flemish School. Such a
response is reinforced by the pseudo-Homeric term 'ox-like' as
well as by the allusion to the engraved portrait by Kirkall in
the preceding passage. In the methodology of burlesque Mrs.
Haywood posed heroically as Juno is a fair equivalent for the
jordan fashionably executed in china. A comparable bit of
satiric imagery drawn from history-painting appears in one of
the Horatian imitations, where Pope scornfully asks if Fortescue
expects him, in order to gain the King's favour, to

> Rend with tremendous Sound your ears asunder
> With Gun, Drum, Trumpet, Blunderbus & Thunder?
> Or nobly wild, with *Budgell's* Fire and Force,
> Paint Angels trembling round his *falling Horse*?[3]

---

[1] *Poems*, Twickenham ed., iv. 227, 29.   [2] Ibid. v. 303–4.   [3] Ibid. iv. 7.

The relationship between the sister arts served Pope as well in his critical as in his satiric writings. As a satirist, in 'Of the Characters of Women' (ll. 185–6), he showed how little the Duchess of Queensberry needed extravagant flattery by saying:

> Poets heap virtues, painters gems, at will,
> And show their zeal, and hide their want of skill.

As a critic Pope had used the same image years before in condemning those whose taste is for 'conceit . . . and glitt'ring thoughts struck out in every line'. In *An Essay on Criticism* (ll. 293–6) Pope had written:

> Poets, like painters, thus unskilled to trace
> The naked nature, and the living grace,
> With gold and jewels cover ev'ry part,
> And hide with ornaments their want of art.

The frequency of the parallel between the arts in *An Essay on Criticism* needs little comment. Sometimes Pope merely emphasizes a simple statement, as when he says (ll. 301–2), referring to both external nature and landscape painting,

> As shades more sweetly recommend the light,
> So modest plainness sets off sprightly wit.

Sometimes, as in a passage which harks back once more to Horace, he builds a more intricate set of analogies.[1] Once, as Miss Manwaring has suggested, he submits a bit of pictorialism which invites us to approve 'brave disorder' in poetry as we admire the bolder touches of an Italian landscape-painting.[2] Further dependence on painting for imagery appears in the preface to the *Iliad*. In discussing Homer's 'descriptions, images, and similes', Pope writes:

His Expression is like the colouring of some great Masters, which discovers itself to be laid on boldly, and executed with Rapidity. It is indeed the strongest and most glowing imaginable, and touch'd with the greatest Spirit.[3]

At this point a useful contrast may be made. With the exception of those from 'Of the Characters of Women' most of the

---

[1] *An Essay on Criticism*, ll. 169–74. For another example, see ll. 19–25.
[2] *Italian Landscape in Eighteenth Century England*, p. 97 n.
[3] *Prose Works*, ed. Ault, i. 233. Cf. pp. 232, 238, where he discusses Homer in terms of history-painting and landscape.

examples of Pope's imagery heretofore discussed have revealed
him in the position of an *amateur* familiar in some degree with
the taste of his time and the theories on which it was based. The
source of his comparisons was the finished picture and the
response which pictures drew from the persons viewing them.
In the passage just quoted from the preface to the *Iliad*, which
was first published in 1715, the words 'laid on boldly, and
executed with Rapidity' imply a different approach to painting
as an art. Pope's concern was less with the amateur's response
than with the creative act itself. Even before he took painting
lessons from Charles Jervas he showed an artist's interest in the
painter's medium and technique. He realized, for example,
that a poem may lose its appeal if its language becomes obsolete,
just as a painting loses its appeal when its colours become dim
with age;[1] and he compares the chances for immortality of
Lord Lansdowne, as a poet, with those, as a painter, of Verrio,
the Italian commissioned by Charles and James to do murals
at Windsor.[2]

Pope's knowledge of the creative processes of the graphic
artist was undoubtedly heightened, during the summer of 1713,
when he became, 'by Mr. Jervas's help, *elegans formarum spectator*.
I begin to discover', he wrote to Gay, 23 August, 'beauties that
were till now imperceptible to me. Every corner of an eye, the
smallest degree of light or shade on a cheek, or in a dimple, have
charms to distract me'.[3] Ten days later he informed Caryll
that he was 'entirely immersed in the designing art' and had
written nothing for some time. 'My eyes', he said, 'have so far
got the better of my ears, that I have at present no notion of any
harmony, besides that of colours.'[4] Pope was among the first
to recognize the unlikelihood that his experiments with painting
would ever produce a masterpiece. Without them, however,
we might not have the lyrical pictorialism of *Eloisa to Abelard*.
Neither should we have the illuminating use of painting technique which contributes so much, as we have seen, to the theme
and the gallery-studio atmosphere in 'Of the Characters of

---

[1] *An Essay on Criticism*, ll. 484–93. A similar comparison occurs in the *Guardian*,
no. 78.
[2] *Windsor Forest*, ll. 283–6, 303–10. An interesting account of Verrio's work, by
Edgar Wind, appears in the *Journal of the Warburg and Courtauld Institutes*, iii.
127–37.
[3] *Works*, ed. Elwin–Courthope, vii. 410–11.
[4] Ibid. vi. 193.

Women'. Even *An Essay on Man* gives evidence, in the following
extended metaphor, of Pope's experience as a practising painter:

> Passions, like elements, though born to fight,
> Yet, mixed and softened, in his work unite: . . .
> Love, hope, and joy, fair pleasure's smiling train,
> Hate, fear, and grief, the family of pain,
> These mixed with art, and to due bounds confined,
> Make and maintain the balance of the mind:
> The lights and shades, whose well-accorded strife
> Gives all the strength and colour of our life.[1]

How deeply Pope became involved in the current ideas which
linked the sister arts philosophically is not entirely clear. He
can hardly have failed to read Dryden's 'A Parallel of Poetry
and Painting', prefixed as it was to the translation of Du Fresnoy
for which Pope wrote the epistle *To Mr. Jervas*. There he found
the long passage, quoted from Bellori, which cites the *Timaeus*
of Plato in pointing out the relative imperfection of nature and
the possibilities open to the artist of creating a higher beauty.
'For which reason', said Bellori, 'the artful painter and the
sculptor, imitating the Divine Maker, form to themselves, as
well as they are able, a model of the superior beauties; and
reflecting on them, endeavour to correct and amend the common nature, and to represent it as it was first created, without
fault, either in colour, or in lineament.'[2] Pope's friend Richardson mentioned Bellori, and in treating the subject 'Of Grace and
Greatness' made the assertion:

Common nature is no more fit for a picture than plain narration
is for a poem: a painter must raise his ideas beyond what he sees,
and form a model of perfection in his own mind which is not to be
found in reality; but yet such a one as is probable, and rational.[3]

Pope's own critical theory, as set forth in *An Essay on Criticism*,
upholds fairly rigidly the notion that art must imitate nature;
but he recognizes a 'grace beyond the reach of art' to which
'great wits' may attain. This he describes as 'a happiness', as
'lucky', and even, in the case of the ancients, as 'celestial'. In
An Essay on Man an extended simile suggests a parallel between
the mysterious ends of divine creation and the combining efforts
of the painter's art.

---

[1] ii. 111–12, 117–22.
[2] Dryden, *Works*, ed. Scott, xvii. 289.
[3] *Works* (1792), pp. 73–5.

> This light and darkness in our chaos joined,
> What shall divide? The god within the mind.
> Extremes in nature equal ends produce,
> In man they join to some mysterious use;
> Though each by turns the other's bound invade,
> As, in some well-wrought picture, light and shade,
> And oft so mix, the diff'rence is too nice
> Where ends the virtue, or begins the vice.
> Fools! who from hence into the notion fall,
> That vice or virtue there is none at all.
> If white and black blend, soften, and unite
> A thousand ways, is there no black or white?[1]

In describing as 'mysterious' the beneficent equilibrium between good and bad human impulses, Pope invites the reader to find the same quality in the artist's handling of light and shade. The image is closely related to the more general one near the end of the first epistle of the *Essay*, in which mysterious nature is equated with 'art, unknown to thee', the art, that is, of God.

Such imagery as this, it is hardly necessary to remark, goes well beyond the purely conventional. Although, throughout his works, Pope shows that he was thoroughly acquainted with the well-known parallel between the sister arts, his experience with the brush enabled him to draw upon the craft as well as the art of painting. That in so doing he produced such varied and subtle effects can be explained only by his own artistic sensibility.

[1] ii. 203-14.

POPE AND DEISM

(*The Dunciad*, iv. 459-92)

ARTHUR FRIEDMAN

IN an attempt to remove the suspicion of unorthodoxy in parts of *An Essay on Man* Pope had, according to a letter written about 1736, altered and enlarged what later was called the *Universal Prayer* in order to reconcile 'Freedom & Necessity';[1] but, if we can believe Warton, when the new poem 'was first published many orthodox persons were . . . offended at it, and called it the Deist's Prayer'.[2] After 1738 Pope's orthodoxy was, for better or worse, defended by Warburton; it was only in the last poem he wrote, *The Dunciad*, Book IV, that Pope tried briefly to clarify his own position by attacking the heterodoxies of others, and this passage would seem to throw some light on the vexed question of his relation to deism.

After the Goddess of Dulness has expressed the wish that 'the Sons of Men' who view nature would

> Learn but to trifle; or, who must observe,
> To wonder at their Maker, not to serve,

there appears an extended address to the Goddess, here quoted in part:

> 'Be that my task (replies a gloomy Clerk,
> Sworn foe to Myst'ry, yet divinely dark;   460
> Whose pious hope aspires to see the day
> When Moral Evidence shall quite decay,
> And damns implicit faith, and holy lies,
> Prompt to impose, and fond to dogmatize:)
> Let others creep by timid steps, and slow,   465
> On plain Experience lay foundations low,
> By common sense to common knowledge bred,
> And last, to Nature's Cause thro' Nature led.
> All-seeing in thy mists, we want no guide,
> Mother of Arrogance, and Source of Pride!   470
> We nobly take the high Priori Road,
> And reason downward, till we doubt of God:

. . . .

[1] See George Sherburn, *Philological Quarterly* (1933), xii. 403.
[2] *The Works of Pope*, ed. Elwin–Courthope (1871), ii. 459.

Oh hide the God still more! and make us see   483
Such as Lucretius drew, a God like Thee:
Wrapt up in Self, a God without a Thought,   485
Regardless of our merit or default.
Or that bright Image to our fancy draw,
Which Theocles in raptur'd vision saw,
While thro' Poetic scenes the Genius roves,
Or wanders wild in Academic Groves;   490
That NATURE our Society adores,
Where Tindal dictates, and Silenus snores.'

Throughout the passage Pope is obviously aiming at various kinds of unorthodox thought, and some of the errors belong to philosophers of an earlier age: Hobbes, Descartes, and Spinoza are named in the Pope–Warburton notes. In a few places, however, there can be little doubt that he had in mind the deists of his own day; this is evident not only from the men mentioned or specifically referred to—Shaftesbury, Tindal, and Thomas Gordon—but also from the deistic positions that are attacked. On lines 485–6 Professor Sutherland has the following note: 'Pope here seems to be at some pains to undo what some of his critics thought he had done in the *Essay on Man*, and to dissociate himself clearly from Deism.'[1] In other lines the dissociation is even clearer.

The plainest of the attacks on the deistic position comes at the beginning of the passage, where it is said of the 'gloomy Clerk' that he is a 'Sworn foe to Myst'ry' and that he 'damns implicit faith', for in relation to the Christian mysteries and 'implicit faith' the frequently vague distinction between deists and 'philosophizing divines' is perfectly sharp.[2] Since at least the time of Toland's *Christianity not Mysterious* (1696) the deists had clearly—if not always quite openly—rejected the revealed mysteries such as the doctrine of the Trinity. Such mysteries by definition could not be discovered or understood by reason, and what could not be understood by reason, so the deists said, could not be believed. The orthodox, however, insisted that

[1] *The Dunciad*, ed. James Sutherland ('The Twickenham Edition of the Poems of Alexander Pope', vol. v, 1943), p. 389. Quotations from the poem are from this edition.
[2] On this topic see Louis A. Landa, 'Swift, the Mysteries, and Deism', *Studies in English, Department of English, The University of Texas, 1944* (Austin, 1945), pp. 239–56. Since Professor Landa gives such complete documentation for both the orthodox and the deistic positions, I have quoted from only a single text to show that the deists' arguments remained unchanged in 1730.

the mysteries could be believed by 'implicit faith' in the testimony of the divine author of the revelation, and such belief was not contrary to reason because the mysteries were above reason. But to the deists nothing could be above reason, and consequently reason must be the foundation of all belief. Thus in Matthew Tindal's *Christianity as Old as the Creation* (1730), when the objection is raised that 'we Christians have two supreme, independant Rules, *Reason* and *Revelation*, and both require an absolute obedience', the author replies:

I can't see how that is possible; for if you are to be govern'd by the latter, that supposes you must take every thing on trust, or meerly because it's said by those, for whose dictates you are to have an implicit faith; for to examine into the truth of what they say, is renouncing their authority: As on the contrary, if Men are to be govern'd by their Reason, they are not to admit any thing further than as they see it reasonable. To suppose both consistent, is to suppose it consistent to take, and not to take, things on trust.[1]

Similarly, in answer to the assertion that there are 'in Religion, propositions to be believ'd, which are above Reason', Tindal says:

If I do not understand the terms of a proposition, or if they are inconsistent with one another, or so uncertain, that I know not what meaning to fix on them, here is nothing told me, & consequently no room for belief: But in all cases, where I am capable of understanding a proposition, 'tis Reason must inform me, whether 'tis certain, probable, or uncertain. . . .[2]

It seems apparent, then, that in the lines on 'Myst'ry' and 'implicit faith' Pope is taking a stand on the fundamental question of the place of revelation in religion and that his attack on the position of the deists could hardly have failed to be recognized by his contemporaries.

In another part of the passage (lines 465-72), though the reference to deism is not open and may therefore be considered more doubtful, Pope is involved in an issue very closely related to the major deistic controversy of the time in which he was writing. In these lines are described two sharply opposed methods of natural religion: (1) the *a posteriori* method, where from the observation of order and design in nature the reasoner is led up to 'Nature's Cause', and the being and attributes of

---

[1] 8vo ed., London, 1731, pp. 166-7.   [2] Ibid., p. 199.

God are inferred from 'plain Experience'; (2) 'the high Priori Road', where the reasoning is 'downward' from supposedly self-evident first principles. The first of these methods—obviously the one favoured by Pope—was not, contrary to what students of the period have sometimes suggested, the characteristic method of the deists. It was rather such staunch Christians as Boyle, Ray, Bentley, Derham, and the other 'physico-theological' writers of the Boyle Lectures who searched for final causes in all the discoveries of the new science and pursued the argument from design through all the works of creation.

The characteristic method of the deists, on the other hand—though in this they did not differ from some of the 'philoso-phizing divines'—was to deduce the being and attributes of God *a priori* from 'the nature and reason of things' and then from God's attributes to deduce man's religious and moral duties. Thus when the deist Thomas Chubb attempts to show 'the *several kinds of evidence*, upon which the truth of God's moral character may be suppos'd to depend', he finds that they may be 'rang'd under these three heads *viz. first*, divine testimony, *secondly*, experience and observation; and, *thirdly*, the nature and reason of things'. Divine testimony, Chubb finds, is entirely unsatisfactory, because it must assume God's truthfulness in order to establish His other moral attributes. The proof from 'experience and observation' is somewhat better, for 'the late discoveries that have been made in *astronomy, anatomy*, and all the parts of *natural philosophy*' display 'the marks of *wisdom*, and *goodness*, that run thro the whole'. But this proof is not conclusive:

. . . tho the repeated instances of God's performing actions, that are productive of much good, . . . are a *strong presumption*, and make it *highly probable*, that such a moral property takes place in him; yet these alone do not amount to an *absolute proof*, that it certainly is so; because the action, tho ever so often repeated, is not sufficient to discover the *motive* it proceeded from.

God may be acting, Chubb says, 'from arbitrary pleasure, or from vain-glory, that he may have the empty praise of his creatures'. But the third method, the argument *a priori*, is completely satisfactory, and Chubb is able to conclude that 'the *nature of things* evidently, and certainly, proves God to be a *wise*, and *good Being*; who prudently exercises his natural properties, to serve the purposes of *benevolence*, and that he

governs his actions by the principles of *reason*'.[1] It was this form
of natural religion, established *a priori* from 'the nature and
reason of things', that became the object of attack by the
orthodox in the decade preceding the publication of *The
Dunciad*, Book IV.

The cause of this attack was to a large extent Tindal's
Christianity as Old as the Creation—a work whose central thesis
Warburton called 'the silliest, and most wretched Error, in an
age of Paradoxes'.[2] By reasoning downward from the divine
attributes ('a most certain way of reasoning'[3]), Tindal had
attempted to show that 'the *Law of Nature*, or *Reason*' is so
complete in the duties it teaches and so plainly intelligible to
all rational creatures as to render revealed religion superfluous.
Earlier attacks on Christianity by the deists, said one of the
replies to the book without great exaggeration, had been aimed
at the prophecies or miracles or some particular doctrine, but
Tindal directed 'his chief Aim at the Foundation of the Whole'.[4]

From God's attributes of power and goodness Tindal had
been able to deduce that all men—even 'the meanest capacities'
—must always have been given sufficient reason to understand
the law of nature.[5] One of the favourite forms of attack on him
was to deny this fundamental point in his argument, by showing
either that men of the meanest capacities could not arrive at
any rational notion of their religious duties or that even the
wisest men could not discover certain important truths without
the help of revelation. And in all cases these critics of Tindal
opposed his abstract reasoning to 'observation and experience'
or the 'facts' of history.[6] It is in this way that William Law
replies to Tindal's assertion of the '*sufficiency*, and *absolute
perfection*, of the light and strength of human reason':

. . . I hope the reader will observe, that this inquiry about the
perfection or imperfection, the strength or weakness, of reason in

---

[1] *A Vindication of God's Moral Character*, in Chubb's *A Collection of Tracts on
Various Subjects* (London, 1730), pp. 251–3.
[2] *The Divine Legation of Moses* (London, 1738), i. 6.   [3] Tindal, p. 31.
[4] John Conybeare, *A Defence of Reveal'd Religion against the Exceptions of a Late
Writer* (London, 1732), p. 4.   [5] See pp. 3, 10, 118, 209, 218–19.
[6] For texts where this opposition is made particularly clear see Thomas Burnet,
The Argument Set Forth in a Late Book, Conference II (London, 1731), pp. 12–13, 16,
26; [Conyers Middleton], *A Letter to Dr. Waterland* (London, 1731), pp. 50–1;
Conybeare, pp. 90, 221–2, 234; Warburton, i. 413–14. See also E. C. Mossner,
'The Decline of Reason', in *Bishop Butler and the Age of Reason* (New York, 1936),
pp. 125–55.

man, as to matters of religion, rests *wholly* upon fact and experience; and that therefore all speculative reasonings upon it, are to be looked upon as idle, and visionary, as a sick man's dream about health; and as wholly to be rejected, as any speculative arguments that should pretend to prove, in spite of all facts and experience, the *immortality*, and *unalterable* state of human bodies.[1]

John Conybeare is even clearer in distinguishing his method from that of his deistic opponent: 'I conceive, it is much safer and more reasonable to argue from known Fact to What is really fit and right for God to do, than to endeavour the Overthrow of What is certain Fact, by uncertain Presumptions what the Divine Attributes require.'[2] And Bishop Butler, finally, in his famous *Analogy* delivers what is probably the most telling blow against the *a priori* method of the deists:

Forming our notions of the constitution and government of the world upon reasoning, without foundation for the principles which we assume, whether from the attributes of God, or any thing else, is building a world upon hypothesis, like Des Cartes. Forming our notions upon reasoning from principles which are certain, but applied to cases to which we have no ground to apply them, . . . is an error much akin to the former: since what is assumed in order to make the reasoning applicable, is Hypothesis.[3]

While critics of Tindal thus attacked the kind of natural religion 'founded on the reason & nature of things',[4] none of them took occasion to object to the other religious argument, from the creation as effect to God as cause. On the contrary, some of them considered the argument from design particularly appropriate because it offered clear evidence concerning God's being and attributes and at the same time presented the same kind of difficulty that Tindal had found with revelation. 'Though the *creation* plainly declares the glory, and wisdom, and goodness of God', Law says, 'yet it has more mysteries in it, more things, whose fitness, expedience, and reasonableness, human reason cannot comprehend, than are to be found in

---

[1] *The Case of Reason, or Natural Religion, Fairly and Fully Stated* (1731), in *The Works of the Reverend William Law* (Brockenhurst, 1892), ii. 124; see also pp. 117–23.

[2] p. 107. See also [Duncan Forbes,] *Some Thoughts concerning Religion, Natural and Revealed* (London, 1735), p. 51.

[3] *The Analogy of Religion Natural and Revealed to the Constitution and Course of Nature* (1736), Introduction, par. 7, in *The Works of Bishop Butler* (London, 1900), ii. 5, and cf. pp. 8, 267.

[4] Tindal, p. 11.

Scripture'.[1]   Thus, as the *a priori* method in the hands of the
deists began to be viewed as dangerous to revealed religion, the
argument *a posteriori* remained a support of orthodoxy.

Both in attacking 'the high Priori Road' to natural religion
and in opposing to it a knowledge of 'Nature's Cause' founded
on 'plain Experience', Pope appears to be writing in the tradition of the replies to the most formidable deist of his day[2]—a
man named by Warburton as a 'Terror' of the age[3] and specifically attacked by Pope in the concluding line of the passage
under consideration.   The passage does not, of course, offer
very satisfactory evidence concerning long-held religious convictions, for it seems to have been written in part under the
influence of Warburton.[4]   But it does at least suggest that at the
end of his literary career Pope was aware of the main issues
involved in the deist controversy and that he was able to place
himself on the side of orthodoxy in a way that his contemporaries
were not likely to misunderstand.

[1] p. 105. For a fuller development of the same point see Middleton, pp. 60–2,
and cf. Butler, pp. 165, 268.

[2] On another point Pope may have been influenced by Tindal's critics. Of those
who take 'the high Priori Road' he says that they 'reason downward' until they
'doubt of God'. None of the deists, of course, had expressed doubt of God, but
some of the replies to Tindal did not hesitate to assert that his scheme actually led
to infidelity or atheism. See Law, pp. 103–4; Burnet, Conference III (1732), p. 43;
Conybeare, pp. 108, 161; Forbes, p. 52.

[3] See *The Divine Legation of Moses* (London, 1741), ii, pp. ix–x.

[4] The three deists specifically alluded to in the passage—Shaftesbury (ll. 487–90),
Tindal, and Thomas Gordon (the Silenus of l. 492)—had all been attacked in the
dedication 'To the Free-thinkers' in the first volume of *The Divine Legation of Moses*
(for Shaftesbury see pp. xi, xxiv–xxv, xxix; for Tindal, p. xix and also pp. 6, 411,
413; for Gordon, pp. x, xix–xx ['the mercurial Writer of the *independent Whig*']);
and John Craig, specified in the Pope–Warburton note as the person ridiculed in
l. 462 for attempting to calculate 'the gradual decay of Moral Evidence by mathematical proportions', is noticed for his 'whimsical and partial Calculation' by
Warburton (p. 2).

THE BACKGROUND OF THE ATTACK ON
SCIENCE IN THE AGE OF POPE

R. F. JONES

IN the three centuries or more that have elapsed since experimental science was first established in England, each period has reacted to it in ways sometimes similar but frequently different. In each there has appeared the eternal struggle between spirit and matter, man and nature, morality and naturalism—the old debate between body and soul. But in each period there have been certain local and temporal conditions that have determined attitudes peculiar to the age. Though the view of science in the nineteenth century contains elements similar to the view expressed in the seventeenth, there were some unique features of the earlier period that fostered attitudes not to be found in the later, features that history has almost forgotten. It is my purpose to analyse the unique features of the opposition to experimental science in the second half of the seventeenth century, largely for the light that may thus be thrown upon literary history, though literature is kept in the background. In the soil of this period the roots of the satire which Pope, Swift, and others directed against science are to be found.

The normal conception of the history of science views it as a record of the discoveries of the past, their significance and influence. Those who make such discoveries are the chief heroes of the narrative and monopolize most of the attention. In short, this type of history presents, for the most part, an unfolding picture of man's increasing knowledge of his natural environment. Yet if one investigates the formative period of modern experimental science in England, he will discover that those interested in science at this time were not so much concerned with great discoveries as with the stream of thought which these discoveries supported or out of which they arose. The main principles found in this thought-current were few and definite. First was the demand for a sceptical mind, freed from all preconceptions and maintaining a critical attitude toward all ideas presented to it. Second, the need of sufficient authentic data was stressed, and observation and experimentation were insisted upon as the only trustworthy means of securing these data. And third, the inductive method of reasoning was to be employed on them. Such were the central or primary ideas in this thought-movement, or, to use an expression borrowed from criticism, the timeless element, for they are as true to-day, though perhaps more generally taken for granted, as they were then. But besides these there was also the time element, or those secondary principles which came into being when the primary clashed with their age. The necessity of opposing the authority of the ancients contributed an anti-authoritarian element. But to undermine the authority of antiquity it was necessary to attack a prevailing theory of the Renaissance, which asserted that modern times represented the old age of the world and the last stages of the decay of nature, in which human powers had degenerated to a level far below that of the ancients, who lived when nature was in its prime. In order to advance new discoveries against established ideas the scientists insisted upon the principle of freedom of thought and discussion. And finally, the belief that knowledge could expand if submission to the ancients were abandoned, and the realization that some discoveries had already shown the possibility of advancement, moved those who had embraced the scientific faith to develop the idea of progress, which indeed joined hands with the opposition to the idea of nature's decay.

These values, attitudes, and ideas, together with a few others, combined to form the scientific movement, and they were expressed by an ever-increasing chorus of voices, not of authentic scientists only, or even chiefly, but of noblemen, state officials, clergymen, and even of the rabble of magicians, astrologers, graceless quacks, and other representatives of the lunatic fringe. Most thought-movements require leaders, and science furnishes no exception. During the first forty years of the seventeenth century it seemed that William Gilbert, author of *De Magnete* (1600), a thoroughly scientific work on terrestrial magnetism, would assume this position. Both by example and precept he had promoted the ideas of induction, observation, and experiment, hostility to ancient authority, and intellectual freedom, and his followers perpetuated his ideas. But when the Puritans secured political power in England, they seized with avidity upon Bacon's philosophy, and enthroned him as leader of the scientific movement, a position he maintained throughout the century. The substitution of Bacon for Gilbert was a happy and, perhaps, inevitable one. In his works Lord Verulam had expressed the idea of science much more comprehensively; some of its constituent elements were primarily due to him. But even more important, his ardent reforming spirit qualified him for leadership, and his eloquence made his leadership effective. In the many references to him during the second half of the century we easily detect the warmth of personal feeling such as the leader of any movement should and does inspire, a feeling of human discipleship.

All the principles which I have represented as constituting the idea of science find varied and eloquent expression in Bacon's works. To these we should add another conception, one peculiarly Bacon's, which, though of no significance to-day, was one of the most important factors, if not the most important, in the development of science at this time. Sir Francis believed that all the phenomena in the universe were the result of the operation of the primary laws of nature, alone and combined. He did not think that these laws were many in number, but just as out of a relatively small number of letters innumerable words may be formed, so any number of phenomena could spring from various combinations of the laws. If man could discover these primary laws, then by combining them he could produce all natural phenomena and be indeed master of nature. But to discover them, Bacon held that it was first necessary to compile a natural history which would include all the data that the earth and the fullness thereof could contribute. The absurdity of such an undertaking is quite apparent to us now, but so eloquently had he impressed upon his followers the need, and possibility, of such a history, that they accepted it with a faith which stifled all misgivings, and which made them eager to undertake an enterprise, the completion of which they could not hope to see. For Bacon had stated that the undertaking could be achieved only by the co-operative endeavours of large numbers of men extended over several ages. So scientists came together to form groups of experimenters, some of which merged to form the Royal Society. The desire to contribute to the natural history intensified their efforts and was largely responsible for the rapid spread of observing and experimenting so characteristic of this period. Again and again we find men declaring that the motive of their scientific activities is a desire to furnish data for the history. The avowed purpose of the

Royal Society, the most important embodiment of the scientific movement, was not to discover natural laws, but to accumulate large stocks of data against the time when the master thinker would have sufficient material for the discovery of primary laws. Robert Boyle ascribed the same purpose to his activities. From this situation, as we shall see later, sprang an exaggerated emphasis upon mere sense-observation and a corresponding distrust of reason.

The thought-movement which I have tried to describe emerged in definite outline in the fifth and sixth decades of the century when the Puritans came into power, and as long as they remained in power they zealously supported it. By appointing Puritan experimental scientists to important positions in the universities, by the encouragement of men engaged in promoting experimentation and spreading propaganda in its behalf, and especially by numerous educational treatises, which proposed turning the universities into scientific and technological institutions, the Puritans launched the scientific movement well on its way. But the asset of Puritan support became a liability in the Restoration for obvious reasons. The strong reaction against the Puritans which followed the King's return made men quick to note the Puritan associations which clung to experimental science and thus to become hostile to science itself. In the next decade the adjective 'Oliverian' (from Oliver Cromwell) was slyly used by enemies of the new philosophy to call attention to this earlier association. The antipathy thus developed would have proved much more serious to the advancement of science had it not been for His gracious Majesty Charles II, who while in France acquired under the influence of Cartesianism an interest in the new philosophy, and who upon his return to England protected the experimenters with his patronage of the Royal Society. The favour shown the scientists by His Majesty is no inconsiderable fact in the history of science, for it discouraged the critics of Baconianism from calling attention too openly to the Puritan past of an organization now sponsored by the King. But the popular preacher Robert South dared to do so in a long oration delivered at the dedication of the Sheldonian Theatre in Oxford in 1669. Of this oration Wallis the famous Oxford mathematician says:

The first part ... consisted of satyrical invectives against Cromwell, fanaticks, the Royal Society, and new philosophy; the next of encomiasticks, in praise of the archbishop, the theatre, the vice-chancellor, the architect, and the painter: the last of execrations against fanaticks, conventicles, comprehension, and new philosophy; damning them *ad inferos, ad gehennam*.[1]

Though unfortunately the oration has not survived, Wallis's words make it plain that Puritanism and science were in conjunction the object of South's wrath.

There was one manifestation of the Puritans' interest in science which did more than anything else to prejudice the Restoration against it. During the period when they were in power there appeared a series of educational treatises by John Dury, John Hall, William Petty, Noah Biggs, John Webster, and others, addressed to Parliament and advocating revolutionary reforms in English universities.[2] Inspired by Bacon, though sometimes indirectly through Comenius, these advocate the most thoroughgoing changes ever proposed for the universities in the same length of time. The writers in most determined fashion urge Parliament to abolish nearly all the subjects taught there and to substitute for them the new science, both the great discoveries that had been published and also the principles embodied in the scientific movement. Even more earnestly they advocate the introduction of all kinds of technological and vocational subjects. They entertained fond hopes that great progress in this direction could be made through Baconian experimentation. They would abolish the study of syllogistic logic, ethics, metaphysics, and religion. They viewed the study of languages only as the preparation of tools whereby the knowledge contained in them might be secured. They dismissed linguistic study pursued for its own sake or for literary purposes as a vain and useless enjoyment. The disputations, declamations, and public lectures, comprising the old methods of training and instruction, were likewise reprehended. Generally speaking, in place of the traditional curriculum they advocated only useful and profitable subjects, to use their own words. First and foremost the students were to be taught the experimental philosophy of Bacon, described by one reformer as

---

[1] See a letter by John Wallis dated 17 July 1669 in Robert Boyle's *Works*, ed. Birch, v. 514.

[2] See Richard F. Jones, *Ancients and Moderns*, chap. v. A few passages from this volume are incorporated in the present article.

demonstration, observation, and experimental induction. Another reformer, John Webster, declares that

It cannot be expected that *Physical* Science will arrive at any wished perfection unlesse the ways and means, so judiciously laid down by our learned Country-man the Lord *Bacon*, be observed, and introduced into exact practice; and therefore I humbly desire, and earnestly presse, that his way and method may be imbraced, and set up for a rule and pattern: that no *Axioms* may be received but what are evidently proved and made good by diligent observation, and luciferous experiments; that such may be recorded in a general history of natural things, that so every age and generation, proceeding in the same way, and upon the same principles, may dayly go on with the work, to the building up of a well-grounded and lasting Fabrick, which indeed is the only true way for the instauration and advancement of learning and knowledge.[1]

Reference is very clearly made to Bacon's natural history, and it is interesting to note that its compilation is made the goal of scientific education.

Chemistry, physics, geography, astronomy (Copernican, not Ptolemaic), botany, anatomy, including vivisection and dissection, and all kinds of scientific instruments were advanced as proper academic subjects. Puritan scientists who had been appointed to various positions at Oxford, and who were influential in the development of the scientific movement, drew up a design for the establishing of a school for the study of magnetism, mechanics, and optics in the university. A proposition published at the end of the Puritan era, entitled *A Modell for a Colledge Reformation*, proposes nothing less than that Christ Church, which was or soon became the most conservative college in Oxford, should be thoroughly overhauled, the dean and canons ousted, and the funds thus released used for training the fellows to be exact experimental scientists in geography, magnetism, mechanics, optics, chemistry, anatomy, and medicine. Special provision was made for a professorship both of Cartesianism and of the Greek atomic philosophy as revived by Gassendi. This proposal differs from other treatises in that it demands that a definite institution be taken over and that its very real funds be diverted from their futile (in Puritan eyes) employment to the support of instruction in experimental science. We are not surprised to find near the end of the century Christ Church lined up solidly with those who were attacking the Royal Society.

[1] *Academiarum Examen* (1654), p. 105.

But even greater emphasis was placed upon utilitarian or applied science than upon pure. Only practical mathematics was to be taught, for as one worthy says mathematics exists only to enable men to build houses and to assist mechanical operations. Another says that physics is to be studied not so much to secure knowledge of nature as to use this knowledge 'for the general good and benefit of mankind'. Medicine, agriculture, horticulture, surveying, and kindred subjects are given a prominent place in the curriculum. Mechanical knowledge is emphasized. In fact one reformer insists that every mechanical art, no matter how humble, should have its professor or lecturer. All these treatises reveal a spirit quite familiar to our academic world to-day, a spirit which insists upon the practical and useful in education, which emphasizes scientific rather than humanistic subjects, and which would load the curricula of our colleges of liberal arts with professional and vocational courses. The modern reader, perusing them for the first time, finds them strangely familiar.

What social sciences were taught at the universities fared better than humanistic studies. History was to remain. In political science, however, Aristotle was no longer to be studied, but in his place Machiavelli and, to quote one writer, 'our own Countreyman master *Hobbs* [who] hath pieces of more exquisiteness, and profundity in that subject than ever the Grecian wit was able to reach unto'.[1] These are indeed queer birds to be recommended by the 'godly men', as they liked to be called. But Hobbes the Atheist had joyfully joined forces with the Puritans in the assault on the universities, and they loved him for it. It is worthy of notice that the most serious attempt ever made in the past to drive humanistic studies from the curriculum to provide space for scientific and technological subjects was made in hearty co-operation with a complete apostle of totalitarianism and with the encouragement of an undisguised dictator.

When the scientific movement emerged from this era, it bore on its face such an indubitable expression of scientific utilitarianism and Puritan Philistinism that authentic scientists themselves became duly alarmed. It is rather amusing to witness the alacrity with which the Royal Society, through its historian Thomas Sprat, sought to assure the world that its

[1] John Webster, *op. cit.*, p. 88.

members had not the least desire or intention to introduce any changes into the universities.

Men are not ingag'd in these *studies*, [he says] till the Course of *Education* be fully compleated; the *Art of Experiments*, is not thrust into the hands of Boyes, or set up to be perform'd by Beginners in the School; but in an Assembly of Men of Ripe years; who while they begin a *new Method* of Knowledge, which shall consist of *Works*, and is therefore most proper for Men: they still leave to Learners and Children, the old talkative *Arts* which best fit the younger Age. From hence it must follow, that all the various manners of *Education*, will remain undisturb'd; because the practises of them, and the labors of this, are not appointed to meet in the same *Age*, or *Persons*.[1]

Joseph Glanvill, a most ardent propagandist of the new science, strenuously denies that he entertains any designs against the schools, and he insists that the development of experimental science will leave them untouched. But one may with little difficulty read between the lines of what Sprat and Glanvill say, and perceive a great dissatisfaction with university education, stifled because of an outraged public opinion. It is quite possible that the Puritan treatises on education had something to do with the delay in the introduction of scientific courses into the curriculum of English universities.

It is not difficult to imagine the resentment over the proposed educational innovations which burned in the hearts of the conservatives, nor to realize the odium that became attached to experimental science because of its association with them. The age was much closer than we are to the great contributions which antiquity had made to the beginnings of modern civilization. With spirits nourished by classical literature and philosophy the conservatives of the period were greatly disturbed by the effort to judge humanistic studies by materialistic and utilitarian standards. Where they made their serious mistake was in trying to maintain the natural philosophy of the past, which the new scientists were tearing into shreds, in not perceiving that the world of nature was the peculiar province of the scientists, and in not realizing that the latter were pursuing the right path to its truth. They were quite correct in repelling the attack on humanistic studies and the exaggerated emphasis upon materialistic values which were characteristic of the Puritans and which continued into the Restoration. The

[1] *History of the Royal Society* (1667), pp. 323-4.

learned Meric Casaubon, prebendary of Canterbury, was severely critical of the materialistic standards by which science would measure utility. If, he says, usefulness were found only in what affords the necessities of life, brewers and bakers, smiths and veterinarians would have to be looked upon as equal or superior to those who have been considered the great lights of learning. Henry Stubbe, a well-known doctor of the day, who waged unrelenting warfare against the Royal Society, scornfully contrasts such vocational subjects as the making of cider, the planting of orchards, the grinding of optic glasses to the logic and moral philosophy taught in the universities. 'What *contempt*', he exclaims, 'is there raised upon the . . . *Ethics* of *Aristotle*, and the *Stoiques*? And these Moral instructions that have produced . . . the *Pompeys* and *Ciceroes*, are now slighted in comparison of day-laboring', and he continues to attack the substitution of the study of mechanical trades, such as the making of wine and the art of dyeing, for the philosophy taught in the schools.[1] Other critics, like Thomas Hall, maintain the same attitude. The resentment against the Royal Society because of the previous attacks of scientific Puritans upon the universities was strong. Peter Gunning, bishop of Chichester, preached regularly against the scientists, and objected to the publication of a volume of verses, simply because it contained a poem in praise of the Society. Though the Society, warned by the strong reaction against the Puritans, honestly disclaimed any intention of meddling with the schools, the values which the members continued to hold were exactly those which would militate against liberal education. The fight was really one between humanism and naturalistic materialism.

But humanistic critics of experimental science began to discover another danger in the emphasis placed upon sense-observation and in the absorbing study of external nature. They began to fear that the world of man would be sunk in the world of nature, that man would seek in nature the laws that govern his being, and would forget the distinction which Emerson was later to make between the law of the thing and the law of man. They had reason to fear. In the history of the Royal Society, which though written by Sprat was an official pronouncement of the whole organization, some remarkable

[1] Henry Stubbe, *Legends no Histories* (1670), preface.

claims are made; such, for instance, as the statement that 'by long studying of the *Spirits* of the *Blood*, of the *Nourishment*, of the parts, of the Diseases, of . . . humane bodies . . . there [may] without question be very neer ghesses made, even at the more *exalted* and *immediate* Actions of the *Soul*'; and again, spiritual truth 'cannot seem incredible [to man] when he perceives the numberless particles that move in every man's *Blood*'.[1] In another passage Sprat asserts, in a manner prophetic of Words- worth, that the pleasant images of nature will purify thoughts and make men morally better than moral precepts will. State- ments like these filled religious souls with fear and resentment. Henry Stubbe, an embittered foe of the experimental philo- sophers, answered that as long as man sought proof of spiritual truth in the material world he would certainly go astray. Meric Casaubon, the most intelligent critic of experimental science, insists upon the difference between the moral and material worlds, ridiculing the belief that science can moralize man, and laughing at Gassendi's claim that he learned to control his passions by observing how all the blood of a louse when angered ran into its tail. Can a louse, he asks, do what philo- sophers and the Bible cannot? Casaubon clearly perceived the danger of placing morality upon a naturalistic basis, by which, he says, reason is prostituted to nature instead of ruling nature, and as an example he cites the justification of sexual freedom on biological grounds. This clash between naturalistic science and humanistic philosophy does much to explain the angry reaction to the attempts of the Puritans to abolish humanistic studies. The critics of science believed that religion, morality, education, and art were so closely associated with the past that a contempt for antiquity, generated by an overweening faith in, and by an exaggerated emphasis upon, the superiority of modern science over all other learning, would tend towards the destruction of the Church, the corruption of education, and the brutalization of man. They viewed with great concern the perils, as regards man's moral and spiritual interests, of a naturalistic philosophy based upon the new science, and they supported the cause of a humanistic culture against the ag- gressive demands of a utilitarian and mechanistic science.

The greatest danger to science, however, and the cause of the most strenuous opposition in religious quarters came from across

[1] Op. cit., pp. 83, 348.

the Channel, where Descartes had developed his mechanistic scheme of things. This mechanical philosophy, as it was called, laid out a pattern for explaining all natural phenomena on the basis of matter, motion, and mathematics, thus at one blow sweeping aside all the specious theories of traditional philosophies. Descartes saw in nature one vast machine filled with innumerable smaller ones. Animals were mere automata, and so were the bodies of men. Light, life, and beauty left nature. But he was pious and sincerely believed in God and men's spirit. He did not try to mechanize the rational soul of man, but postulated for its base a thinking substance, different from the substance of matter; in other words, an immaterial substance. In England the experimental scientists were carrying out Bacon's injunction to observe and experiment, but being human they could not altogether observe his caution against using reason in seeking explanations of the data secured by their scientific activities. More and more they discovered that the mechanical philosophy furnished clearer and more convincing explanations of these data than any which they had inherited or devised. The frequent expressions of this discovery brought it about that the scientific movement became closely associated with Descartes's philosophy, an association which at first promised to be a great asset but which later caused the Baconians many a headache.

All might have gone well had it not been for a certain gentleman whom we have already noticed as a companion of the Puritan brethren. Descartes had saved man's soul and made God's support necessary for the running of the machine. Thomas Hobbes, whose hard-headed philosophy was as rigid as cast iron and as hard as adamant, heartily subscribed to matter, motion, and mathematics, but his dogmatic, unfeeling, and materialistic soul, a soul he would have denied, took from man that spiritual comfort which Descartes's dualism had furnished him in compensation for what the French philosopher had done to nature. By ignoring Descartes's assertion that God's support was necessary to the functioning of the machine, and by means of his famous dictum that there is no such thing as an immaterial substance, Hobbes took God from his heavens and the soul from man. So man's mind as well as his body becomes mechanistic, and mental as well as physical phenomena are explained by the formula of matter and motion.

Inasmuch as Hobbes's philosophy was only an extension of the Cartesian, the latter became suspect. In many minds Hobbes had made Descartes's philosophy atheistic. So here is the situation. On one side the mechanical philosophy was associated with experimental science, and on the other with atheism, so that the Baconians suddenly discovered that they possessed a strange and decidedly unwanted bedfellow.

The alacrity with which they tried to get rid of this bedfellow, to distinguish, at one time between experimental science and Cartesianism, and at another between this science and Hobbes, is at this distance amusing. Two considerations moved them to this action. One was their own genuine alarm at discovering their association with a philosophy now abhorrent to them. We must remember that the scientific movement, as distinguished from scientific discovery, was partly fostered by the clergy. The membership of the Royal Society contained the two archbishops, numerous bishops, and many of lower rank. To discover suddenly that the philosophy which had proved so serviceable to the experimenters had turned atheistic in Hobbes's hands was a rude awakening. The other consideration was a well-justified fear that the charge of atheism would be brought against the Baconians themselves. And it was, though not as vigorously as it would have been had not so many been clergymen. The scientists were on the defensive. Their first step was to keep Hobbes out of the Royal Society, even though he was genuinely interested in science and tried to edge into the organization. This they did with ease. Their next was to discredit him as a scientist. This also they did with ease, Wallis wiping up the ground with him in mathematics and Boyle in physics. Their third step was to refute his dictum that there was no such thing as an immaterial substance. Here they were stumped. In fact they were forced to adopt means which have puzzled some historians of science and caused some scientists to lift their eyebrows. They literally went witch-hunting and ghost-hunting. Richard Baxter, the nonconformist, and Henry More, the Cambridge Platonist, both good friends of experimental science, try their hands at showing the authenticity of witches and ghosts in order to prove the existence of immaterial substances and thus refute Hobbes. But it was Joseph Glanvill, ardent propagandist of the new philosophy, who, egged on by Robert Boyle, was most concerned to free science from the imputation of atheism by gathering all the data he could to support belief in ghosts and witches. No member of the American Society for Psychical Research ever collected occult data with more assiduity than Glanvill sought out witch- and ghost-stories, which he published in 1668 in a book the sub-title of which is 'A full and plain Evidence Concerning Witches and Apparitions'. The great Robert Boyle expressed an emphatic belief in the usefulness of Glanvill's investigation, only cautioning him to use well-authenticated stories. It is quite possible that the desire to refute Hobbes strengthened and prolonged belief in witches. It is indeed strange to find science seeking refuge in ghosts.

There was, however, a more important, and certainly a more rational, way out of the dilemma in which the Baconians found themselves, a dilemma which, as I have said, arose from the fact that the philosophy which they found most useful in explaining experiments had in the eyes of many turned out to be atheistic. The experimentalists could draw, and insist upon, a clear line of distinction between the mechanical philosophy, which was a theory, and the experimental, which rested on sense-observation only. This they did. As we have already seen, Bacon insisted upon the need of extensive and prolonged observation and experiment in order to secure data for his comprehensive natural history, and he had solemnly warned against the danger of employing reason to formulate theories before all the evidence was in. Descartes, on the other hand, had emphasized reason and somewhat discounted the evidence of the senses. The scientists seize upon the difference. They assert that the experimental philosophy demands only that men patiently gather data, the explanation of which may be found elsewhere than in Descartes's philosophy. On the other hand Cartesianism was but a theory or hypothesis, rendered insecure because erected on too slim a factual foundation. They frequently point out Descartes's deficiency in that he did not experiment sufficiently, and where possible they take pleasure in pointing out his mistakes due to his failure to experiment. Boyle also remarks that the Cartesian hypothesis only furnishes delight to reasoning, speculative men, whereas Baconianism deals with nature and confers material benefits upon man. The scientists reduce the matter to a struggle between Bacon and Descartes, with God on Bacon's side. The experimenter who uses his eyes to observe nature may see the goodness and wisdom of God reflected in it; the speculator, unrestrained by sense-observation, is likely to reason himself out of the privilege. Henry More, who had tried to make a synthesis of Cartesianism, Platonism, and Christianity, discovered an alloy in his metal, and hastily shifted his allegiance from the mechanical to the experimental philosophy. He says, 'But the philosophy which they [i.e. experimental philosophers] aim at, is a more *perfect philosophy*, as yet to be raised out of faithful and skilful *Experiments* in Nature, which is so far from tending to *Atheism*, that I am confident, it will utterly rout it and the *Mechanical Philosophy*.'[1] It was perfectly natural that when Sprat, under the supervision of the Royal Society, wrote his history of the Society, he should mention Descartes only once or twice, and that in no very complimentary way.

Sprat realized how dangerous to science was the imputation of atheism to the mechanical philosophy. In fact, when he comes to discuss the relationship of science and religion, he remarks on the 'slippery place' in which he stood. In a manner peculiar to him he met the charge of atheism by exaggerating to an incredible degree the religious nature of experiments and experimenters. Miracles he calls God's 'Divine Experiments', the purpose of which, like that of human experiments, was to convince men through their senses. The Apostles would have made good scientists for they were men of honesty, trades, and business. Furthermore, Christ, like the experimenter, commanded his disciples to believe his works rather than his words. Sprat equates the qualities of a humble Christian with those of a true experimenter: he must judge himself aright, doubt his own thoughts, and be conscious of his ignorance. Certainly, he says, the sceptical, scrupulous, diligent observer of nature is nearer to the modest, meek, severe Christian than the proud speculative man. Moreover, he claims, science and Christianity join in a common humanitarian purpose, for Christ by feeding the hungry, healing the lame, and curing the blind showed that 'it is the most honourable Labour to study the benefit of Mankind; to help their infirmities; to supply their wants, to ease their burdens ... all which may be called *Philosophical Works* performed by an *Almighty Hand*'.[2] Sprat seems to be on the

[1] See Joseph Glanvill, *A Prefatory Answer to Mr. Henry Stubbe* (1671), p. 155.
[2] *History of the Royal Society*, p. 352.

point of inviting God to become an honorary fellow of the Royal Society. Needless to say, religious souls were shocked by his blasphemous enthusiasm, and another demerit was registered against science.

Not only did Restoration science have to struggle against anti-Puritan sentiment and the atheistic reputation of the mechanical philosophy; in an even more fundamental way it ran counter to the age. We have already noticed the distrust of reason which Bacon imposed upon his followers. Sir Francis had noted the misuse of reason conspicuous in the schoolmen and he was familiar with large philosophical systems which men had raised on very flimsy factual foundations. So he had acquired on the one hand an exaggerated idea of the amount of data requisite for true scientific thinking, and on the other a depreciation of reason, which he thought lured men to the airy regions of speculation. Furthermore, he found it especially necessary to warn men against the too ready use of reason if his natural history, the very foundation of his whole *Magna Instauratio*, was to be completed. His followers, who were almost fanatically committed to the history, continued the anti-rational spirit. The age, however, partly under the influence of ancient philosophy, partly under the influence of Descartes, and partly in reaction against Puritan religious fanaticism, was insisting that reason should be basic in religion, philosophy, morality, and æsthetics. So the anti-rationalistic spirit of science ran directly against one of the main values of the times, perhaps the most important. The opposition to science because of its attitude toward reason was so deep-seated and fundamental that it does not find frequent direct expression but plays an almost unconscious part in criticism of science expressed in other ways. It is true some of the scientists themselves were uneasy over the matter. Timothy Clerke, a very intelligent member of the Royal Society, in a manner contrary to the optimism of his fellow members says, 'I rather fear our tumbling into the greatest barbarity and most profound ignorance; the way to solid knowledge by cultivating of our reasons, and inuring them to compare, compute, and estimate well, begins now to be wholly despised.'[1] The hostile reaction to this aspect of the scientific movement, however, is seldom revealed in direct condemnation. It lies at the base of the scorn and satire

---

[1] *Some Papers Writ in the Year 1664* (1670), p. 2.

which literary writers like Shadwell, Swift, **Arbuthnot, and** Pope later directed against the scientists. It is partly responsible for the fact that in spite of the enthusiasm and strenuous activity which characterized science in the early Restoration the experimental philosophy did not capture the imagination of the rising generation. It is true that Newton, a tireless experimenter and a distruster of theories, astonished his age, but his principal work represented a triumph for Descartes and the mechanical philosophy more than for experimental science. Though the observers and experimenters moved along the highest level of the early Restoration they gradually sank to a less important plane and pursued a relatively obscure path, satirized and abused by literary men, until the middle of the next century.

This undervaluing of reason led to yet another condition injurious to the reputation of science. Both the theory of nature's decay and the immense amount of work necessary for the compilation of his natural history compelled Bacon to express a very unflattering estimate of the intellectual qualifications required of scientists. He asserted that the method of observing and experimenting demanded of its operators nothing but the most mediocre mental powers. This idea he passed on to his followers. Though Boyle demurred somewhat, as well he might, to Bacon's estimate of the brains necessary for an experimenter, he, together with other scientists, supported it in another way. Not once but a number of times he declared that he could learn more about nature from humble ignorant people and simple artisans, who were in direct contact with nature, than from the aristocrats of learning. In view of the modest requirements of an experimenter and in view of the tribute paid the most humble by distinguished scientists, was there anyone who could not aspire to be a scientist? When the band-wagon of experimental science began rolling in the Restoration, with men mighty in Church, state, and literature occupying prominent seats, and with trumpets proclaiming the glory of Bacon, observation, and experiment, it was soon surrounded by a mob of tatterdemalions eagerly reaching dirty hands to secure a position on it. The removal of the bars of learning and intellectual competence let loose a crowd of astrologers, empirics, magicians, alchemists, rosicrucians, and a host of others who defy name and classification, all eager to pursue a path that seemed to lead to money, respectability, and fame. Their ways were unlovely and their writings mere jargon, but they could at least despise the ancients, praise the name of Bacon, and shout Experiment! Experiment! Authentic scientists were somewhat confused and inconsistent in their attitude toward them, at one time reaching out helping hands, at another trying to dissociate themselves entirely from them. It is not hard to guess what the intelligent, non-scientific observer of the times thought of a science accompanied by this rabble. The result was that the bad company which the scientific movement kept, in spite of spasmodic efforts to get rid of them, lowered its dignity, which had with difficulty been rescued from the Puritans, and injured its credit with the intelligent public. This fact becomes all the more apparent when we remember that the critics of science had inherited a fastidious aversion to manual contact with material things, a characteristic of aristocratic learning, and did not view those beyond the social pale with any democratic sympathy. There were other reasons for the satiric attack on the experimental philosophy, but the presence of these Ishmaels in the Baconian cohorts increased the contempt with which science was viewed.

The extent to which opposition to experimental science discussed here appears in the anti-scientific literature of the Neo-Classical period can only be suggested now. The atheistic associations of the scientific movement would have produced much more satiric opposition, had so many supporters of the movement not been religious men and had great scientists like Boyle and Newton not remained on the side of the angels. Another reason is discovered in the fact that the charge of atheism was in general diverted from the scientists to the free-thinkers, who had been greatly influenced by science. The anti-rationalistic spirit and the emphasis upon sense-observation characteristic of Baconism played a fundamental part in the satire directed against it. For the chief sin which the satirists find in the experimentalists was the glaring faults of judgement which failed to distinguish between the worth of things and which proposed silly and impossible projects. The importance ascribed to small and insignificant matters by the scientific emphasis upon non-rational observation violated the hierarchy of values upon which neo-classical writers insisted. The naturalistic tendency of the new science and the utilitarian and vocational ideas of education which this science fostered were repugnant to the humanism of Pope's age. And last, the association of science with those low in the social scale and with the much abused Puritans or Dissenters did not recommend it to the undemocratic souls of the neo-classicists. Thus religious, intellectual, and social values influenced the attitude of literature. There were other elements in the scientific movement which inspired satire. The hostility of the new philosophy to the ancients was hardly agreeable to writers who admired them, and the general progressive spirit of Baconianism was antipathetic to the conservatism of the neo-classicists. But those suggested above seem to be the most important.

SWIFT'S EARLY BIOGRAPHERS

HAROLD WILLIAMS

SELECTION and arrangement are essential parts of the biographer's art, and of larger import than the crowded attempt to leave nothing unsaid. Plutarch bids us remember that the very man may often be discerned more clearly in his passing word or in actions of little note than in his great achievements. How many biographers in striving to relate all that a man did fail to show what he was. In our day it has become the fashion to write a man's life immediately upon his death, while recollection is fresh and popular interest unabated. Biographies flood the market, for publishers can count on a remunerative sale if the man or woman portrayed bore a name familiar to newspaper readers, whether for distinction, notoriety, or cheap fame. Further, impatience is fed with lives of the living; and biography, rivalling fiction in popularity, often falls into the same classification.

The life of an *author* calls for the arts of selection and arrangement in a degree beyond that demanded by the recorded achievement of men of action. The story of his life will lie in the written or spoken word, and these are more difficult to appraise than remembered deeds. Nevertheless English literature is enriched by outstanding biographies of writers, as, for example, Boswell's *Johnson* and Lockhart's *Scott*.

Sir Walter Raleigh notes that in earlier days 'a writer was wholly identified with his work'. In the sixteenth century 'there came the first serious attempt to put on record such facts as could be recovered concerning the great writers who had flourished in these islands'.[1] It was in the next century that Izaak Walton, with his rare kindliness of nature, wrote those brief lives containing intimate portrayals matchless of their kind. So we pass by others, including Aubrey and Anthony à Wood, down the steep descent to a commercial realization, in the earlier days of the eighteenth century, of an interest by common readers in lives of contemporaries. Edmund Curll, whom nothing could abash, first seized upon the selling value of cheap, and if possible scandalous, biographies. Few of the

---

[1] *Six Essays on Johnson*, pp. 98–100.

notable, or infamous, in the days of Queen Anne and George I
escaped his net; and many others of earlier date, including
Athanasius and Mahomet, were also gathered in by him. The
quality was poor to disreputable; but the output in biography
can hardly have been equalled since.

If the wits and writers of Queen Anne's day, as well as its men
of action, statesmen, ecclesiastics, and physicians, received their
full share of Curll's attention, it will be more profitable to ignore
him and his coadjutors, as also Giles Jacob's *Poetical Register*,
Cibber's *Lives of the Poets*, and the *Biographia Britannica*, and to
ask ourselves which authors of that time found biographers of
standing before Dr. Johnson embarked on his *Lives of the Poets*.
It will then be discovered that Swift has an easy lead over other
Augustan writers. Addison fares poorly save for Tickell's preface to the works. A dull memoir of Congreve, written perhaps
by John Oldmixon, was published in the year following his
death. Prior, Steele, and Gay must content themselves with
Curll. The memoirs of Pope by Ayre and Dilworth are catch-
penny publications, and Owen Ruffhead's *Life*, although
Warburton lent his assistance, was a tedious performance.
The student of Swift is in far better case.

In the library of Trinity College, Dublin, there is preserved
a manuscript account of his family and early years in Swift's
autograph, extending to twenty quarto pages. This was
evidently intended as a beginning only. So far as it goes it is,
although not wholly reliable, of the highest authority.

The fragment of autobiography was followed by no less than
five publications written by people who had known Swift in
person. In order of date the three volumes of *Memoirs of Mrs.
Laetitia Pilkington* (1748-54) come first. These contain remini-
scences, anecdotes, descriptive passages by a lady, who, if Swift
renounced her friendship later, had often been entertained by
the Dean in his own house. Then comes Lord Orrery's *Remarks
on the Life and Writings of Jonathan Swift* (1752). When the two
met the young peer was about twenty-five and Swift in his
sixty-third year with but a short period in complete command
of his faculties remaining to him. This should be borne in mind
when Orrery writes as if his first-hand knowledge of Swift and
his circle went back much earlier. He describes, for example,
Stella's appearance as if he had long known her, whereas she
had been dead over three years before he paid his first visit to

Ireland. The harsh strictures of an author who posed as Swift's friend won for Orrery's book a phenomenal popularity. It sold in thousands of copies, running into successive editions. Orrery was taken to task in *Observations upon Lord Orrery's Remarks* (1754), written by Dr. Patrick Delany, who had known Swift for thirteen years before his lordship became acquainted with him. Few, however, bought or read Delany's hesitant counterblast. Deference to high birth too often governed his pen. Next came Deane Swift, cousin to the Dean of St. Patrick's, with *An Essay upon the Life, Writings, and Character, of Dr. Jonathan Swift* (1755). Born in 1706 he had the advantage of coming into some slight touch with Swift in early years, but in no intimate way until an even later date than Orrery, indeed hardly till 1738. Deane Swift, it should be noted, although he ranged himself with the defenders of Swift's honour and reputation, entertained a strong aversion to Delany, who, so he believed, had chiefly in mind Mrs. Whiteway, his mother-in-law, and himself among those who sought 'to banish the Dean's best friends from about him, and make a monopoly of him to themselves'. In his knowledge of his distinguished cousin Deane Swift enjoyed an advantage in that original manuscripts came into his possession, including thirty-nine letters forming part of the collection later to be known as the *Journal to Stella*.

Almost thirty years were to pass before another biography, *The Life of the Rev. Dr. Jonathan Swift* (1784), was to appear, written by one who had known Swift, Thomas Sheridan, son of the Thomas who, until his death in 1738, had been a close and intimate friend of the Dean of St. Patrick's and a constant companion of his lighter hours. The younger Sheridan, born in 1719, was Swift's godson. He recalled seeing him in 1735 when on a visit to his father's house at Cavan:

I was there at his arrival, and during the whole time of his continuance there. It grieved me much to see such a change in him. His person was quite emaciated and bore the marks of many more years than had passed over his head. His memory greatly impaired, and his other faculties much on the decline. His temper peevish, fretful, morose, and prone to sudden fits of passion; and yet to me his behaviour was gentle, as it always had been from my early childhood, . . . I loved him from my boyish days, and never stood in the least awe before him.[1]

[1] *Life*, p. 386.

This reminiscence, though written nearly half a century later, has the appearance of exactness and truth. We know that from about this time the failure of Swift's powers brought to a close his life's work. It is of interest, further, to note that Sheridan can justify a statement by reference to Swift himself—'This account I had from his own lips'; or he tells us that Swift recommended to him Sir William Temple as a model of English style.[1] Although Sheridan belongs to the company of those who knew Swift he was writing nearly forty years after his death and must be classed also with the revisers. He reviews and criticizes earlier biographies and supports statements of fact not only from personal knowledge but also from documentary evidence. Before he wrote, Johnson's *Life of Swift* (1781) had appeared, and for this, in the body of his work, he reserved space for a lengthy castigation.

Of these five writers two only can be counted as in any strict sense biographers. Mrs. Pilkington is a vivacious chatterbox, chiefly concerned to win applause, explain away questionable incidents, justify a shady career, and gain a sale for her *Memoirs*. Only two volumes appeared in her lifetime, and of these little more than one-tenth concerned Swift. The third volume, edited by her son and published four years after her death, included further anecdotes. As she was well aware, her recollections of the famous Dean of St. Patrick's could be counted upon to excite interest. She has much to tell of his personal habits and appearance, of the economy of his household, of his friends and dinner parties, of his jesting conversation. If some vivid colouring be removed the essential truthfulness of her picture remains. To dismiss her as a 'lying gossip' is to ignore factual evidence.

Orrery entitled his book *Remarks*, and less than one-third of the volume is devoted to even the semblance of a narrative of Swift's life-story. The reader expectant of gaining some notion of the sequence of events from birth to death will be disappointed.

Delany offers *Observations* as an apologist, contesting Orrery's strictures, correcting mis-statements, defending Swift's character and motives. No dates appear, no chronological order is observed.

Deane Swift called his book an *Essay*, but it is, with all faults, something more. His differences with Orrery and Delany lead

[1] Ibid., pp. 4, 28.

him into tortuous mazes. 'But', as he writes, 'to return from these many digressions . . .'; and he does return to follow Swift through the course of his life.

Sheridan is the orthodox biographer, who, reviewing his predecessors, finds much to condemn and little to praise. His own work is disposed in proper order. About half consists of fairly direct narrative. There follows a full selection 'of such Private Memoirs, as were not meant to meet the publick eye'; and thereafter, invoking the example of Plutarch, he reserves to 'a separate part of the Work, such Anecdotes, Memoirs, and detached Pieces, as could not have been interwoven into the history, without much interruption'.

Meanwhile three compilations had appeared, and of these one deserves commendation. Two may be briefly dismissed. In 1752 J. Cooper, an obscure publisher, brought out the anonymous *Memoirs of the Life and Writings of Jonathan Swift*, a thin duodecimo and now a rare book, made up by an unblushing selection from Orrery's *Remarks*. Six years later came W. H. Dilworth's *Life*, published shortly after the posthumous appearance in 1758 of Swift's *Four Last Years of the Queen*. Dilworth was an industrious compiler of cheap biographies. His book consists of borrowings from Orrery and Delany with a few trivial comments of his own, followed by anecdotes and a culling from Mrs. Pilkington. In contrast, although as an editor he has many shortcomings, the *Life* prefixed by John Hawkesworth to his edition of Swift's *Works* is a creditable performance. Sheridan praised him as a man of 'clear judgment, and great candour', who 'wiped away many of the aspersions that had been thrown on Swift's character; and placed it, so far as he went, in its proper light'. Hawkesworth, who received some help from Johnson, cites authority for his statements and shows critical discrimination. For want of better information he makes mistakes, reproduces errors, and falls into some misunderstandings; but he was far from prepared to accept his authorities upon complete trust, he questions doubtful anecdotes and reasons judiciously. The words with which he concludes his appraisement of Swift's character—'upon the whole it will be found uncommonly steady and uniform'—may fairly be adopted as a judgement of his biography.

In any estimate of the early biographers of Swift it must be remembered that the first three had thoughts ulterior to the mere narration of a life-story. Orrery who, on the strength of his translation of Pliny, counted himself a classical scholar of distinction saw in his friendship with Swift the opportunity to display literary gifts. Inspired by a respect for the epistolary form as an eminently suitable vehicle for persons of rank and quality he adopted for his biography the guise of a series of letters addressed to his son Hamilton, then a 'Student of *Christ-Church* College in *Oxford*'. After covering thirty pages he was led to admit, 'I am making reflections, when I intended to write memoirs'. The intention remained for the most part out of mind. A chain of unnecessary reflections, dull displays of classical erudition, banal criticisms of Swift's writings, and stilted pronouncements on general topics, 'eked out', as Sheridan observes, 'from his commonplace book', encumber his chapters. He plodded slowly through the first eight volumes of Faulkner's edition of the *Works*, deploring every trace of indelicacy or the use of common language, suggesting expurgated versions of writings which offended, impotent as he was to understand Swift's wit and humour, or even his meaning. When discussing *Cadenus and Vanessa* and *Gulliver's Travels* he finds frequent occasion to regret Swift's belittlement of human nature for which *he* entertained an exalted regard. 'The author', he writes, 'was unwilling to lose any opportunity of debasing and ridiculing his own species.' The dense obtuseness of the observation calls for no comment.

It is fair, however, to record entries on the credit side of Orrery's account. He shows modesty and good sense when he abandons the pose of a thinker and turns to draw conclusions from experience. The character-sketch of the first chapter is severe, but he admits that Swift was, when he knew him, 'in the decline of life' and he acknowledges that 'the friendship was an honour'. His account of Swift's passage from the Whigs to the Tories shows acuteness, as also his narrative of the attempt to close the widening rift between Oxford and Bolingbroke. His tribute to Swift as a political writer has merit. He could realize that the prose works showed 'a certain masterly conciseness in their style, that hath never been equalled by any other writer'. His narrative of Swift's rise to power in Ireland is well composed.

It should also be remembered that in his own time Orrery won the regard of the discerning. He was a friend of Pope as

well as of Swift. When Orrery was occupied with his translation
of the letters Dr. Birch took satisfaction in the thought that
Pliny would 'at last have justice done in our language by a
genius equal to his own'.[1] Nevertheless the success of the
Remarks was primarily due to indignant surprise at the 'strange
office' of a writer who sent abroad such harsh judgements upon
a friend. Warburton presumed revenge to be the motive, for
Orrery, he declared, had told him that he 'pursued that friendship so sedulously, that he suffered numberless indignities from
Swift, before he could be admitted to any degree of familiarity'.[2]
The tale may be doubted, for Swift's correspondence shows a
decent regard for Orrery, and he employed him on a trusted
commission with the manuscript of *The Four Last Years of the
Queen*. Another story[3] is that Orrery having one day gained
admission to Swift's library discovered a letter of his own written
several years before, lying still unopened, on which Swift had
written, 'This will keep cold.'

The writer has in his possession a copy of the Dublin *Literary
Journal* for January–February 1752 which was sent to Orrery
by George Faulkner. Orrery had the number specially bound
with title-labels on the front and back covers. On a blank page
he records his opinion of criticisms already published, his judgement of the particular notice, and his readiness to 'review my
performance, and alter & correct in many places'. This modest
and candid observation upon his own book suggests a more
favourable estimate of his character than is commonly entertained. A copy of the *Remarks*, copiously annotated by Orrery
himself, now in the Houghton Library, Harvard, was probably
intended for use in preparing a corrected and enlarged edition.

Patrick Delany raised himself from humble beginnings to a
fellowship of Trinity College, Dublin, ecclesiastical preferment,
reputation as an eloquent preacher, and successive marriages
with two ladies of substance, an advantage which he employed
in cultivating the hospitalities of the dinner-table. His long and
intimate friendship with Swift marked him out as a fitting
antagonist of Orrery. But he was slow to move. Two years
passed before his *Observations upon Lord Orrery's Remarks* appeared,
and he then hid himself behind anonymity. In contradistinc-
tion to Orrery he wrote a lucid, flowing, and eloquent style,

---

[1] Nichols, *Lit. Illustr.* iv. 528.   [2] Nichols, *Lit. Anec.* ii. 232 n.
[3] George-Monck Berkeley, *Literary Relics*, p. xvi.

reminiscent of the pulpit; but, where rougher methods would have served to better purpose, he was finical and precise, for he was needlessly impressed by his lordship's social standing and thought it necessary to gloss his refutations with a tribute to Orrery's capacity to 'set off' mistakes 'with much wit, a fine imagination, and signal sagacity in conjecture', a sequence of gifts to which the author of the *Remarks* could lay no claim. Delany's book, as a whole, although independent testimony presenting some facts and anecdotes at first hand, is of little value, especially when the opportunities he enjoyed, which might well have produced something better, are taken into consideration.

Sheridan, in the introduction to his *Life*, accounting Deane Swift's *Essay* a mere rejoinder to Orrery, asserts that the work, exciting general disappointment, was 'consigned to oblivion.' He adds contemptuously: 'Where let it rest.' This harsh denigration is unjustified. Fantastic Deane Swift was, but not wholly wanting either in competence or in critical ability. He treats Orrery's humourless remarks on *Gulliver's Travels* directly, sensibly, and trenchantly; he is even amusing in the course of his exposure of Orrery's 'lucubrations' on *Cadenus and Vanessa*. His character-study of Swift in the last chapter is well done, far better than anything in either Orrery or Delany, and free from his besetting sin of verbosity. His pages are, however, littered with mistakes in date, in statements of fact, and in annotation, as, for example, in his description of Lady Giffard as Sir William Temple's daughter. Nevertheless he offered contemporaries a more adequate and detailed view of Swift than had yet appeared, making use of autograph manuscripts at the time unpublished, including a considerable body of extracts from the *Journal to Stella*. It is worth noting that Hawkesworth in his able compilation cites Deane Swift as an authority far more often than he does either Orrery or Delany.

As has been noted, Johnson's *Life of Swift* had appeared before that of Sheridan. His *Lives of the Poets* aroused controversy from the first. Defenders entered the lists to contest his 'malignant censures' of Milton and Gray; and Sheridan, characterizing Johnson as a man 'at present of gigantic fame in these days of little men', denounced his attempt to 'scratch out a Life of Swift . . . so miserably executed, as only to reflect back on himself that disgrace, which he meant to throw on the character of the Dean'.

Johnson, as we know, held a poor opinion of Sheridan, declaring that 'vanity and Quixotism obscured his merits'. Although later Johnson expressed a readiness to be reconciled Sheridan avoided the opportunity of a meeting provided by Boswell.[1] There is, however, no reason to attribute to ill feeling his onslaught upon Johnson's *Life*. Even the Doctor's friends, so Murphy tells us, 'trembled for him when he was writing' it.[2] Boswell is constrained to admit 'that he had an unfavourable bias' against Swift.[3] It cannot be denied that, however anxious Johnson may have been to exercise a balanced moderation, he could never altogether get over his dislike. When writing the *Lives* he was, further, too prone to trust to memory and to avoid the labour of looking up his references.[4]

As Sheridan was impelled to champion Swift against the challenges and detractions of Johnson it is worth asking how far he was a fair opponent and how far his thrusts went truly home.

Sheridan maintained that Johnson, holding Swift in 'very little estimation', was in no way 'qualified to give any account of him with the least degree of accuracy'. The first example of careless indifference he selects is Johnson's offhand statement that, although Swift himself claimed to have been born in Dublin, yet Pope told Spence that Swift informed him 'that he was born in the town of Leicester', and that in any event, 'The question may, without much regret, be left in the obscurity in which he delighted to involve it'. With all respect to Johnson it is not easy to excuse this kind of thing. He need neither have been in doubt nor paraded a supercilious indifference to accuracy. Orrery stated emphatically that, although many believed Swift 'a native of *England*', he was undoubtedly born in Dublin. Deane Swift appended to his *Essay* Swift's fragment of biography, printed from the autograph manuscript, as stated both on the title-page of the *Essay* and in a footnote on page 7. In this sketch Swift recorded that he was born in Dublin. Johnson, it is true, does say, 'Jonathan Swift was, according to an account said to be written by himself, . . . born at Dublin.' In what way, however, persisting on a wrong course, was he justified in casting doubt upon the manuscript? Deane Swift said that it *was* written by Swift, and that it had been 'lately pre-

---

[1] Boswell's *Life*, Hill–Powell, iv. 330.   [2] Hill, *Johnsonian Miscellanies*, i. 479.
[3] *Life*, Hill–Powell, iv. 61.   [4] Ibid., 36 n. 3.

sented by the Author of this Essay to the *University* of *Dublin*'. Hawkesworth declares that Swift was born in Ireland, and that he often 'pointed out the house in which he was born'; maintaining, further, that the belief that he was born in England was a 'mistake'. Now Johnson prefaces his own *Life* by commending that of Hawkesworth, whom, so he says, he advised on the 'scheme' and to whom he 'communicated' his thoughts. Is it not a little odd, therefore, that Johnson should profess ignorance about a fact which was not in doubt, and which he had no real reason to pretend *was*?

Sheridan's further observations on Johnson divide themselves into pointing out errors in fact and errors, as he regards them, in opinion. His temper was roused and he grew needlessly wordy; but he does seize upon good fighting points. His attacks go home.

Noting the publication of *A Tale of a Tub* Johnson remarks: 'That Swift was its author, though it be universally believed, was never owned by himself, nor very well proved by any evidence.' Every good Johnsonian knows that this was not the only occasion when the Doctor threw suspicion on Swift's authorship of *A Tale*. Sheridan, commenting on Johnson's doubts, writes: 'Surely the Doctor has never seen the letters that passed between the Dean and Ben Tooke . . . wherein he not only acknowledges himself the author, but gives directions about the publication of another edition.' The reference is to letters which had been printed by Deane Swift in 1765 in his volumes of the London trade edition of Swift's *Works*. These were available to Johnson. In one letter, 29 June 1710, Swift discussed with Tooke the publication of a new edition of *A Tale*, to contain additional matter and be adorned with cuts. He took special note of the fact that in *A Complete Key to a Tale of a Tub*, just published by Curll, the composition of the narrative part of *A Tale* was attributed to his 'little parson cousin', Thomas Swift, rector of Puttenham. He pours ridicule on the whole story. It is true that in so many words he does not claim the authorship. Indeed, he still tries to invest the whole question in some mystery; but nobody reading the letter could suppose that it was written by anyone save an author discussing his own work with a publisher. His letter is, beyond cavil, demonstrative proof. Further, and this is an argument of inescapable force, Tooke in his reply writes: 'As to that cousin of yours which you speak of, I neither know him nor ever heard of him till the Key mentioned him.'[1] Johnson, as a responsible biographer, ought not to have expressed doubts based on internal evidence, which, on his authority, were bound to mislead, when weighty external evidence had long been published confirming Swift's authorship of *A Tale of a Tub*.

Even more is Sheridan aroused to indignation by Johnson's suggestion that the *Battle of the Books* was borrowed from a French work called *Combat des Livres*, and by Johnson's refusal to accept the statement of 'An Apology', prefixed to the fifth edition of *A Tale*, that the author had never 'seen any such Treatise in his Life nor heard of it before'. Johnson's rejection of this statement was in questionable taste, as there is not the least probability that he had ever seen the French book, which he refers to by a title it never bore. This is what Johnson says: 'The improbability of such a coincidence of thoughts without communication is not, in my opinion, balanced by the anonymous protestation prefixed, in which all knowledge of the French book is peremptorily disowned.' Johnson takes the plagiarism for granted and refuses to accept the disclaimer because it is anonymous, whereas, as Sheridan quite reasonably remarks, nearly everything Swift wrote was anonymous. He concludes with charging Johnson with such 'gross prejudice and want of candour, as should make the reader cautious how he gives any credit to the many other misrepresentations' of Swift and his character.

It was William Wotton who first, in 1705, in some 'Observations upon the Tale of a Tub', suggested that Swift's *Battle* was a borrowed piece of work. 'I have been assured that the *Battel in St. James's Library* is *Mutatis Mutandis* taken out of a *French Book* entitled, *Combat des Livres*, if I misremember not.' This is casual. Surely Wotton ought, before making such an assertion, to have looked up the French book and collated it to see what parallelisms he could discover? To begin with he would have failed to discover a French book of the title. It is probable that Wotton's informant alluded to a book by François de Callières published anonymously in 1688. Its title was *Histoire Poëtique de la Guerre nouvellement declarée entre les Anciens et les Modernes*. Others besides Johnson have followed Wotton, and among them Sir Walter Scott,[2] who has no hesitation in asserting that

---

[1] *Correspondence of Jonathan Swift*, ed. F. Elrington Ball, i. 183–6.
[2] *Memoirs of Swift* (1814), pp. 45–6.

Swift took 'The idea' of his *Battle* from 'a spirited poem' by 'Coutray'. Scott got the title of the French book correctly, but it was not written by an author called Coutray, and it isn't a poem. As a witness for the prosecution, therefore, Scott is an embarrassing liability. Wotton, Johnson, and Scott had never seen the book they called in evidence with such airy dogmatism. It is, of course, just possible that Swift at some period did have the book in his hands for a short time. During his years in Temple's household he read industriously and widely. Nevertheless his assertion that he had never seen it was quite sincere. In the essentials, which make the *Battle of the Books* what it is, its wit and its satiric irony, the work is Swift's and his only. All in all it is probable that he was wholly justified in disclaiming knowledge of De Callières's book, for the slight parallelisms belong to the subject rather than to independent invention or to borrowing.

To pass on—Johnson is fairly caught out by Sheridan when, writing of the *Examiner*, he asserted carelessly that, 'With regard to wit, I am afraid none of Swift's papers will be found equal to those by which Addison opposed him.' Disregarding the questionable judgement on respective gifts of wit the blunder to be noted is that Johnson completely forgot that Addison's last *Whig Examiner* was published on 12 October 1710 and Swift's first *Examiner* on the second of the following month.[1] It is true that the *Examiner* began to appear on 3 August 1710, but it was then written by other hands. This brought into the field an opposition *Whig Examiner*, 14 September–12 October 1710, of which, however, only five numbers appeared, all written by Addison. Swift and Addison did not, as Johnson avers, come into conflict. There was no overlap of their respective papers.

Sheridan's next quarrel with Johnson is his reflection upon Swift's disinterestedness and independence of spirit, which he describes as 'a strain of heroism . . . in his condition romantick and superfluous'. He followed this up with an illustration which the reader was invited to accept as evidence that Swift was not always as disinterested as he claimed for himself or as others claimed for him. Johnson writes: 'He refused, indeed, fifty pounds from Lord Oxford, but he accepted afterwards a draught of a thousand upon the Exchequer, which was intercepted by

[1] Sheridan says 'the 10th of the following November', a mistake on his part.

the Queen's death, and which he resigned, as he says himself, "multa gemens" (with many a groan).' The inference the ordinary reader would draw from this is fairly put by Sheridan —'that though Swift rejected the offer of so paltry a sum as fifty pounds, he was not proof against so large a bribe as that of a thousand.' I shall not follow Sheridan in detail, for I think if it had been put straightforwardly to Johnson he might, possibly might, have been induced to admit that he was bringing into conjunction two disconnected and incomparable incidents, and that in quoting Swift's words, 'multa gemens', he had given them a wrong turn and jumped over a sundering gap in Swift's life. In the *Journal to Stella* Swift declares that he was so offended by Oxford's offer of a bank-bill for £50 that he could hardly be reconciled to him. This may have seemed to Johnson, and not unjustifiably when he thought of his own penurious days, a superfluous strain of heroism. But Swift's position in relation to the Tory Ministry was on a different plane. He had come to London carrying a commission from the Irish Archbishops and Bishops. He was received on familiar social terms by Harley and St. John. Oxford's offer of £50 placed him, so he felt, on a level with hired party scribblers. He was genuinely injured in spirit. The only recognition he was prepared to accept was ecclesiastical preferment. As we well know, the best that could be done in the end was the Deanery of St. Patrick's, Dublin. And this is where the £1,000 to which Dr. Johnson alludes comes in. When Swift was presented to the Deanery of St. Patrick's he found himself faced with heavy charges. His predecessor, Dean Stearne, had built for himself a fine new deanery house. On account of the house Swift was obliged to pay £800, and, in addition, £150 in respect of first-fruits, and £50 in respect of his patent, which all adds up to £1,000, a staggering demand to meet for one whose income ran to something between £200 and £300 a year. The induction grant, which Swift might reasonably have expected, he never received, although the Exchequer order seems to have reached him. Thirteen years after his installation he wrote ironically to Pope: 'I forgave Sir Robert Walpole a thousand pounds, *multa gemens*.' The complaint was not serious. He wrote jestingly. He never had much hope of the money. The casual allusion was penned many years after his rejection of Oxford's bank-bill for £50. The two sums had no relationship to each other. Dr. Johnson forced them into an unnatural conjunction, coupled with an unfair reflection on Swift's standards of honour with regard to money matters.

Sheridan was roused to his fiercest indignation, and not without cause, when he reached the passage in which Johnson alludes to a letter addressed to Queen Caroline in June 1731, written on behalf of Mrs. Barber, a minor versifier and wife to a woollen-draper of Dublin. She was, further, known to be a protégée of Swift's. The letter purported to be of the Dean's composition and concluded with the signature 'Jonath. Swift'. The letter, says Johnson, 'has all the appearances of his diction and sentiments', although he admitted that it was not in the Dean's hand. 'When he was charged with this letter', continues Johnson, 'he laid hold of the inaccuracies, and urged the improbability of the accusation, but never denied it: he shuffles between cowardice and veracity, and talks big when he says nothing.' It is difficult to understand how Johnson allowed himself reflections so unpleasant, so harsh, and so unjust. The 'diction and sentiments', grotesque and exaggerated to the last degree, couched in the worst taste, bear no resemblance to anything Swift can be conceived to have written. When the letter came to him from Pope, who had received it from the Countess of Suffolk, he replied at once disclaiming all con-nexion with the counterfeit document; and seven days later he wrote to the Countess of Suffolk in much the same terms. No candid reader of these letters could find any justification for the charge that Swift shuffles 'between cowardice and veracity'. His denial could scarcely be more vigorous. As Sheridan says, it is difficult to understand how such an imputation was thrown 'upon such bad grounds'.

The original letter may be seen in the Forster Collection, South Kensington. It is written in a large hand, very likely that of a woman. The signature is a crude, unpractised imita-tion of Swift's hand. The origin of the forgery has never been explained. It has been suggested that Swift himself in jest wrote the letter, which was then copied and sent to the Queen. The suggestion may be dismissed. Had he attempted anything of the kind he could hardly have failed more miserably. Another suggestion is that Mrs. Barber herself composed the letter. From all that we know of her this appears most improbable. It must have been the work of some third person, whose identity was not then discovered, and is unlikely to be now.

It is not always that we show at our best, not always that we occupy ourselves with a congenial task. Johnson was out of sympathy with Swift; he could not wholly overcome a measure of dislike. The *Life* he wrote, however, cannot be accounted either careless or perfunctory, although it is only about one-third the length of that devoted to Pope, half the length of Savage's, shorter than Addison's, less than half Dryden's, and about the same as Cowley's. Nevertheless he was at some trouble and gathered relevant and informative facts. If, as he says, he communicated his thoughts to Hawkesworth, when the latter was occupied with his *Life of Swift*, he was clearly not attempting to write upon an author to whom before he had given no consideration. On the other hand Sheridan is not to be dismissed as the irascible friend; or as counsel for the defence seeking to put his adversary in the wrong. His objections are fair comment, he covers the ground well, and Johnson comes out of the encounter rather rumpled and shaken.

On the other side of the question it must not be forgotten that a long list can easily be gathered of Johnson's generous and appreciative tributes to Swift's character and genius. Two examples must serve, one near the beginning of the *Life*, the other at the end. Commenting upon Swift's failure to make the best use of his undergraduate days Johnson tells us that, in contrition, he resolved to devote eight hours each day to study, 'and continued his industry for seven years'. He then continues: 'This part of his story well deserves to be remembered; it may afford useful admonition and powerful encouragement to men whose abilities have been made for a time useless by their passions and pleasures, and who, having lost one part of life in idleness, are tempted to throw away the remainder in despair.' And none could ask in praise more than Johnson's concluding words: 'Perhaps no writer can easily be found that has borrowed so little, or that in all his excellences and all his defects has so well maintained his claim to be considered as original.'

SWIFT'S SUPPOSED INGRATITUDE TOWARD HIS UNCLE GODWIN: A SURMISE[1]

ARTHUR E. CASE

'. . . THE Reverend Dr. Whittingham, Archdeacon of Dublin, a bold and ready talker, used to be forward to shew his colloquial courage where few would have chosen to exercise it, by attacking Dean Swift, and that with great rudeness and severity. At a visitation dinner, they chanced to be placed nearly opposite to each other at table, when Dr. Whittingham suddenly asked, "Pray, Mr. Dean, was it not your Uncle Godwin who educated you?"—Swift affected not to hear this insulting question. At length it was twice repeated, with a loud and bitter accent, when the Dean answered abruptly, "Yes. He gave me the education of a dog." "Then," answered Whittingham, grinning and clenching his hand, "you have not the gratitude of a dog." '

Thus Sir Walter Scott, on the authority of Theophilus Swift, on the authority, in turn, of Mrs. Whiteway. The story has often been repeated in one form or another. It is dear to historical novelists and popular biographers, especially those who enjoy the spectacle of Swift occasionally getting his comeuppance. It pleases those, too, who conceive Swift as the eternal paradox, and who like to contemplate ingratitude in the man who, in *Gulliver's Travels*, denounced that vice as a capital crime. The provenience of the anecdote is perhaps not the most reliable in the world, but it has been accepted by several respectable biographers, and the element in it which chiefly concerns me at the moment has independent evidence to confirm it: Swift was dissatisfied with the education given him by his Uncle Godwin and did not scruple to say so.

But the scholar, given one fact, always wants to know more. *Why* was Swift dissatisfied? As we all know, the factual material dealing with Swift's early life is scanty, and conjecture has had

---

[1] The Editors feel privileged to include this essay by permission of Mrs. Arthur E. Case, and thus to make the gesture of friendliness to Professor Sherburn which the late Professor Case undoubtedly would have made were he living.

to be called upon to fill gaps. There can be no quarrel with conjecture so long as it is not labelled as fact. Unfortunately, some conjectures about Swift have been repeated so often that their conjectural nature has been forgotten. It has been said, for example, that Swift's grievance was that at the age of six he was torn ruthlessly from his mother and sent to a boarding-school. As the sending of very young boys to boarding-school was and is a common practice among the well-to-do classes in Great Britain, and as this is generally regarded as a high privilege for the child, especially if, as in Swift's case, the school is a good one, this explanation of Swift's anger is not very plausible. Along with this theory often goes the implication that at the time Swift was sent to Kilkenny Mrs. Swift went back to England. For this there is no evidence whatever. It is safe to assume that when Jonathan, at the age of four, was brought back from Whitehaven by the nurse who had kidnapped him three years earlier, his mother was still in Dublin. But I know of no definite *evidence* that she returned to Leicester before Swift was twenty, though it is generally assumed that she did so some time in the middle of her son's boyhood.

Other suggested explanations of Swift's dissatisfaction have to do with his being sent to Trinity College, Dublin, as a pensioner, and with the supposed neglect of him by his uncle's family during his seven years of college life. There is more to support these theories than there is to support the one first mentioned. Swift's own words in his *Autobiography* are: '. . . in the university at Dublin . . . by the ill treatment of his nearest relations, he was so discouraged and sunk in his spirits that he too much neglected his academic studies. . . .' But this does not specify the nature of the ill treatment, nor does it completely account for the bitterness and tenacity of Swift's feelings about his education.

Puzzling lately over the phrase 'the education of a dog', I began to make new conjectures to explain it. I rejected the supposition that Mrs. Swift had left Ireland when her son was six, partly for the reasons already given, partly because Swift's *Autobiography* hints of no dissatisfaction with Kilkenny School, and partly because I could not believe that the strong bond between Swift and his mother could have been formed if she had been in charge of him only from his fourth to his sixth year. The next question was, obviously, 'When did Mrs. Swift leave

Ireland, and why?' Gradually I evolved a possible theory, with variations, which I now set forth.

Mrs. Swift had never felt at home in Ireland. She had accepted the partial support of her brother-in-law Godwin while Jonathan was a boy, but always with the idea that when he grew up he would be an Englishman. It was she who fostered his love for England and coincidentally his contempt for Ireland, which she either could not or did not wish to conceal from him. When he left Kilkenny it seemed to her that the time had come for him to prepare for his English heritage by going to an English university. She proposed to Godwin Swift that he should supply the means. But Godwin was beginning to feel a financial pinch, though he did not wish the world to know it; besides, he felt that Ireland, which was good enough for him and his family, should be good enough for his sister-in-law and her son. He refused to send Jonathan to Oxford or Cambridge, but offered to send him to Trinity College. Mrs. Swift felt aggrieved and said so plainly: Godwin stood firm, and buttressed his position by offering to pay for the college education of young Tom Swift, the son of another of Godwin's brothers, only if he would enter Trinity. This was a stiffer condition than that applied to Jonathan, for young Tom had been born and reared in England and his father was an Oxford graduate, so that he had a better claim than Jonathan to be sent to an English college. Mrs. Swift had to give in, not being able to finance her son's education herself, but she felt so bitterly about the affair that she could no longer live on her brother-in-law's bounty, and so returned to England to live with her family. She succeeded, however, in convincing Jonathan that both he and she had been wronged by a cold and parsimonious man who owed his nephew the best of educations, i.e. an English one, and that that man was responsible for the parting of mother and son. It is not hard to imagine the impression that such talk would have made upon a sensitive boy of fourteen, devoted to his mother, the only close and thoroughly affectionate relation he had. His ideas about his education, his uncle, and the relative merits of England and Ireland would have been given an emotional colour which it would have been almost impossible to change. Whether or not Oxford was, in the 1680's, a better university than Trinity, whether or not Godwin Swift could or should have undertaken the expense of giving Jonathan an English education—these were questions to which Jonathan would never be able to give a reasoned answer. Then and forever, in his eyes, he had been given 'the education of a dog'.

There are possible variations on this theme. For example, the impetus of Mrs. Swift's request may have been an addition to her small independent income through some gift or legacy from her own family, which led her to feel that she could once more afford to live in that expensive country, England, though she would not be able to support Jonathan at Oxford. The chief point at issue would, however, have remained the same, and so would the result of the argument between her and Godwin Swift.

Is there enough evidence to justify publishing this theory? A man is notoriously incapable of valuing his own theories accurately, so I hesitate to express an opinion. At the moment I am inclined to say no. There are more than enough conjectures about Swift on the market already. Why, then, do I inflict another? To answer this I must ask leave to compare my conjecture with one which I have fabricated solely for the purpose of contrast. I present it with a great deal of trepidation. I do not believe in it for a minute. But it may have a temporary usefulness, after which I hope it can be completely forgotten. I may plead in partial excuse that it deals, not with an eighteenth-century subject, but with an early nineteenth-century one, the sailing venture in which Shelley met his death. It runs thus. Shortly after Shelley, his friend Williams, and their crew of one set out from Livorno it became evident that a storm was brewing. Shelley always reacted emotionally to storms. This one moved him suddenly to confess to Williams that he was in love with Williams's wife Jane, that he had declared his love to her (cf. the poem, 'We meet not as we parted'), and that the only thing for Williams to do, on a really high plane, was to resign his interest in Jane to Shelley. This, not unnaturally, startled Williams into remonstrance. Shelley persisted, and in order to devote himself to his argument with less hindrance, made fast the sheet, which had been in his charge, and came forward. The wind was rising; Williams attempted at the same time to calm Shelley and to reef the sails, as a nearby ship's-captain was shouting to him to do. But Shelley, concerned with what he deemed a more important matter, restrained Williams's arms: the sails remained aloft and unreefed, the sheet remained fast. A few minutes later the squall struck the *Don Juan* and all was over.

Well, there it is. So far as I can tell it does not conflict with any of the known facts about Shelley or the manner of his death. Psychologically it is quite arguable. It even has a certain ghastly melodramatic attraction about it. If an historical novelist got hold of it, and I should protest against his using it because he couldn't prove its truth, he would probably retort that I couldn't disprove it either.

Now I do not want to compare these two theories on the score of their relative probability. Both depend, not on simple probabilities, but on possibilities resting on possibilities resting on possibilities. It would be convenient if there were some mathematical formula for solving problems of this kind. I am reminded of a sentence quoted by Professor Henry A. Beers from an old-fashioned algebra: 'It is 3 to 1 that A speaks the truth, 6 to 1 that B does, and 1 to 3 that C does. What is the probability that an event took place which A asserts to have happened and which B and C deny?' But, I repeat, I am interested at present not in the comparative likelihood of my two theories, but in their comparative usefulness. The Shelley theory, it seems to me, has two serious faults. In the first place, even if it were true it would be of no significance. It would add nothing to what we know of Shelley's character, his mind, or his work. And secondly it leads nowhere. It can neither be proved nor disproved. The actors in the drama are dead and cannot speak; moreover, they died before they could leave any record of what happened on that tragic voyage. No other person saw or heard what passed. Nothing could come of such a theory (if anyone took it seriously) but fruitless bickering and wasted time. It is worse than a dead issue—it is a mischievous one. It should probably never have been broached, even frivolously.

But the theory about Swift, I submit, may have some value. If there is any truth in it, it may help to shed light on the influence of Mrs. Swift upon her son, a matter about which we should like to know more than we do. And it has this additional advantage over the Shelley theory: it provides leads for further investigation, and therefore may be regarded as being possibly fruitful. Several means of testing it suggest themselves.

Are there any records of Mrs. Swift's sources of income, or of gifts or legacies to her? Is there any untraced correspondence with or about the Thomas Swift connexion which may prove of value? Other lines of investigation may become evident to those who chance to meet with my conjecture. In any event, it is the sort of conjecture for which a wide net must be flung if it is to be proved or disproved. So I give it to the public, hoping that someone, in the course of time, will find means to settle the questions it raises.

SWIFT'S *MECHANICAL OPERATION OF THE SPIRIT*

JAMES L. CLIFFORD

CURIOUS readers in the year 1704, coming upon the sensational new book, *A Tale of a Tub*, were generally amused and also severely shocked. If they had stomach enough to read the volume quite through, as doubtless many did, the most severe shock of all may well have been administered not by the *Tale* itself, but by a separate *Discourse Concerning the Mechanical Operation of the Spirit—A Fragment*, which came at the end. Well aware of the importance, for emphasis, of the last word, twentieth-century readers sense immediately the strategic significance of this so-called *Fragment*. It occupies the place in the book most effective for achieving a climactic effect, the position most certain to colour the reader's opinions as he puts the book aside. Yet, strangely enough, until very recently there has been very little critical discussion of this piece and of its function in the design of Jonathan Swift's first published volume. It has received short shrift in the lengthy analyses of the main allegory and digressions of the *Tale* proper and of the *Battle of the Books*.

Perhaps one reason for the comparative neglect of this part of the book has been the basic nature of the satire. The harsh reduction of all religious enthusiasm to physical causes and the openly indecent sex symbolism offended from the start most readers. Puzzled and upset, many critics have preferred to pass by what they could not openly discuss in print, possibly rationalizing their neglect by the excuse that the *Fragment* was really not an integral part of the *Tale*.

There is scarcely any mention of *The Mechanical Operation of the Spirit* in the more important nineteenth-century discussions of Swift's works. It is not surprising that Thackeray, who found the *Tale* itself a 'wild book', was content to lash out at Swift in general without going into details; but Hazlitt would not normally have been revolted by the flagrant sex symbolism and might have been expected to see the superb power and wit of the concluding piece. Indeed, he called the whole *Tale* 'one of the most masterly compositions in the language'. It was undoubtedly the prudery of the age that kept even the author of the *Liber Amoris* from coming to grips with the ideas of Swift's devastating satire.

Forster, Craik, Moriarty, and others studiously avoided any analysis of the *Fragment*. Henry Morley (as did some other editors) left it out completely from one reprinting of the *Tale* and the *Battle of the Books*, though including the spurious 'History of Martin'. Only Churton Collins, in 1893, was willing to call it 'a singularly powerful satire', when discussing 'the cataclysm of filth and vitriol with which the scorn and contempt of Swift overwhelmed' the fanatics. Along with the savage fourth book of *Gulliver* and many of the poems, *The Mechanical Operation of the Spirit* was meat too strong for the stomachs of Victorian readers.

Fortunately the attitude is beginning to change. Modern critics, while rediscovering the merits of Swift's corrosive, naturalistic verse and of the voyage to the land of the Houyhnhnms, have given some serious consideration to the final piece of the *Tale of a Tub* volume. A. C. Guthkelch and D. Nichol Smith have provided a superb annotated edition (1920). Émile Pons in *Swift: les années de jeunesse et le 'Conte du tonneau'* (1925) has discussed many of the basic themes. In an important series of articles, Clarence M. Webster has shown how conventional for his own time were many of Swift's explanations of the physiological origin of enthusiasm and his insistence on the abnormal sex life of the zealots.[1] And finally Ricardo Quintana, in his *Mind and Art of Jonathan Swift* (1936), has commented on the canny artistry of Swift, who perceived how effectively the terminal position of the *Fragment* 'would cope the two great satires preceding it'. But neither Quintana nor any other of the recent commentators on *A Tale of a Tub* has analysed carefully the significance of the order of the pieces in the 1704 volume.

It is not my intention in the present study to investigate the sources of the ideas in *The Mechanical Operation of the Spirit*—its obvious relationship to the popular mechanical concept of nature of his day, so ably described by Mr. R. F. Jones in an earlier paper in this volume—the many echoes of Cervantes, Hobbes, Marvell, Henry More, Locke, and others, though such a detailed study might well be rewarding. Instead, I should like

---

[1] See in particular *P.M.L.A.*, xlviii (Dec. 1933), 1141–53, and l (March 1935), 210–23.

to attempt some evaluation of the reactions of contemporary readers to the piece, and to make tentative suggestions concerning Swift's reasons for placing it at the end of the 1704 volume. Although the justification for yoking together the two diverse inquiries may not at first appear obvious, it will be my purpose to show that the way in which early readers were affected by the 1704 volume sheds some light on Swift's structural plan, even when those readers themselves failed to understand the hidden design.

That the volume containing the three kindred pieces was widely read on its first appearance we know from letters of Charles Davenant and Bishop Atterbury, and from the number of early editions. Contemporary references to it are fairly numerous, but unfortunately not many of the commentators discuss the work in great detail. In the few published attacks, however, the *Fragment*, or the ideas contained in it, have a prominent place. Thus William King, who found it expedient to disclaim publicly authorship of the inflammable volume, tells in *Some Remarks on the Tale of a Tub* how he came upon the work. 'I never gave over till I had read his Tale, his Battle, and His Fragment.' Finding distinct unity in the three parts of the volume, King adds: 'The true reason why I do not descend to more particulars is, because I think the three treatises (which by their harmony in dirt, may be concluded to belong to one Author) may be reduced to a very small compass . . . .' The author's chief aims, according to King—and his indictment is clearly applied to the *Fragment* as well as to the *Tale*—are to be profane, to show proficiency 'at hectoring and bullying, at ranting and roaring', to 'exceed all bounds of modesty' in the search for the lewdest images, and to evince 'great affection for everything that is nasty'.

William Wotton's more celebrated attack in 1705, included in the third edition of his *Defense of the Reflections upon Ancient and Modern Learning*, goes even farther. The volume, he insists, is 'one of the Prophanest Banters upon the Religion of *Jesus Christ*, as such, that ever yet appeared'. For Wotton *The Mechanical Operation of the Spirit* is the worst of all: 'In the *Tale*, in the *Digressions*, in the *Fragment*, the same Spirit runs through, but rather most in the *Fragment*, in which all extraordinary Inspirations are the Subjects of his Scorn and Mockery.' Wotton, indeed, finds no excuse whatsoever for this last section of the book. Other parts, particularly the attacks upon himself and Bentley, may be explained as the result of personal spite and vituperation. But 'even that Excuse will not serve in the *Fragment*, which is levelled at no particular Man that I can find whatsoever'. In this section the real purpose of the work becomes evident: 'the Mask is more plainly taken off in the *Fragment*'.

Much the same attitude toward the profane and degrading imagery of the *Fragment* may be found in other pamphlets of the day when the *Tale of a Tub* volume is mentioned. In *A Morning's Discourse of a Bottomless Tubb, Introducing the Historical Fable of the Oak and Her Three Provinces*, written by 'a Lover of the Loyal, Honest, and Moderate Party', which appeared in 1712, the *Tale of a Tub*, or 'this Romantick Piece', is first called 'frivolous' or rather 'Bottomless', and only bantering references are made to the author's 'Mechanick Method'. Warming to the topic, however, the anonymous writer insists that 'a judicious Scanner' of the book,

upon a second Reading, will hardly let him scape from a severe Censure, for in Conclusion, as I was saying before, he now turns Cousin *Neptune* in good Earnest, questioning and lessening in his Fragment, the Divinity and Inspiration of the *Apostles* and *Prophets*, and with an Assurance only proper for a Critick of his Kidney, calls it a *Religious Enthusiasm, and a lifting up the Soul and its Faculties above Matter*, then pounding his Opinions together, mixes it with the Devils possessing People, and to crown his Admirable Topick, affirms, *That the Corruption of Sences is the Generation of the Spirit, That Men establish a Fellowship of Christ with Belial, and such is the Analogy between Cloven Tongues and Cloven Feet*: And lastly, to prove a particular Transport in his Prophane Lunacy, affirms, *That a Debate has continued this Hundred Years whether the Deportment and Cant of our* English *Enthusiastick Preachers* was Possession or Inspiration.

Similarly, in the scurrilous parody of Swift, usually assigned to young 'Tom' Burnet, called *Essays Divine, Moral, and Political: By the Author of the Tale of a Tub* . . ., printed in 1714, much of the attack is centred upon these same ideas. The method in this instance is to paraphrase and quote from Swift's works, producing a *pot pourri* of scandalous statements, the cumulative effect of which is much worse than Swift originally intended. After a disagreeable dedication to 'Prince Posterity', in which Swift is personally maligned, there comes Essay I, 'Of

Religion in General', largely a burlesque of the 'Digression on Madness', making all religions come from fumes. Included is some discussion of the refining of '*Carnal* into *Spiritual* Extasy', of the use of female priests, and the debate whether the 'Deportment of Enthusiastick Preachers is *Inspiration or Possession*'. But it is in Essay II, 'Of Christianity', that the *Fragment* is chiefly parodied. One long passage is merely a pastiche of mangled quotations. For example:

In the Beginning of *Christianity*, the Operations of the Spirit were esteem'd Supernatural; but of Late, that Operation is purely Mechanical, and wonderfully perform'd by our *British* Workmen. *The lifting up the Soul above Matter, either by Inspiration, Possession, or Natural Causes (such as the Effect of a strong Imagination, Spleen, violent Anger, Grief, Pain, and the like)* may serve for a Definition of Enthusiasm, which is call'd *The Operation of the Spirit*. But the Enthusiasm, or Spiritual Operation of our *Christian Sectaries*, of which I speak at present, is a Trade, the effect of Art, which after several Advancements and Refinements, by Cultivating Hands, is, at last, brought to its utmost Perfection, Building always on this Foundation, *That the Corruption of the Senses is the Generation of the Spirit.*

There are further elaborations on the theme, effectively used by Swift, of Mahomet going to Paradise on his Ass, with the added almost direct quotation concerning Indians who pray from fear: 'they are put upon their Knees by their *Fears*, and we by our *Desires*'.

Swift's manner is mocked throughout, as when the author remarks:

This would best appear by describing and deducing the whole Process of the *Operation*; and this I have explain'd from great Reading and Observation; but I don't think it safe and convenient to Print it, least it might be made use of as an Argument for the *Abolishing of Christianity*, which, in my Opinion, is not of that absolute Necessity which some People would perswade us.

Readers familiar with Swift's works were sure to see the point; and the insidious part was that by the ingenious and unscrupulous use of his own phrases and themes was fashioned a much more revolting set of ideas, which Swift with justice would undoubtedly have rejected. And this particular nasty attack was given wider circulation by its being reprinted intact in Jonathan Smedley's *Gulliveriana* in 1728.

Swift's first biographer, his friend the Earl of Orrery, in 1752 showed clearly his horror over the *Fragment*, in which 'the author has revelled in too licentious a vein of sarcasm: many of his ideas are nauseous, some are indecent, and others have an irreligious tendency'. Orrery found the piece not equal in wit and humour to the rest of the book, but on grounds that to us would seem flimsy.

I should constantly choose rather to praise, than to arraign, any part of my friend *Swift's* writings: but in those tracts, where he tries to make us uneasy with ourselves, and unhappy in our present existence, *there*, I must yield him up entirely to censure.

When it is remembered that Orrery forced himself to discuss the fourth voyage of Gulliver 'with great reluctance', and was heartily tired and disgusted with it, we need not take his critical opinions very seriously.

It should be evident from these examples that Swift's contemporaries were well aware of the scandalous implications of the ideas in the *Fragment*, and generally not afraid of coming directly to grips with the distasteful themes. Indeed, they seem to have provided much of the subject-matter for the attack.[1] What, then, was Swift's real purpose in placing this combustible material emphatically at the end of his first published work?

Before an attempt is made to answer this question, however, there are other important considerations. How certain are we that the *Fragment* was written by Swift? And can we be sure that he alone was responsible for the placing of the piece where it is in the volume?

For modern scholars (as well as for early readers of the *Tale*) there has been no doubt whatsoever of Swift's sole authorship of the *Fragment*. Indeed, the claim in Curll's *Complete Key to the Tale of a Tub* in 1710 that not Jonathan, but his cousin Thomas Swift was responsible for *The Mechanical Operation of the Spirit* and the main allegory of the *Tale* has been so clearly discredited by Guthkelch and Nichol Smith in their edition that there is no need to go over the evidence again. Nor can there be any real doubt that the printing of the piece was exactly as Swift wished. Despite all his typical attempts at mystification—

---

[1] It may not be far-fetched also to see oblique hits at the themes of the *Tale of a Tub* volume in Defoe's railing against blasphemous anonymous pamphlets in the *Review* for 8 Nov. 1705. Other later attacks which may be mentioned appeared in the *Medley* (1710–12) and in *Gulliveriana* (1728), pp. xix, 6–7, &c.

the devious explanations of the background of the manuscript
and bland claims of ignorance of authorship in the bookseller's
advertisement, the use of asterisks and marginal annotations
to indicate censored omissions, even the later excuses in the
'Apology'—the evidence appears fairly clear. As Guthkelch and
Nichol Smith put it, 'It is not rash to assume that the *Discourse*
appeared exactly as Swift meant it to appear.'

Moreover, there is no evidence that the position of the
Fragment in the volume was not carefully premeditated. The
signatures in the first edition are regularly in order, the same
paper is used throughout the volume, and there is nothing to
show that any portions were printed separately or were late
additions. To be sure, the *Fragment* has a separate title-page,
but so has the *Battle of the Books*, and in each case the pagination
throughout the volume is exactly as one would expect if the
whole book had been set up at one time. Later editions printed
by Nutt follow the same order. And although we have no
direct evidence that Swift himself was responsible for the
arrangement of these early editions, his correspondence with
Benjamin Tooke in 1710 shows clearly that Swift was in close
touch with the printing of the revised fifth edition. If he had
been displeased with anything in the earlier versions, he could
easily have changed the order at this time. But in all the
authorized editions in Swift's lifetime the *Fragment* came last in
the volume, after the *Battle of the Books*. Only in the so-called
Dutch edition of 1720 (which first contained 'The History of
Martin' and other dubious matter) and in editions deriving
from it, is the order changed. And for these versions we may be
certain Swift was not responsible. He put the *Fragment* last
because he wished it to be there, and despite early attacks he
kept it in this emphatic position.

Much more difficult to ascertain is the date of composition of
the *Fragment*. Was it an early piece which Swift hated to discard
and so tacked on uncomfortably to the end of his book? Or
was it written contemporaneously with the great digressions of
the *Tale*, some time after the original allegory? Scholars have
long disagreed. W. D. Taylor in his *Jonathan Swift, a Critical
Essay* (1933) intimates that the *Fragment* is a preliminary version
of Sections VIII and IX of the *Tale*; and Mrs. Miriam Starkman in a recent study of the background of the *Tale* suggests
that the work is perhaps an early rendering of the themes

embodied later in his larger satire.[1] Hone and Rossi (1934)
advance the hypothesis that the *Fragment* merely completed the
religious irony 'by criticising another type of dissenters who
could not very well be fitted into the scheme of the *Tale*'.
Herbert Davis in his recent edition offers the interesting suggestion that the piece 'might very well have been a part of one
of the "Treatises speedily to be published," announced at the
beginning of the book—*An Analytical Discourse upon Zeal,
Histori-theo-physi-logically considered*', but volunteers no guess
concerning the probable date of composition. Guthkelch and
Nichol Smith, on the other hand, explicitly place it later than the
Battle—in the same period as the later sections of the *Tale*. 'It
is the product of the same mind, and in the same phase, that
gave us the greater but not stronger "Digression concerning
Madness" and the section on the Aeolists.' To this Quintana
and Clarence M. Webster agree, the latter calling it 'one of the
most brilliant and revelatory of his works, one never surpassed
by him for unmistakable statement that Man was carnal'.[2]
Despite Pons and others to the contrary, there are many who
feel that the style and wit of the *Fragment* are fully as brilliant
and powerful as of the passages in the *Tale* traditionally more
admired.

But why should Swift concoct this bewildering *Fragment* after
the main portion of his work had been completed? Webster,
in the article just quoted, suggests that in the *Tale* proper Swift
was not ready to be definite and explicit about the causes of
enthusiasm and reserved that analysis for the final 'Discourse'.
But may not the decision have been solely the result of Swift's
artistic sense of climax? What would appear to be at least a
tenable supposition is that once all the maze of preliminary
matter and digressions had been interwoven with the religious
allegory, the original 'The Conclusion' appeared to Swift too
weak, and the *Fragment* was designed as the shocking end to the
volume. Or it may be that at this time 'The Conclusion' was
specifically revised to make it inconclusive, so that it would act
merely as a transition to the *Battle* and the final stinging
Fragment.

Although exact dates of composition for the various sections
of the *Tale* are difficult to ascertain, it is generally accepted that

---

[1] Being published by the Princeton University Press.
[2] *P.M.L.A.*, xlviii (Dec. 1933), 1152.

the allegory of Peter, Martin, and Jack was begun early in Swift's career and probably completed in 1696–7; that the *Battle*, together with some of the critical digressions, was the product of the period between June 1697 and March 1698; and that some of the preliminary matter and certain inserted passages may have been written as late as 1702–3. From evidence given by Guthkelch and Nichol Smith much of 'The Conclusion' would appear to have been written between June and September 1697. On the other hand, internal evidence in the *Fragment* puts it after September 1697 and possibly much later, for the reference to Sir Humphrey Edwin could not have been written earlier. But since Swift was possibly adding and changing passages throughout, up to the last minute, all such attempts at dating must necessarily be inconclusive. Barring the discovery of some hitherto unknown bit of evidence, the only solution to the problem would appear to lie in an analysis of the structure and plan of the 1704 volume itself.

Casual readers are apt to assume that *A Tale of a Tub* is a disorganized Gothic profusion of ideas, carelessly thrown together by Swift as a parody on the similar loose structure of the works of Burton and various writers of Swift's own day. Certainly parody of his contemporaries was in Swift's mind, but a careful study of the organization of the material will reveal the intricate and careful design of the whole piece.[1] Like James Joyce's *Ulysses*, underneath the bewildering exterior is a carefully knit unified framework, tied together by a multitude of cryptic allusions and cross-references. Long acquaintance with the volume serves only to increase our admiration for the art of this masterpiece.

It has long been recognized that the work which began merely as a satire on the abuses of the Church was turned after 1697 into a double satire on the abuses of religion and modern learning. But sufficient attention has not been given to the superb parallel structure which Swift then devised for his work. There are two dedications, a 'Bookseller to the Reader' and an author's 'Preface'; for each of the sections of religious allegory (II, IV, VI, VIII, XI) there are parallel digressions, much more closely tied together in spirit and content, as Mrs.

[1] For a recent popular discussion of Swift's complex art, using the *Fragment* as an example, see Edwin Honig, 'Notes on Satire in Swift and Jonson', *New Mexico Quarterly Review*, xviii (Summer, 1948), 155–63.

Miriam Starkman has recently pointed out,[1] than has been hitherto supposed. To list all the verbal connexions, the hidden allusions which subtly lead the reader back and forth from one theme to the other, until they almost fuse in the later sections (VIII to XI) would require too much space. Even near the end, if we stretch a point and consider Section X, called by Hawkesworth 'A Further Digression', as a unit with Section IX, the back-and-forth parallel structure is maintained up to 'The Conclusion', which ironically purports to end the work.

But for readers of the 1704 volume this did not end the discourse; if their interest had not flagged they were carried back-and-forth once more—to the literary quarrels of the Ancients and the Moderns, in the *Battle of the Books*, and back again to religious fanaticism in the final *Fragment*. Thus even after the *Tale* was ostensibly over, Swift provided one last bit of parallelism between the absurdities of learning and of religious enthusiasm. And while it is true that there is much evidence to support the belief that Swift was just as deeply aroused (if not more so) by the corruptions in literature as by those in the Church, the fact remains that he chose to end the volume on the religious theme.

That Swift thought of the *Fragment* as an integral part of the work is shown conclusively by the list of 'Treatises writ by the same Author, most of them mentioned in the following Discourses; which will be speedily published', which faced the title-page in the first four editions. Almost all of these eleven 'treatises' are directly referred to at various points in the book, the first eight in the *Tale* proper, and the last, 'A Critical Essay upon the Art of Canting, Philosophically, Physically, and Musically considered', in the *Fragment*. The titles are sprinkled throughout the pages, like mysterious clues in a treasure-hunt. If there is any cabalistic significance in the order of the treatises and the sections in which they appear, no one yet has found it out. But they do serve to hold the whole work together more compactly; and to bind the *Fragment* securely to the *Tale* with a long cord of allusion.

The innocuous 'The Conclusion' which ostensibly brings the *Tale* proper to an end is playfully arch in 'the Modern Way', with witty sallies over the Bookseller, the 'Profound Writers' of his day, the author's 'short Fits or Intervals of Dullness', the use of commonplace books, &c. Swift amuses himself over the difficulty of ending his work. He plays fancifully with the idea that the close of a Treatise, as with Human Life, should be like the end of a feast—conducive to dozing away the rest of the day in perfect repose. When he finally writes *Finis* it is only after a vague hint of the necessity of taking up his pen again. It is all in the mock-serious vein of his lighter moments.

But it would not have been characteristic of Swift, with his basic savage indignation, to end the book on such a trifling note. Elsewhere, it is well to remember, he showed himself a master of emphasis—witness the fourth voyage of *Gulliver*, the superb irony of the last phrases of the *Argument against Abolishing Christianity* and of *A Modest Proposal*. He well knew the art of building up to an overwhelming climax by easy stages. If the volume had ended with the so-called 'The Conclusion', or even with the *Battle of the Books*, the reader would have been left merely with the impression of playful parody, of literary trifling. And it is inconceivable that this could have been Swift's desire.

What Swift wanted to do—even this early in his career—was to 'vex' mankind, to attack human weakness at a vulnerable point—man's irrational susceptibility to phantasies of enthusiasm, his gullible acceptance of absurd claims to an 'inner light' as opposed to reason. Swift wished to expose what one critic has called 'the pathology of religious exaltation'; he was determined to show that the religious imagination out of control is only a corruption of the senses. These are undoubtedly the ideas Swift hoped the reader would remember. To make certain, he deliberately chose to end his attack with the most revolting bits of imagery. No one would ever miss his point, enforced so vigorously by all the devices of shock and surprise. The degrading symbols, the indecent suggestions, the puns where no terms were too sacred to be used, were all chosen with one aim in view—to make Swift's basic themes unforgettable.

The *Fragment* is thus the summation of one of Swift's chief themes—the shocking suggestion that all spiritual visions of the 'modern saints' are nothing but what we recognize as Freudian phantasies, blocked sex drives, and mob psychology. The operation of the spirit is wholly physical. It is significant that the *Fragment* ends with the story of the philosopher who, 'while his Thoughts and Eyes were fixed upon the *Constellations*, found himself seduced by his *lower Parts* into a *Ditch*'. With all the brutality and obsession with sex of Sinclair Lewis's *Elmer Gantry*, the piece is a forerunner of twentieth-century dissections of human nature. And a more up-to-the-minute exposé it would be hard to find. As W. D. Taylor points out, 'Jack Leyden followed about by a community of women' finds his counterpart in twentieth-century life itself. And 'As to the flesh playing leap-frog with the spirit', where can we find it 'better exemplified than in *Lady Chatterley's Lover?*'[1]

There is no evidence that Swift considered this theme more important than his violent attacks on false learning. But he may have thought that a final exposure of the sectaries would make the most indelible impression on his readers. And the reactions of Wotton, Burnet, and others of his contemporaries, show that this is exactly what happened. Though not completely grasping Swift's plan, they nevertheless sensed that in the *Fragment* might be found the kernel of his most horrifying ideas. Cleverly hidden as it is by the apparent Gothic wildness of design, Swift's keen sense of climax had thus led his readers from one knife-thrust to another, up to the last devastating shock. Is it, then, too far-fetched to suggest that the *Discourse Concerning the Mechanical Operation of the Spirit* was meant to be the true ending of the whole complex system which we think of as *A Tale of a Tub?*

[1] *Jonathan Swift, a Critical Essay* (London, 1933), pp. 64–5.

THE MANUSCRIPT OF SWIFT'S SERMON ON
BROTHERLY LOVE

HERBERT DAVIS

WE do not know what prompted Swift in January 1720 to write *A Letter from a Lay-Patron to a Gentleman Designing for Holy Orders*;[1] but we do know that it was the first thing he published after six years of retirement at the Deanery at St. Patrick's, where his only public activity had been to preach to his congregation as required by his office. It might well be assumed therefore that what he has to say about the duties of preaching and the preparation of sermons arose from his own experience during those years. Moreover, the circumstances of his earlier life had provided him with the general training and apprenticeship which he here recommends for all who would enter into Holy Orders. For he had been able to lay in a competent stock of human learning as well as some knowledge of divinity before he took orders. He had had the opportunity of learning to read and to speak in a small country parish before addressing himself to a city congregation. It is also clear from a perusal of the sermons that have been printed that he never allowed himself to forget the 'two principal Branches of Preaching' as here set down: namely, 'to tell the People what is their Duty; and then to convince them that it is so'; and that he was always careful to give the simplest shape to his discourses, dividing his topic into separate parts and 'expressing the Heads of each Division in as few and clear Words' as possible, so that it might be easy for his hearers to retain them.

But it has not, I think, been hitherto pointed out that the autograph manuscript of Swift's sermon on *Brotherly Love*, which is now preserved in the library of Trinity College, Dublin, provides very conclusive evidence that he was actually describing his own practice when he gives such detailed and rigorous advice concerning the methods of preparing a sermon,

---

[1] The title of the Letter, as it was first printed by E. Waters, Dublin, 1720; afterwards reprinted in London, 1721, as *A Letter to a Young Gentleman, Lately enter'd into Holy Orders*.

copying it out, reading it over, and practising how it should be spoken, before finally delivering it from the pulpit.

The method he recommends was one which had been successfully used by

a Clergyman of some Distinction, who appeared to deliver his Sermon without looking into his Notes; which, when I complimented him upon, he assured me, he could not repeat six Lines; but his Method was to write the whole Sermon in a large plain Hand, with all the Forms of Margin, Paragraph, marked Page, and the like; then on *Sunday* Morning, he took care to run it over five or six Times, which he could do in an Hour; and when he delivered it, by pretending to turn his Face from one Side to the other, he would (in his own Expression) pick up the Lines, and cheat his People, by making them believe he had it all by Heart. He farther added, that whenever he happened, by Neglect, to omit any of these Circumstances, the Vogue of the *Parish* was, *our Doctor gave us but an indifferent Sermon to-day*. Now among us, many Clergymen act so directly contrary to this Method; that from a Habit of saving *Time* and *Paper*, which they acquired at the University, they write in so diminutive a Manner, with such frequent Blots and Interlineations, that they are hardly able to go on without perpetual Hesitations, or extemporary Expletives: And I desire to know what can be more inexcusable than to see a Divine, and a Scholar, at a Loss in reading his own Compositions; which, it is supposed, he hath been preparing with much *Pains* and *Thought*, for the Instruction of his People.

. . . .

Let me entreat you therefore, to add one Half-Crown a Year to the Article of *Paper*; to transcribe your Sermons in as large and plain a manner as you can, and either make no Interlineations, or change the whole Leaf: For we, your Hearers, would rather you should be less correct, than perpetually stammering; which I take to be one of the worst *Solecisms* in *Rhetorick*. And lastly, read your Sermon once or twice, for a few Days before you preach it: To which you will probably answer some Years hence, *That it was but just finished when the last Bell rang to Church*; and I shall readily believe, but not excuse you.

A careful examination of Swift's manuscript proves that he himself carried out every step in the procedure he recommended.

The sermon itself is written in a large, formal hand on ten quarto leaves, each page carefully numbered at the top right-hand corner from 1 to 20; and at the top of the first page he began by putting down the date when he started to write it,

Nov^{br} 24, 1717 (o.s.), that is to say, on the Sunday one week before it had to be delivered. Then he sets down in the middle of a clear space at the top of the page the four words of his text with, above it, the reference to the Epistle to the Hebrews and the chapter and verse from which it was taken. Each page of the manuscript consists of from twenty to twenty-two lines evenly and clearly written in a large round hand with equal margins and the end of the lines also neatly filled out in a formal copyist's manner.

Nevertheless the manuscript is evidently not a fair copy of an earlier rough draft, for it contains on almost every page some corrections and additions; and on the last page, where the text had originally ended about three-quarters of the way down, the lower space has been completely filled in by the last three sentences written in a smaller hand and covering the whole width of the page. Later Swift fastened the ten leaves between two blank leaves and on the outside of the first wrote simply the title *Brotherly Love* and the date 1717, and on the inside at the top left-hand corner 'Finisht Nov^{br} 29, 1717'; and on the outside of the last leaf, similarly, 'At St. Patricks Dec^{br} 1st 1717'.

The dates on the manuscript alone would seem to show that Swift began on Sunday, 24 November, to compose the sermon and to write it out on these sheets, and that he completed the twentieth page, including all the corrections and additions, on the following Friday, 29 November, two days before he delivered it at St. Patrick's. But apart from the indications of these dates, some of the corrections and deletions prove that Swift was composing as he wrote it down. For the corrections are made as it were within the space of the sentence, showing the shifting of his thought as it moves into its final shape. For instance, on the second page he first wrote:

> The last Legacy of Christ was Peace and mutuall
> Love; the primitive Christians accepted the
> Legacy, and their followe—

breaking off in the middle of the word as he remembered the other portion of Christ's legacy and the completion of the paradox that He would leave peace and the sword. So he puts his pen through these last nine words and substitutes:

> but then he foretold that he came to send a
> Sword upon the Earth;

This provides him with a perfect foundation for the foursquare compact structure of the whole sentence which states the immediate effects of Christianity and the unfolding of those effects throughout history.

> The primitive Christians accepted the Legacy,
> and their Successors [*instead of the word that
> had first suggested itself to him* 'followers']
> down to the present Age have been largely full-
> filling his Prophesy.

The weight of such a sentence, however, at the end of what is only an introductory paragraph to be followed by a very simple statement of the theme of the discourse, offers a considerable problem. How is he to return to the direct homiletic style, the main purpose of the preacher as Swift conceived it, namely, to tell his hearers what is their duty? And we see him struggling with the opening of the following sentence, or possibly coming back to it again and finding it awkwardly fitted on to what had preceded it and requiring alteration. He had first written a sentence which is weak and redundant:

> However the Duty still remains in force, and
> there is none more incumbent upon Christians
> than that of brotherly Love.

He changes the first phrase so that it fits in firmly with the preceding statement and still keeps before us the two contrasted standards of the general practice of mankind and of the Christian profession, changing the weak 'however' into

> But whatever the practice of mankind hath been
> there is no Duty more incumbent upon those who
> profess the Gospel.

And finally he inserts after 'hath been' a further addition, a characteristic Swiftian emphasis and completeness, the phrase 'or still continues'.

Most of the pages that follow are so free from alterations and corrections that they might almost seem to be fair copies from an earlier draft. And it may be of course that Swift himself put into practice what he recommended and changed the whole leaf if it had become too much defaced by corrections or interlineations. Nevertheless on several of these pages there remain some very slight corrections which still seem to be those of a man composing as he writes. For example:

p. 5. the great want of brotherly Love *among us* [deleted] is owing to the Weakness and Folly of too many among you

p. 6. 'tis to be doubted whether Doctrines are not sometimes delivered *which produce a quite differ* [deleted] by an ungoverned Zeal, a desire to be distinguished, or a View of Interest, which produce quite different Effects

p. 7.   among the *lower Sort* [deleted] trading People, which *they* [deleted] hath been industriously instilled into them

p. 9. lay open *the sad* [deleted] some of the sad Effects

p. 15. desire you will consider, *whether it is for your sake* [deleted] when any of you make use of fair and enticing words to draw in Customers, whether you do it for their sakes or Your own:

p. 17. He is ready to defend *his L* [deleted] with his Life and Fortune the *true* [deleted] Protestant Succession

p. 20. For *if they* [deleted] if the Reasonable Men

There are other changes which are made between the lines or in the margin, or substitutions of single words which just as clearly show him at work, reading over the whole sermon and revising it, after he had written it out. For example:

> And yet this very Notion he publisheth as *the Test of his Loyalty*

This last phrase is deleted and replaced by the following, which is written in the margin at the foot of the page:

> his best Argument to prove him a most loyall Subject

And in the following sentence the passage between brackets is an interlineation stuck in later to clarify and intensify the meaning, or perhaps to point at some particular persons whom he had in mind:

> And others again
> [whom God had formed with mild and gentle Disposition]

think it necessary to put a Force upon their own
Tempers, by acting a noisy, violent, malicious Part,
as a Means to be distinguished.

We have seen that Swift not only wrote in the date 29
November, at the foot of the last page of the sermon, but also
wrote again on the verso of the first blank leaf, 'Finisht Nov^{br}
29, 1717'; we may assume therefore that the revisions and
corrections had all been made two days before the sermon was
to be delivered. He had then still plenty of time to follow the
procedure that he recommends and read it over once or twice to
become familiar with it before preaching it. And here again
we find in the manuscript actual proof that he did take the
trouble to do this and that he read it through with the intona-
tions of the words in his ears as he intended to speak it. For on
several pages of the manuscript he has accentuated with a broad
sloping penstroke certain words which he evidently wished to
be spoken with ironical emphasis, and this mark is again
repeated in later passages when he reiterates the characteristics
of a really moderate churchman. For example:

But the most moderate and favored Divines dare not

own, that the word Moderation with respect to the

Dissenters can be at all applyed to their Religion,

but is purely Personall and Prudentiall.

or again:

to preach Moderation to the first, and Patience
to the other, would perhaps be to little purpose.

It is impossible to study the pages of this manuscript without
realizing that Swift did not think lightly of his duty to preach
at St. Patrick's, whatever remarks he may sometimes have
made about his sermons. For we get a glimpse of him here
actually at work taking great pains not only to prepare a
discourse which in the clarity and force of its argument and in
the simplicity of its style should be fitted to the needs of his
congregation, but also to study and perfect his delivery of it in
such a manner as best to edify his hearers.

Some of his friends, indeed, at the time of the eclipse they had
all suffered after the death of Queen Anne, had been inclined

to envy him because the satisfaction of preaching was still left
to him. Dr. Arbuthnot had written in November 1714:[1]

I cannot but say, I think there is one thing in your circumstance,
that must make any man happy: which is, a liberty to preach. Such
a prodigious privilege, that if it did not border upon simony, I could
really purchase it for a sum of money. For my part, I never imagine
any man can be uneasy, that has the opportunity of venting himself
to a whole congregation once a week. And you may pretend what
you will, I am sure you think so too, or you do not judge right.

And a couple of months later Swift had confessed in a letter to
Knightley Chetwode:[2]

I hear they think me a smart Dean; and that I am for doing good.
My notion is, that if a man cannot mend the public he should mend
old shoes if he can do no better; and therefore I endeavour in the
little sphere I am placed to do all the good it is capable of.

Nevertheless I do not imagine that he always had as much
satisfaction in his preaching as he did on that morning of
December 1st, 1717, when he preached this sermon. And one
reason why this manuscript was preserved by him may well
have been because he rather liked what he had written.

Professor Landa has remarked that 'No reader will miss the
irony in the title of this violent and uncharitable invective
against the dissenters'. And we may be sure that Swift was
careful that none of his hearers should miss his intention or be
misled by the text he had chosen. It must have given him some
sardonic pleasure when he had finished it finally to inscribe on
the outside of his manuscript just the title *Brotherly Love*, and
beneath it the date 1717. At some later time when he had
picked up the manuscript and looked over the pages again, he
had evidently felt that this innocent title needed some slight
gloss and he had scribbled in just under the word 'Brotherly',
'Politicall', and this later annotation may well signify that he was
willing to have this sermon preserved as one of the 'preaching
pamphlets' in which he had 'exerted himself in the pulpit'; and
that he did not think of it as merely an old, useless sermon.

He had also been careful at the time he preached it to make
sure that his congregation should understand this, for he added

---

[1] *The Correspondence of Jonathan Swift*, edited by Elrington Ball (London, 1910–14),
ii. 255.
[2] Op. cit. ii. 265.

the concluding paragraph which is crowded into the space at
the foot of the last page as though it had been an afterthought:

> I have now done with my Text, which I confess to have
> treated in a manner more suited to the present Times,
> than to the Nature of the Subject in generall.

He then proceeds to excuse himself for this very neatly by
quoting the Apostle to the Thessalonians,

> As touching Brotherly Love ye need not that I write
> unto you for ye yourselves are taught of God to love
> one another.

And finally he commits them to the mercy of God, who can
alone restore and continue among them this gift of charity
which is 'the very Bond of Peace and of all Virtues'. Swift does
not hide his scepticism even in the pulpit. Indeed it is this
which gives such strength to his sermons and it is this which
keeps them fresh. He knows that God alone can implant in the
heart of man the real virtue of Christian charity, but the Dean
of St. Patrick's can at least use his pulpit to warn those under
his care to beware of party hatred, malice, and uncharitable-
ness even towards their Teacher. It is true that he speaks with
his usual vehemence about 'the Insolence of the Dissenters as a
principal Cause of all that Hatred and Animosity now reigning
among us'. But he has always a more positive purpose than to
express his own feelings. He is concerned as a preacher to
address himself directly to the actual congregation sitting before
him in St. Patrick's. His aim is to influence them at that time
in a manner which he frankly admits is political. Though they
have the advantage of belonging generally to 'the middle and
the lower sort of people', where what little religion there is in
the world chiefly resides, they are in danger of being made use
of by political leaders for their own purpose. They are even
led to suspect him and 'call him by a Name which they tell
you signifyes some very bad Thing'. It is his duty to make clear
to them that they are not properly concerned in the quarrels
of political parties and that they might well live amicably
together. With their interests as tradesmen, there is no reason
why their personal friendships or their religion should be affected
by party considerations. And so he will set before them what
he regards as the marks of a really *moderate* Churchman, which
are no other than those he had formerly proclaimed as an

impartial *Examiner*, a position midway between the fanatics and the dissenters. This strong statement of his political beliefs gives considerable interest to the one document which we possess from the middle of this period of silence. It shows that by the end of the year 1717 Swift once again felt himself secure enough to speak his mind in public, at least within the shelter of his own cathedral, and to bear witness to those principles which he had upheld in the last years of Queen Anne. He claims the right to be regarded as a loyal subject of the Crown in the new reign of George I, while firmly declaring himself still a Tory and a Churchman.

But this manuscript possesses still further value in its subsequent history when some years after Swift's death it came into the possession of George Faulkner, the Dublin printer. It may well have been, as Mr. Harold Williams suggested,[1] one of the 'Three Sermons in ye Dean's Hand found by Mrs Ridgway in his Study before I recd ye Key' listed in the Abbotsford Manuscript among 'Mss: found in the Dean's Study'. They were probably found in 1744, but they were not included in the sale of Swift's library, and it is not until ten years later that we hear of the manuscript again. For in March 1754 it was published by Faulkner in Dublin with this prefatory note:

> The original Manuscript may be seen with the Printer,
> in the Dean's own Hand Writing.

And in the London edition which was published at the same time by R. & J. Dodsley there is a similar advertisement. There can be no doubt that this is the very manuscript which is now in the library of Trinity College, Dublin.[2]

This presents us with a situation unusual even in dealing with eighteenth-century texts. For we have this manuscript[3] providing us with the text in its final corrected form in the author's own hand, and the printed versions first published in 1754 in Dublin and in London, both claiming to have been printed

---

[1] *Dean Swift's Library* (Cambridge, 1932), pp. 33-5.

[2] Mr. Joseph Hanna has kindly informed me that there is a note in the Manuscript Catalogue that the manuscript was presented to Trinity College Library on 2 April 1754.

[3] This manuscript was not available during the war, when Professor Landa was editing the *Sermons* in vol. ix of my edition of Swift's *Prose Works*: the text was therefore printed, like that of the other Sermons, from Faulkner's edition of the *Works* (1762), vol. x.

from this original manuscript which was then to be seen in George Faulkner's shop in Dublin. Swift had died nine years before and there can be no question of an editor's correcting or revising proofs. Therefore by comparing the printed text with the manuscript we can find out exactly what happened to an author's text when it was being prepared for publication by George Faulkner in Dublin in 1754.

The autograph manuscript was certainly not used by the printer, as it bears no sign of having been touched in any way after it had been completed by Swift. A copy must therefore have been made from it, and it is probable that in this copy Swift's spelling and capitalization were already normalized and possibly some changes made in the punctuation. The copyist may also have been responsible for certain changes in word order in passages where interlinear additions have been made. One or two minor errors may also have been introduced by the copyist, but the final changes as they appear in the printed version, whether due to the copyist or to the compositor, may be taken as indicating the regular printer's usage.

These changes are as follows:

Such abbreviations as occur, rarely indeed in the manuscript, are printed in full. Swift's peculiarities of spelling are normalized throughout: his use of the plural form '—yes', e.g. *Enemyes, Partyes, Bodyes*; and of '—y' in endings such as *signifyes, qualifyed*; his doubling of the final consonant in words like *naturall, generall, criminall, robb, sett*; his preference for 'or' in such words as *favor, neighbor*; his elimination of the 'e' in *destroyd, falsly, wondred, immediat*; and on the other hand his consistent use of *onely, extream, acknoledged*.

The printer has also attempted to normalize Swift's rather inconsistent capitalization. These practices had been followed in the early volumes of Faulkner's collected edition, which had begun to appear in 1735, when Swift himself was certainly given the opportunity of correcting the sheets. And there are two other practices which we know that Swift was in part responsible for: namely, the insistence on preserving the already old-fashioned ending '—eth', and the use of a heavier and more formal system of punctuation than he was ever accustomed to introduce into his manuscripts. But I doubt whether Swift would have approved the printer's tendency to use the ending '—eth' at every possible opportunity, which has led him to introduce it in these few pages fourteen times where Swift did not have it in his manuscript. Also the increase in the heaviness of the punctuation by adding frequent commas, and by substituting semicolons for commas, goes a good deal further than any of the examples we have of Swift's own usage in providing a more formalized punctuation for the printed page.

These are, however, matters of smaller importance. It is of much more interest to use our opportunity to test how far we can rely upon the accuracy of Faulkner's printer, in setting up his copy from a manuscript.

We find first that on two occasions an interlinear addition has not been printed in exactly the right place:

MS.	*1754*
p. 2. by extinguishing Brotherly Love have ʌ been the Cause	by extinguishing Brotherly Love have been the Cause
p. 9. upon that Account And truly ʌ I have thought	And truly, I upon that Account have thought

There are also nine actual errors in the text introduced into this version, which, duly copied by the London printer, were thus carried into the main stream of the London collected editions, beginning with Hawkesworth in 1745. They are as follows:

MS.	*1754*
p. 4. those Adversaries	these Adversaries
p. 10. vulgar	irregular
banded	Handed
p. 11. And this occasion the Fanaticks lay hold on	And this occasions the Fanaticks to lay Hold on
p. 12. betwixt	between
p. 13. Rudenesses	Rudeness
p. 16. warping	varying
p. 19. other	last
p. 20. As touching	Touching

This list of errors might be considered sufficient to make us doubt the accuracy of any pieces printed by Faulkner without the supervision of author or editor. But we must not be in too great a hurry to join with his London competitors in condemning him. For here, in the printing of this very sermon, we have the proof that he was concerned, as he claimed in his address *To the Reader*, to make his edition of Swift as accurate as possible. For, when he reprinted the sermon in 1762 in the tenth volume of the *Collected Works*, the text was entirely reset, and though two other errors were then introduced, all these misprints were corrected.

We should have expected the printer to use for his copy-text the edition of 1754; but I have not found a copy in which these errors had been corrected, nor have I seen one with a list of Errata. Faulkner, however, had advertised that 'if there should be any Errors in (his volumes) he will be glad to be set right, and will with Pleasure, print an Errata for that Purpose, to render this Edition as correct as possible'. And it may well be that after his 1754 text appeared, someone had taken the trouble to compare a copy with the manuscript then in his shop, and to correct those errors in it.

At any rate the fact that they were corrected when the sermon was reprinted in Volume X of the *Works* proves that Faulkner continued to be concerned that these later volumes also should be as correct as possible. Thus once more when we are able to verify and check his reliability, we find that his claim that the Dublin edition has greater authority than those printed in London is fully justified. And we must admit that 'he hath some Degree of Merit with the Publick by the Publication of these Works, which would never have been collected together, had he not been favoured with the Author's Friendship and Intimacy'.

SWIFT'S DEANERY INCOME
A NEW DOCUMENT

LOUIS A. LANDA

SWIFT's tendency to present a situation in its darker aspects, however well it served as a literary manner, is likely to be misleading if taken seriously with respect to his personal affairs. His correspondence offers certain instances in point, none more striking than the persistent gloom with which he represents, in the last decade of his active career, the state of his finances. When writing to various friends, or even to acquaintances where reserve on such a topic is normally expected, he bemoaned his lowered income and—bad prophet that he was— his impending poverty. Typical is the lament in May 1729, to one of his correspondents, that like all men in Ireland dependent on tithes and rents he is on 'the high road to ruin'. 'I do expect,' he adds, 'and am determined in a short time to pawn my little plate, or sell it for subsistence.'[1] Three years later he wrote to Gay in a similar doleful strain, again announcing that he is on the verge of ruin: '. . . all my revenues which depend on tithes are sunk almost to nothing, and my whole personal fortune is in the utmost confusion. . . .'[2] Charles Ford, Arbuthnot, Barber, Pulteney, Lord Oxford, and Pope heard the same tale.[3] It was Pope particularly who after Gay's death received the burden of these woes: 'I know not any man,' Swift wrote to him in 1733, 'in a greater likelihood than myself to die poor and friendless.'[4] When Pope showed this plaint to the Duchess of Queensberry, that pleasant, forthright lady wrote to Swift: 'I differ with you extremely that you are in any likelihood of dying poor or friendless.'[5]

As we well know, Swift did not die poor; and he undoubtedly realized after his appointment to the deanery that he was to

[1] To Knightley Chetwode. See *The Correspondence of Jonathan Swift, D.D.*, edited by F. Elrington Ball (London, 1910–14), iv. 81. Cited subsequently as *Corres.*

[2] Ibid. iv. 351.

[3] *The Letters of Jonathan Swift to Charles Ford*, edited David Nichol Smith (Oxford, 1935), pp. 142, 163; *Corres.* iv. 150, 219, 316, 351; v. 107, 223.

[4] Ibid., p. 380.

[5] Ibid., p. 399.

possess a life-long comfortable income.[1] It is true that he had
financial difficulties of a certain kind, but there was only one
serious threat to his fortune. This occurred in 1725 when John
Pratt, Deputy Vice-Treasurer of Ireland, who had £1,200
belonging to Swift in his possession, was imprisoned for
defalcations amounting to over £70,000. Fortunately Pratt
proved a man of honour, and Swift 'miraculously escaped being
perfectly worth nothing'.[2] What touched Swift more were the
vexatious delays in rents and interests, and particularly the
reduced return from tithes. Doubtless these occasioned momen-
tary pinches and account for his troubled words—for example,
the reiterated statement between 1733 and 1735 that his
income had been reduced by £300.[3] Yet his prophecies of ruin
are belied by the steady accumulation of that sizeable fortune
remaining at his death to endow his hospital. The fact is, that
with respect to his income, as elsewhere, Swift writes more
darkly than the situation warrants, indulging himself—surely
half seriously—in remarkably obvious distortion of the realities.
It is probable that he did not expect to be taken literally. Nor
is it likely that his friends were perturbed: report had it that the
deanery made a good return. Nevertheless it is not possible to
speak with any finality concerning Swift's financial affairs: they
have never received careful investigation, not even the easily
available documents, such as the account books. Though
doubtless many revealing documents are lost beyond recovery,
I have recently found a manuscript which sheds light on the
exact return from the deanery. This document, which has
escaped the notice of modern scholars, offers further testimony
that Swift's income was ample. It is an undated and unsigned
manuscript among the records in St. Patrick's Cathedral,
Dublin, inscribed 'Of Dr Swift's Effects'; and it sets forth item
by item the sources—rents, tithes, and fees—from which Swift's

---

[1] Shortly after his appointment he writes to Stella of the heavy initial expenses
for the deanery house, the First Fruits, and the Patent, amounting to £1,000 (cf.
Journal to Stella, 23 April 1713), but a year later, in a letter written to Archdeacon
Walls, filled with calculations, he is obviously feeling secure financially. See
Corres. ii. 147.

[2] Swift wrote to Ford that Pratt 'owed me all and something more than all I had
in the World'. He was proud of the resignation he displayed in the face of this great
loss: 'I despaired of every Penny, and yet I have legall Witness that I was a great
Philosopher in that Matter.' See *Letters of Swift to Ford*, ed. David Nichol Smith,
pp. 121, 125; *Corres*. iii. 241, 251, 252.

[3] Ibid. v. 107, 163, 223.

annual deanery income was derived, with the amount each returned.[1] After careful comparison of the hand with that of the Reverend John Lyon, the Prebendary of St. Patrick's to whose care Swift was committed in 1742, I am convinced that the document was compiled by Lyon; and I surmise from the evidence immediately following that it was prepared in 1742 for the Commission of Lunacy which found Swift to be 'a person of unsound mind and memory'.

The writ under which the Commission acted, dated 12 August, directed an inquiry not only into Swift's sanity but also. if he were found insane, into his income and possessions: '. . . what lands and tenements, goods and chattels, the said Doctor Jonathan Swift was possessed of at the time he became of unsound mind and memory, or at any time since, and what is the yearly value thereof. . . .'[2] The report of the Commission a few days later showed that Swift possessed as of 20 May 1742, and did still possess, 'lands, tithes, and tenements of the clear yearly value of eight hundred pounds sterling' as well as goods and chattels estimated at ten thousand pounds sterling.[3] The manuscript under discussion has the heading, 'The Yearly Value of Lands, Tithes, Ground Rents & Fees belonging to the Dean of St Patrick's Dublin', and the figures totalled at the end amount to £807, which corresponds to the 'clear yearly value of eight hundred pounds sterling' mentioned in the report of the Commission of Lunacy. That the Reverend John Lyon should be asked to compile the document for the Commission was fitting in view of his position at this time as Swift's almoner and of the important additional fact that he had perhaps a better knowledge of the chapter records than any other member of the Cathedral. It was natural therefore that he should be chosen to draw up an account of deanery income, just as he was the obvious person to be entrusted with the care of Swift once the affirmation of lunacy had been made, and later to act as secretary to Swift's trustees. There is further evidence that Lyon was given the task of compiling a list of Swift's effects at this juncture: there exists a catalogue of Swift's books in his hand drawn up apparently as a result of the proceedings of the

[1] For permission to use this manuscript I am greatly indebted to the present Dean of St. Patrick's, the Right Reverend David F. R. Wilson, a staunch admirer of his predecessor. I am also greatly obliged to the Dean's Vicar, the Reverend J. W. Armstrong, who patiently dug through masses of manuscripts for my benefit.

[2] *Corres.* vi. 183.   [3] Ibid. 184–5.

Commission—so Mr. Harold Williams, who discovered the document, thinks.[1]

In attempting to discover the circumstances which gave rise to a document concerning income and possessions, one must at least examine the hypothesis that this newly discovered manuscript dates from Swift's death—that it was prepared for his executors who would, of course, need the information it sets forth. The tone of the document at certain points, with the reference to Swift in the past tense and to his executors, at first glance faintly suggests that it was prepared at the time of his death. This tone, however, is just as appropriate for one who was already known to have lost his faculties and who, though physically alive, was dead in the eyes of the law, as Swift was according to the report of the Commission. The allusion to Swift's executors will not be puzzling when it is recollected that his will was made and witnessed long before 1742 and was easily available to Lyon and the Commission. But the evidence is final at least on this one point, that Swift was alive when the document was drawn up: the reference (see the eleventh item below) to the 'present Bishop of Clogher', to 'the present Dean', and their financial settlement concerning the deanery house which both occupied permits no other interpretation. The Bishop of Clogher can be no other than John Stearne, Swift's predecessor at St. Patrick's and afterwards Bishop of Clogher from 1717 to 1745. Since he predeceased Swift by a few months in 1745, the mention of him gives us one terminal date and proof that Swift was still alive. The latest date mentioned in the manuscript is 25 March 1741, which thus establishes that it was written between 1741 and 1745.

If, then, we take into account the circumstances, the nature of the document, and the various pieces of evidence—that the Commission of Lunacy was directed to make a valuation of Swift's income, that its report of the annual return of his 'lands, tithes, and tenements' tallies with the sum given in the manuscript under discussion, that the hand is that of John Lyon, an obvious choice to serve the Commission, that Swift was alive

---

[1] *Dean Swift's Library* (Cambridge, 1932), pp. 10, 13. From this same period is extant an inventory of Swift's personal property. From a photostat of the original in Swift's Hospital I find that though most of the items listed are in an unknown hand some are in the hand of Dr. Lyon, a further indication that he was making an accounting of Swift's possessions at this time. This inventory has been reprinted by T. P. Le Fanu in *Proceedings of the Royal Irish Academy*, xxxvii, sec. c (1927), 263–75.

when the document was compiled—we may reasonably assume that the manuscript was prepared by John Lyon in 1742 for the Commission of Lunacy. It appears to be, however, not an official return so much as a rough or preliminary draft, as is indicated by words crossed through and interlinear corrections. In what follows I propose to quote each item in the document in its order, and to make notations where these may be relevant. As already stated, the document is headed 'The Yearly Value of Lands, Tithes, Ground Rents & Fees belonging to the Dean of St Patrick's Dublin'.

The first item is concerned with deanery possessions in County Kildare:

The Lands & Tithes of ye Manor of Kilberry & Cloney near Athy in ye Co: of Kildare yield now p[er] Ann: £200—N: The Lease was renewed from March 25: 1741 to J: Stopford Esq And 400£ paid as a Fine. Mr Stopford owns these Lands to be worth to him 500£ p[er] Ann: The Vicarage is Non-Cure of 60£ p[er] Ann: is in ye Dean's Gift. The Dean appoints his Seneschal in this Manor.

Swift paid a visit to County Kildare in January 1714–15 to make a personal appraisal of the worth of these deanery lands. In a letter written soon after he lists his holdings in this region, including, to use his phrase, such 'cursed Irish names' as Tullygorey, Shanraheen, and Clonwannir; and he calculates that the entire holdings at full rent are worth £475 per annum.[1] Since he was receiving only £120 yearly, he proposed to revise his leases upward; indeed, he had written from London six months earlier to his agent that no land rents from deanery holdings should be accepted pending a review of leases.[2] The Cathedral records show four leases of these lands in the period of Swift's deanship, with increasing rentals from an annual return of £150 in a lease of 1716 to the £200 mentioned in this manuscript.[3] His well-known insistence upon an increased rental at each renewal is exemplified in his dealings with Stopford; and Stopford's significant admission that the lease was worth £500 annually to him, whereas Swift was returned only £200, is evidence in support of what Swift and other Irish

---

[1] *Corres.* ii. 266.   [2] Ibid., p. 148.
[3] See the register of leases in St. Patrick's Cathedral, Dublin. My information is taken from the section headed 'The Dean's Property'. For the lease to J. Stopford listed in the first entry, see the 'Chapter Minute Book of St. Patrick's Cathedral, Dublin, 1720–1763', f. 116 v. The lease was confirmed by the Chapter at a meeting on 15 May 1741.

clergymen constantly maintained, that a churchman is fortunate to receive half the value of his lands.

The second item concerns deanery lands in County Dublin:

The Lands of Dean Rath, Priest Town, Ballibane & Angerstown containing 357 Acres near Clondolkan yield p[er] Ann. £90. This Lease was renewed from 25: Decr 1740 And £   was paid by way of Fine. N:B: Mr Pearson the Tenant pays 20^s p[er] Acre for these Lands.

Swift's predecessor, Stearne, had leased these County Dublin holdings in 1709 for an annual rental of £54. Swift appears to have induced the lessee to surrender this lease in 1720 for one returning a rental of £70 annually. In addition he reserved to himself during the last eleven years of the term of the lease thirty acres of Priest Town and 'all the Tythes for some time'. The lease on these lands was re-negotiated or renewed at least twice before Swift's death, and by 1740 he had almost doubled the yearly sum returned when he first became dean.[1]

The third item is concerned with tithes:

The Rectorial Tythes of Tallaght, Esker, Clondolkan, Tassagard & Rathcool, which ye Dean in his own Accompts rates at 420£ p[er] An: com[m]unibus Annis deducting all charges We reckon only at £400. Mem: A Piece of Land near Tallagh Ch: belonging to ye Dean called ye Dean's Croft is now inclosed with ye Gardens as I am informed of his Grace of Dublin.

The places mentioned are in County Dublin, and the tithes due from them account for approximately one-half of the total deanery income. It was here that Swift's revenues were most vulnerable: as he wrote to Pope, '. . . although tithes be of divine institution, they are of diabolical execution', and he regularly registers complaints about the difficulties of collection.[2] The whole matter of tithes was extremely complicated by, among other things, conflicting claims and divided ownership. For example, in three of the above-mentioned parishes Swift had claims to only portions of the tithes. In Tallaght all tithes were in the hands of lay impropriators except the great tithes, which were appropriate to the deanery of St. Patrick's; from Rathcool also Swift received only the great tithes, from

---

[1] See 'The Dean's Property' in the register of leases in St. Patrick's Cathedral; see also the 'Chapter Minute Book, 1720–1763', f. 100 v.

[2] *Corres.* iv. 127; cf. also iv. 81, 150, 219, 316, 351; v. 107.

Tassagard two-thirds of all tithes.[1] Tassagard and Rathcool are of some interest for the early relationship between Swift as dean, and his Archbishop, William King. A month after his installation, these two parishes being vacant, Swift appealed to King 'as a personal favour' to give the benefices to his curate at Laracor, Thomas Warburton—an appeal as little successful with the Archbishop as the one Swift had made a few weeks earlier in behalf of Thomas Parnell.[2]

The fourth item:

The Tenements East & West of ye Deanery are in Lease viz: Worrall from 25 Mar: 1732 for 40 Years at 5£ p[er] Ann. Mr J^n Connly for his Holding East of ye Deanry pays £9 p[er] Ann. Whose Lease was renewed from 25 Mar: 1732 for 39 Years.

The first-named lessee, John Worrall, held a portion of deanery property located in St. Kevin Street and Deanery Lane.[3] He was a member of the Cathedral chapter; in fact he had a longer connexion with St. Patrick's than Swift, having begun as a minor canon in 1690 and then serving as Dean's Vicar from 1695 to well beyond Swift's death.[4] His relations with Swift were the subject of some controversy among the early biographers, but there can be no doubt that for a long period Swift's feeling toward him was friendly and companionable and that he was trusted with Swift's personal affairs as well as with Cathedral business.[5] That portion of the item concerning Connly is crossed through; nevertheless the annual return of £9 is figured in the total at the end of the manuscript, and rightly so as indicated by a clause in Swift's will leaving the profits from Connly's lease to Anne Ridgeway, deanery housekeeper in Swift's last years. The holding consisted, we learn from the will, of two houses.

The fifth item:

Mr Goodman for his Holding West of ye Deanry pays £10 p[er] Ann: Whose Lease was renewed from— .

---

[1] See a parochial return—an uncatalogued manuscript—in the Register of the Diocese of Dublin, dating from 1725. Tassagard (or Saggart) meant more than tithes to Swift: Vanessa had a bower there. [2] *Corres.* ii. 56; 23–4.

[3] See the 'Chapter Minute Book, 1720–1763', f. 68 r., for 28 Nov. 1732, and 'The Dean's Property' in the manuscript book of leases.

[4] Hugh Jackson Lawlor, *The Fasti of St. Patrick's Cathedral, Dublin* (Dundalk, 1930), pp. 203, 216.

[5] See *Corres.* iii. 263 *et passim.* It was to Worrall that Swift gave credit for saving the money in Pratt's hands in 1725. See *Corres.* ii. 251–2.

This property is described in Swift's will as 'two houses or more lately built'. The lease, which was for a term of forty years, he bequeathed to his cousin Mrs. Whiteway. I have not been able to supply from existing documents the date of the renewal left blank in the manuscript.

The sixth item:

The Residentiary House yields £5 which is paid by yᵉ Proctor of yᵉ Oeconomy—who also pays yᵉ Dean's Duties reserved in all chapter Leases worth £10 p[er] Ann:

This item is of more than ordinary interest. It involves the two-way transaction which brought Swift the land for his famous garden, Naboth's Vineyard. The Residentiary House, deanery property located in Deanery Lane, was so named because it served as a place of residence for visiting canons when they came to serve their turns in the Cathedral. It was leased with clauses calling for a certain number of rooms to be kept free for this purpose.[1] In 1721 Swift agreed to renew a lease of the Residentiary House to the chapter of St. Patrick's for the sum of £5 annually; in return the chapter granted to Swift and his successors a lease on two acres of land belonging to the economy of the Cathedral, to run for a term of forty years provided that the lease of the Residentiary House should continue in force.[2] The two acres thus secured Swift turned into Naboth's Vineyard, the garden which he prized so highly and which served as a place to stable his horses and entertain his friends.

The seventh item:

The Dean's fees by renewing Leases, Burials & other Contingencies worth £10 p[er] Ann.

The eighth item:

There is also a small Tenement somewhat ruinous now in Deanery Lane or Mitre Ally worth £3 p[er] Ann.

The ninth item:

The Dean's House Garden & Excellent offices all in very good Condition we value but low at £70.

[1] See the lease in the records at St. Patrick's Cathedral, Dublin, between John Rous, Verger, and John Stearne, Dean, 1711.
[2] See the 'Chapter Minute Book, 1720–1763', f. 18 r.; cf. also f. 57 r., 17 April 1730, when the chapter sublet the Residentiary House to its sexton for £12 per annum.

This item refers to the annual rental—the estimated valuation of the deanery house as a place of residence—and is considered part of the revenue of the dignity, though no actual monetary return as such is involved.

The tenth item:

There was £20 p[er] Ann: paid to yᵉ Dean out of yᵉ Oeconomy by way of Repairs, because he laid out above £200 in improving yᵉ Deanry-House, no part [of] wᶜʰ if I mistake not, he has charged to his Successors.

I have found no record of any single undertaking by Swift involving repairs to the Deanery for the amount mentioned. It is possible that the chapter granted him this annual sum to compensate for cumulative repairs, such as those entered in his accounts for 1718.[1] This annual grant of the chapter to Swift is not totalled with the other figures at the end of the manuscript.

The eleventh item:

'However there is yᵉ Sum of £300 to be paid to yᵉ Dean's Executors being yᵉ Third of what the present Bp of Clogher Expended in building yᵉ Deanry—The present Dean having paid his L[ordshi]p £600.'

This is a reference to the deanery house built by Swift's predecessor John Stearne when Swift was only a prebendary of St. Patrick's. The construction, which Swift watched with great interest, was begun in 1707 and ranged over four years. It was in December 1711 that Swift, then in London, wrote to Stearne: 'I reckon your hands are now out of mortar, and that your garden is finished.'[2] Within two years Stearne was translated to the bishopric of Dromore (later to Clogher) to make way for Swift as Dean of St. Patrick's. When Swift took possession of the deanery house he became Stearne's debtor. According to this item in the manuscript he paid Stearne £600 and Swift's executors were to receive £300, stated to be a third of Stearne's expenditure.[3] This arrangement was not the result

---

[1] See 'Personal Expenses and Income of Jonathan Swift, 1717–1718', Forster Collection, MS. 510. 48. D. 34/6, Victoria and Albert Museum.

[2] *Corres.* i. 311; for other references see pp. 82, 85, 91, 124, 181, 311.

[3] In the *Journal to Stella*, under entry of 23 April 1713, Swift writes to Stella that he had expected to pay £600 for the deanery house but had been informed by St. George Ashe that the sum would be £800. This manuscript confirms that Swift's original expectation was right. See also *Corres.* ii. 124, 147.

of free bargaining between Stearne and Swift but was neces-
sitated by an Irish statute passed in the reign of William III
(10 Wm. III, c. 6) to encourage the building of houses and
other improvements upon church lands. It provided that any
clergyman who built a residence should receive two-thirds of
the expenditure from his immediate successor and that this
successor (or his heirs) in turn should receive one-third of the
original expenditure from the next successor.[1] Thus of the £900
spent by Stearne to construct the deanery house Swift paid him
£600, the two-thirds demanded by statute, and Swift (in this
case his executors) could expect £300, the one-third of the
original disbursement as demanded by the statute. This sum
of £300 is not figured in the final total in this manuscript,
properly so because it was to accrue at some future date whereas
this compilation is concerned with the *annual* return from
deanery possessions.

The twelfth item concerns Naboth's Vineyard:

> The Dean took about 2 Acres of Land adjoyning ye South side of
> ye Cabbage Garden which he called Naboth's Vineyard from y^e
> Chapter subject to £3 p[er] An: besides 5^s Dean's Duties & 3^s
> Proctors fees. Which Ground (except a Garden being part thereof
> leased to one White at 5£ p[er] Ann:) was enclosed by a good
> Stone Wall ye South side of which is lined with Brick & plantd with
> ye best Fruit trees, & is separated from ye remainder laid out for
> pasture by a quick Set Hedge—To which ye Servants have access
> by a Gate at ye West end. This Naboth's Vineyard with White's
> Garden, the Dean has bequeathed to his Successor[s], provided they
> pay £300 to his Executors towards building his Hospital—otherwise
> ye Interest of it is to be sold to ye Highest Bidder.

Naboth's Vineyard, we learn from this item, was leased to
Swift for a rental of £3 per annum, probably a fair rental in
its unimproved state. After Swift had built the 'cursed wall'
which cost him over £600, planted the fruit-trees, the quickset
hedge, and made other improvements, its value was so en-
hanced that his trustees could lease it in 1743 for four times that
sum.[2] Naboth's Vineyard is the subject of a clause in Swift's
will in which he expresses the earnest hope that his successors

[1] *The Statutes at Large passed in the Parliaments held in Ireland from ... 1310 to ... 1786*
(Dublin, 1786), iii. 473 ff.
[2] See the lease between Arthur Lamprey and Swift's trustees, dated 25 Dec.
1743, in the records of St. Patrick's Cathedral, Dublin.

will preserve it—'to be always in the hands of succeeding Deans during their office'. Thus, though he empowers his executors to sell the remainder of the lease to the highest bidder, he directs them to give his successor in the deanery the first refusal. This item in the manuscript concerning Naboth's Vineyard, like the preceding item, has strictly speaking no place in a list touching on annual income; and it presents no figure to be totalled with those from rents, tithes, and fees. Its inclusion is puzzling, unless the intention was to supply information concerning Swift's 'goods and chattels' which the Commission of Lunacy was also directed to evaluate.

The manuscript concludes with a column of figures, the total of which constitutes Swift's deanery income from the various sources—lands, tithes, ground rents, and fees. The total set down is £807; but one annual return, of £5, was apparently omitted inadvertently, and with this added we find that Swift's annual revenue from the deanery was £812. Thus St. Patrick's was not the most valuable deanery in Ireland in point of income (those of Derry, Raphoe, and possibly Down returned more); nevertheless it was a satisfactory one—and in point of prestige a surpassing one. Swift could have held no other with the same satisfaction. A qualification must be made concerning Swift's income from the deanery: it was reduced, as he complained, by arrears and defaults. To what extent, it is difficult to determine. That there were such we know from the scattered accounts available, but I am inclined to believe that Swift suffered less in this respect than most clergymen in similar positions; in any case, less than his constant complaints would indicate. He was too much a master of the art of persuasion and of applying pressure to forgo his rights. It would have brought some satisfaction to Swift's enemies to learn that his deanery income was not so high as they believed. They reported it to be £1,000—far too much for a divine hardly suspected of being a Christian, who nevertheless barely missed being a bishop:

> A Place he got, yclyp'd a *Stall*,
> And eke a Thousand Pounds withal,
> And, were he a less *witty Writer*,
> He might, as well, have got *a Mitre*.[1]

[1] [Jonathan Smedley,] *Gulliveriana; or, a Fourth Volume of Miscellanies* (London, 1728), p. 109.

'What Pretence', asked the anonymous author of an attack on
Gulliver's Travels, 'has he more than any other Man, to a
Thousand a Year for doing nothing, or little more than strutting
behind a Verger, and Lording it over men honester, and more
deserving than himself . . .?'[1] Although the deanery income was
substantial in itself, it was of course not the whole of Swift's
annual income. Since the manuscript under discussion is concerned with deanery possessions, it does not include Swift's
income from the three parishes he held along with the deanery
—Laracor, Rathbeggan, and Agher. Swift, one must remember,
was a pluralist. Doubtless the tithes from these additional
benefices decreased from the pleasing figure of £200 for which
they were set in 1708 and 1714;[2] still the decrease came at a
time when it could not seriously affect Swift's standard of living.
Finally it should be observed that when Swift was most vocal
and uneasy about his financial affairs he was accumulating
that substantial sum which by 1736 amounted to £7,500. This
money drew interest at rates ranging from 5 to 6 per cent.[3] As
a matter of fact, ready money he found rather troublesome—so
he indicated in an Advertisement in 1738 announcing that he
'is now able to lend two thousand pounds at five per cent upon
good security'. His complaint is that since he cannot purchase
a good estate for endowing his hospital, he is forced to keep
his fortune in mortgages on lands and the like securities.[4]

On the whole, then, Swift deserves no great sympathy when
he cries out his financial woes. The clue to his attitude is not so
much in the actual state of his finances as in his temperament.
It may be the truth, as he wrote to the Earl of Oxford in 1735,
that his revenue had decreased by £300; but he adds a more
significant truth with characteristic understatement: '. . . with
good management I still make a shift to keep up, and am not
poor, nor even moneyless'.[5]

---

[1] *A Letter from a Clergyman to his Friend, with an Account of Capt. Lemuel Gulliver*
(London, 1726), p. 20. For another report that the deanery was worth £1,000
annually see E. Curll's *Dean Swift's Literary Correspondence, for twenty-four years; from
1714 to 1738* (London, 1741), p. 16.

[2] See Forster Collection, MS. 505. 48. D. 34/1, 'Private Expenses of Jonathan
Swift, 1708–1709'. See also *Corres.* ii. 147. Swift's accounts for 1717 and 1736 show
decreases, but apparently they do not give full information.

[3] *Corres.* vi. 87 n. But entries in his accounts for 11 April 1737 show arrears in
interest. See Forster Collection, MS. 512. 48. D. 34/8.

[4] *Corres.* vi. 86–7.

[5] Ibid. v. 223.

SOME ASPECTS OF DEFOE'S PROSE

BONAMY DOBRÉE

IN very few ages could you dare say, as Pope did to Spence, 'There is nothing more foolish than to pretend to be sure of knowing a great writer by his style.' Pope, it may be, wished the stress to be upon 'great', as though you might indeed spot the 'Burnets, Oldmixons, and Cookes'; but in any case so strong a family likeness runs through certain prose forms of the early eighteenth century that it is notoriously hard to tell one hand from another. You do not easily find the challenging disparity you get between, say, a Bacon and a Donne, or a Carlyle and a Landor; only the foolhardy will guarantee to distinguish essays by Addison, Steele, Berkeley, or Tickell—and even, one may venture, Bolingbroke and Chesterfield some years later. They were all, to a greater or less degree, masters of the middle style. They had to be, since men at that time prided themselves on speaking with the voice of society rather than with their own individual speech: it would offend against taste for a man to be known by the way he wrote.

Yet if the ideal seems to have been to write prose to resemble, as Professor James Sutherland puts it, 'the unhurried conversation of an eighteenth century gentleman' (one might add 'at its best', remembering Swift's *Polite Conversation*), this would seem to apply only to occasional essays of the elegant kind, perhaps a little too self-consciously easy and well-mannered. Moreover the law of primitive survival operates here as elsewhere, and Roger North writing *The Musicall Grammarian* in about 1730 might well be first cousin to Sir Thomas Browne. But what is more to the point, here are survivals on another level, the level of Tom Brown and Ned Ward, whose *Amusements Serious and Comical* and *The London Spy* smack much more of the prose of Nashe or Dekker than they do, say, of Steele's. The most important thing, however, is that in the *Tatler* and papers at that level, from the *Mercuries* of the previous century to the *World* of the 1750's, the writers spoke with a tone of authority, with the calm and sometimes infuriating assurance of a dominant class; we feel that they were confident they knew what they were talking about; they were superior. Compare those with, say, the writers of the *Miscellany Letters* culled from Mist's weekly journal in 1722, and at once it strikes you that though the style is 'middle' enough it lacks this sense of authority. Sometimes, however, it seems to strive for it.

Where does Defoe stand in all this? His prose is often admirable, yet it seems to miss calm assurance, especially after the humiliation of prison and pillory; it certainly never has the least whiff of the patronizing. But naturally on turning to him from *Spectators* and *Guardians* we are at once reminded that more than the fashion of a time goes to determine how prose is written; and that the generalization we may have agreed to above too much smooths over the fact that prose is functional, that it is meant to do something. It is intended to produce varying emotional effects, some leading to action, others to a pleasurable pensiveness. Defoe from the early stages of his career as a writer understood this very well. Thus we read in *An Essay on Projects*[1] (1697):

> As for such who read books only to find out the author's *faux pas*, who will quarrel at the meanness of style, errors of pointing, dulness of expression, or the like, I have little to say to them. . . . As to language, I have been rather careful to make it speak English suitable to the manner of the story, than to dress it up with exactness of style; choosing rather to have it free and familiar, according to the nature of essays, than to strain at a perfection of language, which I rather wish for, than pretend to be master of.

We can only guess at what he meant by 'essay'—he was capable of calling anything an essay, even a doggerel poem—but he clearly meant something unaffected, unstilted, possibly un-rhetorical. Yet as you listen to the way he varies the end of his clauses—always an important place in prose—the passage strikes you as written by a man who is by nature a stylist: it is a pleasure to the ear; both the vowels and the incidence of stress are well modulated. His statement might too easily be made to imply more than he really meant; nevertheless it contains a principle: language must be 'suitable to the manner of the story'. There is then no one style for him; his subject-matter will to some extent dictate what his style is to be.

But prose is moulded by yet another factor which Defoe was

---

[1] Quotations have throughout been modernized in spelling, &c.

always conscious of: you must suit your way of saying things
to the kind and number of people you are talking to. He had
made up his mind as to his audience by the turn of the century;
this statement of the principle, however, is taken from a work
composed near the end of his life, *The Complete English Tradesman*
of 1725. He tells us:

If any man were to ask me, which would be supposed to be a
perfect style, or language, I would answer, that in which a man
speaking to five hundred people, of all common and various
capacities, [idiots or lunatics excepted,] should be understood by
them all [in the same manner with one another, and] in the same
sense in which the speaker intended to be understood [,this would
certainly be a most perfect style]. (2nd ed. 1726.)

It is true that Defoe was here telling tradesmen about the
best style for them to write in; yet he has the air of laying down
a general principle. At all events, taking the two statements
together, one would conclude that Defoe's style is to be judged
as a vernacular one, as journalism if you like, speech, that is,
addressed to any and every reader. It will be of the street and
not of the boudoir as Addison's is, or even of the coffee-house
as Swift's aimed at being; it will tend to the tub-oratorical. His
is to be a classless way of writing; there will be no appeal to the
snobbery of learning, no titillating of the ear of the refined, no
truckling to genteel forms: but an honest-to-God, Dissenter's,
market-place utterance.

Alas! when you have no guide, only the excitement of the
moment, when you write with the astonishing output of about
ten machines, so that you never have a minute to 'polish or
refine'; when you never have leisure to be intensely conscious
of what you are doing, it is hit or miss, and you are bound to
become prolix. Of this, some of Defoe's contemporaries were
aware. The editors of the fourth (1738) edition of *The Complete
English Tradesman* thought it convenient to prune the work,
saying in the Preface:

The Author of this Work was the celebrated Mr. Daniel De Foe
whose extensive knowledge in all the branches of the British Trade
and Commerce is sufficiently known. But one thing we take the
liberty to observe of his Writings, that, generally speaking they are
too verbose and circumlocutory; insomuch that it has been well
observed of them, That to have a complete work come out of his
hands, it was necessary to give him so much *per* sheet to write it in

his own way; and half as much afterwards to lop off its excrescences, or abstract it: And then, especially if it were on a trading subject, no Author of his time could produce a more finished performance.

Thus, for example, in the extract quoted earlier, the passages between hooks were left out. Do the omissions weaken the statement? It would seem not. Had Defoe, then, no style? Or a bad style? One might think the worst; but then one remembers the perfect unstressed realism of *Mrs. Veal*, the thousand felicities in *Moll Flanders*, the brilliant satire, and sometimes perhaps subtler irony, in some of his political writing. The conciseness, often terrifying, in the *Journal of the Plague Year*, or some magnificences, such as the 'roaring lion' passage in *Captain Singleton*, spring to the mind; so that if one can indeed say that Defoe has no style it is because he has a hundred. Here, as in everything else, he shows a staggering variety, at almost every instant making his words 'suitable to the manner of the story', so that you may get two or three styles on the same page. Can we find a common denominator? Is there throughout his styles some hall-mark of personality which might enable you to hazard boldly when faced with a disputed work, 'This is—or is not—by Defoe?' A task beyond the scope of this essay: but to talk about it may entertain, and help to clear the ground.

It must be confessed that it seems unlikely, in spite of various scattered remarks, that Defoe ever thought about style in the way that Addison, or Pope, or Swift, or Bolingbroke thought about it. His great strokes of artistry—and he abounds in them —seem entirely unconscious. Take, for instance, the semicolon, made famous by Coleridge, which occurs when Crusoe is rummaging about the abandoned ship before she breaks up. Going through the drawers in the cabin, he notes with complacency that he owns many useful articles such as razors, knives, and forks; then he comes upon

... about thirty-six pounds value in money, some European coin, some Brazil, some pieces of eight, some gold, some silver.
I smiled to myself at the sight of this money. O drug! said I aloud, what art thou good for? Thou art not worth to me, no, not the taking off the ground; one of those knives is worth all this heap; I have no manner of use for thee; even remain where thou art, and go to the bottom as a creature whose life is not worth saving: However, upon second thoughts, I took it away; and wrapping all this in a piece of canvas . . . .

Upon which Coleridge: 'Worthy of Shakespeare!—and yet the simple semicolon after it,[1] the instant passing on without the least pause of reflex consciousness, is more exquisite and masterlike than the touch itself. A meaner writer, a Marmontel, would have put an ! after "away", and have commenced a fresh paragraph.'

Well, frankly, one wonders. Defoe is so abominably careless. A few days (or a page or so) earlier Crusoe had stripped naked to swim to the ship, and then—filled his pockets with biscuits which he found aboard! Did Defoe know what he was doing? Was the punctuation art, or a touch of grace beyond the reach of art? The stroke is, of course, as we would say, true: but then Defoe had such an uncanny way of getting inside the skin of the people he was imagining himself to be, that one asks whether, while writing, he ever stopped to consider at all, or ever thought in terms of 'presenting' anything or anyone. And yet, think of *Mrs. Veal, The Shortest Way, And What if the Pretender Should Come?* Only a consummate writer, only a master ironist, could possibly, you say to yourself, have written these things, so convincing, so economical, so very much the opposite of what *The Complete English Tradesman* was to be.

But look again at *The Shortest Way*. Is it possible to classify it? Purposeful parody, yes: but of what sort? Can you call irony what is so nearly burlesque? If it is ironical, it is irony carried so far that it ceases to be itself. Yet what are you to call it? For it isn't satire, which attacks frontally; it isn't invective, except perhaps inversely, which might reconstitute it a branch of the ironic; nor is it sardonic. However, let us look at a little of it:

If one severe law were made and punctually executed, that whoever was found at a conventicle should be banished the nation, and the preacher be hanged, we should soon see an end of the tale, they would all come to church, and one age would see us all one again.

We, of course, living in our so gentle age, regard the brilliant thing as a monstrous phantasy; to us the whole magnificent spoof is obvious. Yet anyone at all familiar with the violent controversy of the period who should come across Defoe's paper for the first time might well take it at its face value. We need only look at it again to see how it was that a young parson of the Church of England could write to a friend that he valued the work next the Bible and the Commandments, and fervently

[1] Actually, in the first edition, a comma.

pray that the Queen would act on its recommendations; we can see how it was that the Dissenters should be panic-stricken. To us, who are in the secret, Defoe is *playing* the shocked pietist to perfection; indeed, as far as he was concerned, to disastrous perfection.

His fault was not to realize that such a form of attack is safe only if people know who you are, and understand your gambit: otherwise you must somehow tip the wink. You can do this either by exaggerating so outrageously that no one can take you literally, as Swift did in *A Modest Proposal*; or else you must carry your argument not merely to the point of common-sense absurdity—for that much Defoe did—but to a point of logical absurdity which no one can mistake, as when Swift says in the *Argument Against the Abolishing of Christianity*:

Nor do I think it wholly groundless, or my fears altogether imaginary, that the abolishing Christianity may perhaps bring the Church in danger . . . ,

or when Pope in *Guardian*, no. 40, tells his readers that Philips's feeble rival often 'deviates into downright poetry'.

Defoe was too single-minded, too simple-hearted; once the demon of imaginative creation got hold of him, he was as one obliviously possessed: he was, in *The Shortest Way*, the high-flyer in person: he never learnt the lesson of detachment, and in his anti-Jacobite pamphlets was as dangerously Jacobite as he had been high-flying over ten years earlier. It was this faculty —the one which constitutes him a genius of the first order— which made *Mrs. Veal* so beautifully convincing. He could not be ironical, we think. Take that astonishing, incomparable masterpiece, *Moll Flanders*: it is full of delicious irony so long as we keep outside Moll. But, given his absorbed interest, could Defoe do so? We are almost forced to think that here too it was unconscious as it was in *Robinson Crusoe*. Yet, we say, surely not in the Preface:

. . . When a woman debauched from her youth, nay, even being the offspring of debauchery and vice, comes to give an account of all her vicious practices . . . an author must be hard put to it to wrap it up so clean as not to give room, especially for vicious readers, to turn it to his disadvantage.

'Vicious readers'! It is easy to pass this over carelessly, but what a superb little stroke of ironic satire it is; as lightly

brushed in as Swift's complaint at being held up in writing
his panegyric on humanity because he found his commonplace
book fill much slower than he had reason to expect. But yet one
doubts: with Defoe one never quite knows. What, for instance,
is happening in this little passage culled from a discussion about
wind at the beginning of *The Storm* (1704)?

'The winds', says the learned Mr. Bohun, 'are generated in the
intermediate space between the earth and the clouds, either by
rarefication or repletion, and sometimes haply by the pressure of
clouds, elastical virtue of the air, etc., from the earth or seas, as by
submarine or subterraneal eruption or descension or refilition from
the middle region.'

All this, though no man is more capable of the inquiry than this
gentleman, yet to the demonstration of the thing, amounts to no more
than we had before, and still leaves it as abstruse and cloudy to our
understanding as ever.

Defoe, we think, must be having a little quiet fun with the
learned Dr. Bohun. Yet on reading the whole page one cannot
be at all sure.

But where one can be sure with Defoe is in the studied
rhetorical effects of his political polemics. It would be enlightening to know whether Morton, the Head of Newington
Academy who so wisely added training in English to the usual
classical-mathematical curriculum of the day, actually taught
formal rhetoric. For Defoe often used set rhetorical figures
which he infused with all the spontaneous vigour of a man
shouting in the street. Here, for instance, is one from *A Challenge
of Peace* (1703), when he is ringing the changes on the Queen's
phrase about desiring peace and union among Christians:

First, Sacheverell's bloody flag of defiance is not the way to peace
and union. . . .
New Associations and proposals to divest men of their freehold
right . . . is not the way to peace and union.
Railing pamphlets, buffooning our brethren as a party to be
suppressed, and dressing them up in the bear's skin for all the dogs
in the street to bait them, is not the way to peace and union—

the refrain gathering a maddening intensity as he follows up the
attack:

Railing sermons, exciting people to hatred and contempt of their
brethren because they differ in opinions, is not the way to peace and
union.

Then he begins to vary the refrain:

Shutting all people out of employment, and the service of their prince and country, unless they can comply with indifferent ceremonies of religion, is far from the way to peace and union—

and it becomes '. . . cannot tend to this peace and union', or '. . . cannot contribute to peace and union'. He is, of course, whipping up the mob to a frenzy; he knows the enormous emotive force of the reiterated drum-beat, as Mark Antony knew it when he spoke over Caesar's corpse.

Compare this with the sort of effect Swift was to get in *The Conduct of the Allies* some ten years later. Swift, we realize in reading, was a more sophisticated person, yet in his English political period (which some of us who love him may be allowed to deplore) he was appealing to much the same mob emotions as Defoe played upon; perhaps, however, the reading populace was, after ten years of political tension exacerbated by journalistic fury, itself becoming sophisticated. Here at all events, the appeal seems to be to reason. Whereas Defoe is shouting 'You over there on the pavement, can't you see . . .?', Swift is saying, 'Well, of course, we sensible men sitting round the table can see . . . .' Here he is piling one 'if' clause upon another:

But if all this be true: if, according to what I have affirmed, we began this war contrary to reason: if, as the other party themselves, upon all occasions, acknowledge, the success we have had was more than we could reasonably expect: if, after all our success, we have not made that use of it, which in reason we ought to have done: if [and here one watches the clauses lengthen out] we have made weak and foolish bargains with our allies, suffered them tamely to break every article, even in those bargains to our disadvantage, and allowed them to treat us with insolence and contempt, at the very instant when we were gaining towns, provinces, and kingdoms for them, at the price of our ruin, and without any prospect of interest to ourselves: if we have consumed all our strength in attacking the enemy on the strongest side, where (as the old Duke of Schomberg expressed it) to engage with France, was to take the bull by the horns; and left wholly unattempted, that part of the war, which could only enable us to continue or to end it: if all this, I say, be our case, it is a very obvious question to ask, by what motives, or what management, we are thus become the dupes and bubbles of Europe?

Swift, we would say, is the more persuasive; but who can judge which was the more effective at the time? For one thing we do

not know how far they spoke to the same audiences. Yet we are
sensible that Defoe is arguing with equals: Swift is informing
his reader with the voice of authority.

Defoe in his bewildering variety of styles—the philosophic,
the (perhaps) ironic, the narrative, the fiery-polemical, the
brutally scourging, the oil-on-the-troubled-waters style, the
patiently and brilliantly expository, or, most astonishing of all,
the devastatingly polite—seems so often to be verging upon
someone else's manner, that it is impossible to say where in his
'higher vernacular' he is at his most characteristic. In one sense,
perhaps, it is from about 1700 to 1715, during the controversial period, where you feel, at all events onward from *A
New Test of the Church of England's Loyalty*, that he is speaking
from a platform. Perhaps at first he was a little stiff, but the
continuous practice of the *Review* made him more flexible. He is
—as far as this manner goes—at his best perhaps in the 1705
phase, before the freshness had worn off, and before feelings
became so dangerously embittered. The numbers beginning
14 July on 'this mighty, this deplorable thing, the *Danger of the
Church*' are enormously entertaining; and even now, without
needing to understand much about anti-Marlburian faction, we
can laugh at:

> Never was there equal danger, never a time of such unaccountable
> distress of the Church of England; the Protestant religion, of which
> the Church of England is the principal bulwark, is at the last gasp,
> is at the brink of destruction.
>
> Well, gentlemen, and what is the matter?—Truly, matter enough,
> and reason enough: Why, the matter is, the Duke of Marlborough
> has beat the French. . . .

It could not be done all of a sudden: it had to be led up to
through four numbers: but then it is perfect in its blandness,
and Defoe can go on to hoist himself into a high-Anglican
pulpit, and deliver a glorious balloon of a discourse which he
suddenly pricks with a superb effect of deflation.

But even when the acerbity was heightened, as in the autumn
elections of 1710, he is still magnificently controlled. How
genuinely he was shocked with the violence at the polling it
would be unwise to suggest, but he lets fly in a fine flurry of
virtuous scolding:

> Well, Gentlemen Citizens of London, is this what you call an
> election of Members of Parliament? And if I should address myself

to you, Gentlemen, of various other parts of England—you have met, mobbed, rabbled, and thrown dirt at one another; the horse have trampled down the foot, the foot have stoned and hurried the horse, men's heads, arms, and legs, have been broke, some come home bruised, some bloody—Northampton, Whitchurch, Coventry, London, Westminster, Norwich, Marlow—and innumerable other places, the fighting, the rabbles, tumults, and extravagancy, are not to be enumerated—Now, pray, what do ye call this?—Shall we call this a free choice?—No man will, I believe, pretend to it.

It is, as often with Defoe, so urgent as to be breathless; the construction tends to get out of hand, and has to be recalled to order by some desperate means. Yet he himself has not been run away with: he has pulled himself up; the rating tone of a magistrate reproving a mob becomes judicial: 'Now, Gentlemen, before we enter into particulars . . .'; and the number (24 October) develops into a beautifully argued plea for calmness. His tones, however, are infinite, and he can be really shocked and grieved, in dignified prose, at treachery;

Never open your mouths after this about public faith, the honour of treaties, justice to allies, the standing fast to confederacies and the like; whoever may complain of these things, it is not for those I am speaking of to open their mouths about it now.

It is all too rarely, perhaps, that Defoe attains that level of dignity.

But dignified he can be, especially when violently attacked, and once, certainly, he had the advantage of his most redoubtable opponent. Swift, in *Examiner* 15 of 11 November 1710, commented on 'two stupid and illiterate scribblers, both of them fanatics by profession: I mean the *Review* and *Observator*', and embroidered the theme by referring to 'rough, dirty hands', 'outrageous party writers', and 'idiots'. On 14 December Defoe answered:

Besides, among all the authors of whom the streets abound—with my humble service to Mr. Examiner, I recommend it to him, to answer this civil question—If, Sir, you have so much learning, how came you to have so little manners?

Again, while Addison in *Count Tariff* calls Mercator 'a false, shuffling, prevaricating rascal', Mercator (we assume him to have been Defoe) on 26–9 September 1713 refers to the Guardian as 'a man whose sense and good manners qualify him to be a match for any man, provided his cause be good, and who it is hoped will handsomely yield a cause up if it be other-wise'. At particular moments, then, amazingly, Defoe is more urbane than Addison himself, more wholly an educated gentle-man than Swift!

We can turn by way of contrast to a quite different aspect of Defoe's writing, where he is struggling to be a philosopher. We can look again at the disquisition with which he preludes *The Storm*. He is, as we see, trapped in the religious dilemma of the day, engaged in what has been described as filling up the gaps in scientific knowledge—one way by which God makes himself known—with chunks of revelation:

'Tis apparent, that God Almighty, whom the Philosophers care as little as possible to have anything to do with, seems to have reserv'd this [the cause of the winds], as one of those Secrets in Nature which should more directly guide them to himself.

Three paragraphs develop this; then:

In this search after Causes, the Philosopher, tho' he may at the same Time be a very good Christian, cares not at all to meddle with his Maker: the Reason is plain; We may at any time resolve all things into Infinite Power, and we do allow that the Finger of Infinite is the First Mighty Cause of Nature herself; but the Treasury of Immediate Cause is generally committed to Nature; and if at any time we are driven to look beyond her 'tis because we are out of the way: 'tis not because it is not in her, but because we cannot find it.

No one would claim this to be admirable prose or delightful writing: yet it does enable you to follow the workings of Defoe's mind; it does not at all get in the way. Here, for comparison, is Addison (in *Spectator* 531) dealing with much the same problem—from the 'optimistic' angle—but by his authoritative utterance ('the unhurried conversation of a gentleman') a little veiling the difficulty:

I have here only considered the Supreme Being by the light of reason and philosophy. If we would see him in all the wonders of his mercy, we must have recourse to revelation, which represents him to us not only as infinitely great and glorious, but as infinitely good and just in his dispensations towards man.

The passage is admirable balanced English, so balanced and admirable that it ceases to be real. It has about it that faint flavour of sham that clings about Addison when he is most

Mandeville's 'parson in a tye-wig'. He is not only superior, he is the Superior Person. You do not follow the workings of a mind. It is refreshing to turn back to Defoe, and, skipping one paragraph, read:

Thus in Nature the Philosopher's Business is not to look through Nature, and come to the vast open Field of Infinite Power. . . . Philosophy's a-ground if it is forc'd to any further Enquiry. The Christian begins just where the Philosopher ends; and when the Enquirer turns his Eyes up to Heaven, farewel Philosopher; 'tis a Sign he can make nothing of it here.

Deftly and concisely put: there is no shilly-shallying or evasion, no glozing over the difficulty; you are stark up against it, and in direct contact with Defoe's mind.

At that time (1704), though already too prolix, he still had the leisure to be economical where he wished. It is tempting to think that but for the unceasing, relentless torrent of words he was compelled to produce (partly by his own nature, it is true) from 1704 onwards, he might have learnt to castigate his prose. When later on he became a speculative moralist he was much more long-winded—but then moralizing lends itself to prosiness. Here we have him in Crusoe's *Serious Reflections* . . . of 1720. The section sets off in a brave *Spectator* manner: 'Conversation is the brightest and most beautiful part of life; 'tis an emblem of the enjoyment of a future state. . . .' Then, after a somewhat wordy description of the conversationalist who is a good man, we get:

But take this with you in the character of this happy man, namely that he is always a good man, a religious man: 'tis a gross error to imagine, that a soul blacken'd with vice, loaded with crime, degenerated into immorality and folly, can be that man, can have this calm, serene soul, those clear thoughts, those constant smiles upon his brow, and the steady agreeableness and pleasantry in his temper, that I am speaking of; there must be intervals of darkness upon such a mind; storms in the conscience will always lodge clouds upon the countenance; and where the weather is hazey within, it can never be sun-shine without; the smiles of a disturbed mind are all but feigned and forged; there may be a good disposition, but it will be too often and too evidently interrupted by the recoils of the mind, to leave the temper untouched, and the humour free and unconcerned; when the drum beats an alarm within, it is impossible but the disturbance will be discovered without.

It must be confessed that it is structureless and repetitive; it lacks bone: it does not get us into contact with Defoe's mind; it does not really do anything. It should be edifying; it is merely ineffective.

No doubt at sixty or so, after a life of sometimes daring and sometimes pusillanimous duplicity, abstract moralizing, preaching the beauty of holiness, may seem a little unreal. At all events the matter lacks urgency, so we get none of that sense of the importance of hitting hard here and now which gives pungency to the early Occasional Conformity tracts. It might be well for a man to forget that he had been 'set apart' for the ministry. But Defoe was always a product of the Stoke Newington Academy; moralizing was in his blood—and in the rest of him, in his bones and in his nerves, there was the terrific imagination which made him be what he created, created out of fact. That is why his best prose, we may think, is where he can moralize in the first person through the mouths of his creatures—the narrator of the *Journal of the Plague Year*, Crusoe, Moll Flanders, and so on: it is no longer abstract moralizing; it is practical morality.

It is the same when he is moralizing directly from what may have been a ruffling experience of his own. The manner is beautifully direct; but is it not—in 1725—going away from the 'polite' prose of the previous quarter of a century back to the basis of the other colloquialism of Tom Brown and Ned Ward? Take this from *Everybody's Business is Nobody's Business*:

Being at a coffeehouse t'other day, where one of these ladies kept the bar, I had bespoke a dish of rice tea; but madam was so taken up with her sparks, that she had quite forgot it. I spoke for it again, and with some temper, but was answered after a most taunting manner, not without a toss of the head, a contraction of the nostrils, and other impertinencies too many to enumerate. Seeing myself thus publicly insulted by such an animal, I could not choose but show my resentment. Woman, said I sternly, I want a dish of rice tea, and not what your vanity and impudence may imagine; therefore treat me as a gentleman and a customer, and serve me with what I call for: keep your impertinent repartees and impudent behaviour for the coxcombs that swarm round your bar, and make you so vain of your blown carcase.

It is brilliant 'higher vernacular', an instrument evolved from infinite practice, which closely follows the sinuosities of Defoe's

mind (or temper), in exactly the same way as when that mind
undergoes various avatars in his type-personages. Thus it is
that, for example, Moll Flanders' veracious unveracity, her
unconscious, innocently amoral self-betrayals, are among the
most enchanting things in literature. It does not matter here
his not being able to stop to polish or refine—he certainly lacked
any vestige of the art to blot—because there is no construction.
Since Defoe is the object, nothing comes between the object
and you; no moralizing is forced on you from outside.

It is then, we may think, in the great six-years period of
creative writing, in the works with which most people are
familiar, that Defoe made his contribution to English prose; for
there the style which he now found it easiest to write was
beautifully 'suitable to the manner of the story'. Treatises on
trade, histories of the Devil, handbooks on servants, journalism
on street robberies and all those later works are no longer read,
because they all needed a style more concise and more detached
than Defoe now found it in him to write. So long as the matter
was to hand for his superb impersonations, and his experiences
to give them the verisimilitude of reported fact were un-
exhausted, his prose seemed to form itself naturally to give
substance to the image which presented itself, one may well
think, simultaneously with the emotion, moral or artistic, which
inspired him. The prose itself is seldom economical, but there
are such leaps as in the *Robinson Crusoe* passage quoted. It is not
arrow-swift, but it bustles over the ground at a tremendous
pace; it is neither unhurried nor authoritative, but it impels you
to follow at its own speed; it seldom ravishes the ear, but it
hardly ever offends it. Good-mannered because it never makes
assumptions about you, the reader, it is also modest, and rarely
fatigues. And because it is always true to the movements of
Defoe's mind, without that mind containing any reservations,
undistorted, as Coleridge might say, by the least pause of reflex
consciousness, it is immensely effective so long as you take care
to remain alert.

THE SONGS IN STEELE'S PLAYS

RAE BLANCHARD

STEELE campaigned so heartily against Italian opera and so often deplored the trend of entertainment away from drama pure and simple that the prominence given to music in his own comedies may be overlooked. No playwright, however, at the turn of the century paid more attention to incidental songs and their performance than he; and incidental music—overture and act-tunes—was composed expressly for two of his plays. On this evidence one may believe that he bowed to the fashionable taste for theatrical music and endeavoured in the production at Drury Lane of *The Funeral or Grief-à-la-Mode* (1701), *The Lying Lover* (1703), and *The Tender Husband* (1705) to please an audience that loved music as a decorative accessory to their bill of fare. And his last comedy, *The Conscious Lovers*, produced in 1722, also had its musical moment. In the four plays there is a generous handful of songs, fourteen to be exact; and it may be of interest to consider them briefly: their range and variety, the dramatic purposes they serve, their musical settings, the singers who sang them, and their fortune through the century as lyrics to be read and recited and songs to be sung.

Variety in their themes and forms is a marked characteristic. The love songs enhancing the courtship of Lady Sharlot, Lady Harriot, Victoria, Penelope, and Biddy Tipkin compliment youth and beauty in various moods and themes including a serenading song and an epithalamium. Deeper notes are struck in the patriotic themes: a call to arms, a commemoration of Blenheim, a lament for the fallen English soldiers, and tributes to King William and Queen Anne. There are laughter and conviviality in a mock song for a comic role and a drinking song. Moreover, they have considerable technical variety; and though not one was intended to be spoken only, it is apparent that Steele wanted to make them shapely lyric poems, harmonious in form and movement with their themes. The line with four accents predominates; but dimeter, trimeter, and pentameter metres vary the design. With a single exception they are short, having one unit or, at the most, two or three stanzas. Two are single units of four couplets. Another pair consist of two quatrains each. Three have a pattern of six octosyllabic couplets in two stanzas. Of the others, no two are exactly alike in form. The longest, possibly intended as an ode, is about fifty lines in length and is formal and intricate in structure. An irregular strophic pattern is used for three: one of twelve lines consists of an iambic quatrain, a ballad stanza, and a tetrameter quatrain; another of sixteen lines has an introductory tetrameter quatrain followed by two stanzas of three octosyllabic couplets each; a third of ten lines has a ballad stanza followed by two tercets of tetrameter lines. The comic song is in quatrains with emphatically marked time-beat and rhyme. The drinking song has two graceful five-line stanzas of anapestic dimeter and trimeter lines. One of them, the spinet song, is in madrigal form with eleven lines rhyming *aa, bbb, ccdd, bb* in an arrangement of four- and five-stressed lines. As lyrics, they have a definite sense of design. Conscious artistry, metrical precision, and a quiet mien, hall-marks of eighteenth-century light verse at its best, are not lacking in Steele's songs.

The unusual number of them in the three early plays seems to indicate that he sought openings for music; but, unlike his fellow playwrights who merely gave the direction 'Here a Song', he tried to make them a part of the action. True, *The Funeral* has a conventional ending, 'Here a dance and the following songs': whereupon 'Arise, arise, great dead for arms renowned' and 'On yonder bed supinely laid' were sung by musicians awaiting their cue in the wings. Likewise *The Lying Lover* ends formally with the singing of a compliment to Queen Anne, 'The rolling years the joys restore'. But in the main the purpose of Steele's songs is not merely to mark a pause or create a moment of diversion; they serve to highlight a character or a situation or are episodic in themselves. In *The Funeral*, for example, 'Let not love on me bestow', intended by its author Campley to introduce his declaration to Lady Harriot, is talked about in two scenes before it is heard: why it was written, how it has been practised to the spinet, what the air is like, what the rhyme-scheme is, who is to sing it, and where. And in a dramatic episode the paper of verses is made to conceal a cheque presented to the insolvent Lord Hardy by his friend Campley. When the expected moment arrives there is a difference of opinion as to whether the song, now declared to be set to 'an excellent air of old Mr. Lawes's', shall be performed to the spinet or the lute. Then, with the paper propped before her upon someone's hat, the clowning Mrs. Fardingale (Dicky Norris) by Steele's direction 'Sings and squalls it'; and finally, to impress his beautiful audience, Campley (Wilks) sings it himself. The serenading song in *The Tender Husband*, 'Why, lovely charmer, tell me why', is appropriately sung at the window of the romantic Biddy Tipkin. In *The Lying Lover* Young Bookwit mentions his song to Latine, who loves music 'immoderately', before directing his musical equipage to perform 'Venus has left her Grecian Isles' for the flattery of the reluctant Victoria. 'With studied airs and practised smiles' in *The Tender Husband* is related to the artificial beauty and Frenchy manners of Mrs. Clerimont (Mrs. Cross) and introduced during a conversation about her face, 'very prettily designed today'. She first hums the song, 'à-la-Française', with affected gestures, and then mockingly sings it like an Englishwoman. Whenever possible Steele made his song an organic part of the play.

His insistence that the words be clearly understood is not surprising when we remember his objection to Italian opera: that listening to it was a purely sensuous experience, that English ears heard only the music. Of his own songs his view seemed to be that each had its distinct lyrical value as poetry. In the marriage of music and verse the beauty and meaning of the verse should not be overshadowed. To make sure, therefore, that the words were fully appreciated several of the songs were recited either before or after they were sung. Lady Sharlot read aloud from the paper 'Let not love' before it was performed for Harriot's benefit. 'To Celia's Spinet' Penelope declaimed part by part with comment on each section before it was sung. 'With studied airs' was first recited by Mrs. Clerimont before her music-master sang it. And this particular one was hummed or sung twice more. After the singing of 'Venus has left' Bookwit recited the last tercet in order to enforce the meaning. Captain Clerimont knew 'Gentle Parthenissa' by heart and, as he painted Biddy's portrait, recited it for her before asking his servant to sing. There is precedent in earlier drama for this technique, but Steele more than his contemporaries seems to have found it useful and agreeable.

The lute, for a long time the chosen instrument to accompany stage songs, he designates in only one instance, and for a song performed humorously: Mrs. Fardingale sends her servant to fetch a lute, to which she plays an accompaniment for her 'squalling'. It is regarded facetiously also in the burlesque song, 'Cynderaxa', composed by Trim (Pinkethman) in honour of his cook-maid sweetheart and performed, by the stage direction, to a 'Pair of tongs', which he calls his lute. A number of the settings are written 'within the compass of the flute' with instrumental parts for the common or the German flute; and possibly several were sung to one of these instruments played off stage or to the band of strings furnishing the act-tunes. Either arrangement may have been followed for those formally intro- duced into the text and according to Steele's caption sung by named musicians; and likewise for those sung by 'The Boy' at Lord Hardy's summons and by Captain Clerimont's servant. A flautist or a violinist may have stood in the wings when Bookwit entered 'with bottle and glass singing'. String music may have accompanied 'Venus has left', for the foppish Bookwit calls upon his band of fiddlers to 'strike up' for the song.

But the most interesting point to note is Steele's liking for the spinet. In each of the early plays there is a spinet scene. In *The Funeral* Campley and Mrs. Fardingale declare they have prac- tised 'Let not love' to this instrument; and, when the moment arrives for singing, Lady Sharlot says rather pointedly—'There is the spinet, Mr. Campley; I know you're musical.' For the spinet song in *The Lying Lover*, the 'master' is summoned 'from the next room', and the direction follows, 'Here the song is performed to a spinet':

> Thou soft machine that dost her hand obey,
> Tell her my grief in thy harmonious lay.
>
> .   .   .   .
>
> Speak in melting sounds my tears
> Speak my joys, my hopes, my fears—
>
> .   .   .   .   .   .

In *The Tender Husband* Mrs. Clerimont's 'spinet-master' arrives opportunely and plays and sings 'With studied airs'. Steele is more explicit in his directions than any other playwright of the period. He may have been partial to keyboard music, or he may have sought to evoke in these episodes the social atmosphere of chamber music. The spinet or small harpsichord was a popular domestic instrument, and his play scenes with the characters clustered about it are reminders of the informal portraits of the century with groupings of musical friends in the drawing-room.

Very lively incidental music was composed by William Croft for the first performances of *The Funeral* and *The Lying Lover*. The suite for each play, in addition to an overture, consists of airs and dances to be used, presumably, for special effects within the play itself. There is no reason to think that Croft's music had anything to do with the programme of miscellaneous dancing and singing given between the acts. But one can only guess at the purposes it served, as no directions are given in the text or the score. It would indeed be enlightening to know to what extent the theatre management, Steele, and Croft conferred upon the composition and use of this music. At a time of many competing entertainments Steele would be aware of its contribution to his plays and its value in alluring public interest.[1] Croft is now remembered as a famous organist at Westminster Abbey and a composer of cathedral music, his name being revered for the beautiful setting of the Anglican Burial Service and St. Anne's Tune, to which we sing Watts's hymn 'O God, our help in ages past'. But, when this theatrical music was composed, he was in his early twenties, his career at its beginning; and he was following the illustrious example of Henry Purcell. In the form preserved the music for both plays is scored in four parts for first and second treble, tenor, and bass, the instruments not designated, with eight sections in each suite. *The Funeral* music consists of Overture, Scotch Aire, Slow Aire, Jigg, Slow Aire, Aire, Aire, and Chaconne. The Scotch Aire testifies to the popularity of Scotch music and the Chaconne, a slow Spanish dance in triple time, the longest section in the suite, also to the taste of the moment. The music for *The Lying Lover* has even more variety and sprightliness: Overture, Hornpipe, Aire, Round O slow, Aire, Trumpet Aire, Minuet Round O, and Chaconne. The first casts included players who could dance and sing and also the matchless comedians Pinkethman, Norris, and Bullock (all three in *The Funeral*); and undoubtedly the merriment in Steele's comedies, as well as the musical

[1] G. A. Aitken quotes in the *Life of Steele* (1889), i. 72, the advertisements: 'Next week will be published Mr Croft's his new Musick in the Comedy called *The Funeral* ... Written by Mr Steele', in the *Post Boy*, 11 to 13 Dec.; and 'This Day ...', 16 to 18 Dec. 1701. The publication of the play itself 'As it is Acted' was advertised for 18 to 20 Dec. 1701; the date is 1702 on the title-page.

atmosphere, would be heightened by the orchestral performance of Croft's act-tunes.[1]

The music for the songs as first performed was written by theatrical composers of the day—Daniel Purcell, William Croft, Richard Leveridge, Lewis Ramondon, and John Ernest Galliard —all of them good musicians. At mid-century the names of Thomas Arne, (——) Sullivan, and (——) Bagley were added to the list and in the final decades that of John Stafford Smith. Three settings are by unnamed composers. Several of the songs were sung to popular tunes, for example to a minuet by Francesco Geminiani, the violinist, and to airs composed for other lyrics by Maurice Greene, George Monro, and J. C. Pepusch. At least in the first run of the early plays certain of them may have been performed by the actors themselves. In the roles of Campley, Bookwit, and Captain Clerimont, Robert Wilks, said to have had a fine singing voice, may have sung 'Let not love' and 'Since the day' and probably on occasion 'Why, lovely charmer'. Mrs. Letitia (?) Cross, cast as Mrs. Clerimont, and Mrs. Lucas as Lettice the maid, were singers as well as actresses. Mrs. Cross doubtless sang 'With studied airs'; and Mrs. Lucas, as she was in the scene, may have performed 'To Celia's Spinet'. But also associated with the singing are the names of professional musicians who had nothing at all to do with the action. Richard Leveridge, James Bowen, (——) Pate, Lewis Ramondon, Francis (?) Hughes, Mrs. Harris, Mary Anne Campion, and, later in the century, Kitty Clive and 'Mr.' Sullivan sang Steele's songs in the play performances and, sometimes, in the music-hall as favourite airs.

The settings are preserved on folio half-sheets or whole sheets

[1] Croft's work is preserved in a book of manuscript music at the Library of Congress, Division of Music (M 1515. A 11 Case), *Play House Aires*, oblong folio, calf binding, no imprint: the music for *The Funeral* on pp. 109–32 and for *The Lying Lover* on pp. 390–412. This book was purchased from the library of William H. Cummings (d. 1915), founder of the Purcell Society. It appears to be a complete copy of the book listed in the *Catalogue of the Sacred Harmonic Society of London* (1872), where it is described as *Theatre Music Overtures and Act Tunes by Various Composers for English Plays Produced at the End of the Seventeenth and Commencement of the Eighteenth Century . . .*, 4 vols., oblong folio (London, [*c.* 1700–4]). An analysis of the contents of this printed book tallies with *Play House Aires*. Music for some twenty plays is included, for two others by Croft. Aitken knew about this music and published the first treble of the score for the Overture and Scotch Aire of *The Funeral* music in *Life*, ii. 369–72, but gave no idea of the nature and extent of it. A portion of Croft's music for Steele's plays is listed in the *First Supplement* of the *Catalogue of Printed Music in the British Museum*.

engraved with words and music—found in single song-sheet editions and in book collections—and also in various types of song-books. In some versions only the melody for the voice is given and in others the complete accompaniment. Occasionally the instrumental form appears alone. The paragraphs following contain brief accounts of the music, the composers, and the singers; the notes at the end (pp. 196 ff.) describe the forms in which the settings are found and also give a list of miscellanies in which are printed the lyrics without music: a partial list intended only to suggest the nature and extent of their circulation during the century.[1]

Four of the five songs in *The Funeral* were set by Daniel Purcell: 'Let not love', 'Ye minutes bring', 'On yonder bed', and 'Arise, arise'. Purcell, though lacking the original genius which his great brother had possessed, was a talented musician in demand for theatrical compositions. Within this twelve-month London audiences had applauded his settings for incidental songs, his act-tunes for a play or two at Drury Lane, his music for a portion of Dryden's *Secular Masque*, and his prize setting for Congreve's masque, *The Judgment of Paris*. His settings for Steele's songs are bright and spirited and melodious, but ornate in style. These are not home-spun, artless airs: they are written for trained voices; they abound in shakes and graces, slides and turns; and their accompaniments also have ornamental features. The fifth song in the play, 'Cynderaxa kind and good' (shades of Dryden's Lyndaraxa!), according to one tradition, was set by William Croft. But in the absence of any such setting, may we not surmise that Pinkethman romped through his merry verses and buffoonery with the kitchen tongs to the music of a dance tune in Croft's suite? 'Let not love' had a second setting. At the end of the century John Stafford Smith (of *Star-spangled Banner* fame) used Steele's words, without indicating their source, however, in one of his glees for mixed voices.

---

[1] My search has been limited to the libraries of Baltimore and Washington, the Boston Public Library, and Houghton Library at Harvard University. From playbills read at the Folger Library and in the Theatre Collection at Harvard I have found various details not given in the standard reference books on the history of eighteenth-century music and theatre. For his stimulating interest I am indebted to Professor Emmett Avery and for substantial assistance, kindly given, to Mr. W. N. H. Harding of Chicago, possessor of a great collection of eighteenth-century songs.

The men and women who sang the songs of *The Funeral* were well-known singers, some of whom undoubtedly were members of the Drury Lane Company. Steele would consider it a triumph to secure the virtuosos Jemmie Bowen and Mr. Pate to sing the lyrics that brought the play to a climactic close: in the printed text their names are given above the nuptial song 'On yonder bed' and the solemn, patriotic 'Arise, arise'. There may be obscurity in the facts of Pate's life, but no doubts can be held of his prestige or the merit of his performances, for example, in Henry Purcell's *Fairy Queen* or Motteux's operatic *Island Princess*. And young Bowen, in demand as 'The Boy', sang his grace notes so skilfully that he had earned the praise of the great Purcell himself. Two women singers also sang *The Funeral* songs, Mrs. Harris and Miss Campion. Of Mrs. Harris little seems to be known; her name appears on a song-sheet edition of 'Let not love' that may have served on some occasion as *entr'acte* entertainment. We know that Miss Campion had a voice of exceptional beauty and delighted her audiences from about 1702, when she sang in a revival of *The Island Princess*, to 1704, when she left the stage; and that a promising career was cut short when she died in 1706 at the age of nineteen. 'Sung by Mrs. Campion' heads a song-sheet version of 'Ye minutes bring' (assigned to the Boy); and as she was with the Company in 1703, it is not inconceivable that she stood in the wings awaiting her call at the revival of *The Funeral* on 28 May, 1 November, and 15 December of that year.

Of the four songs in *The Lying Lover*, 'Venus has left' was set by Daniel Purcell, 'Since the day' by Richard Leveridge, and 'To Celia's Spinet' by William Croft. The setting for the fourth, 'The rolling years', is unfortunately not to be found, nor is the composer's name on record. The three known settings are tuneful airs to hum or to pick out on the piano, but their effectiveness would depend on a good voice and an instrumental accompaniment. Particularly Croft's spinet song, rich in *agréments* and musical frills, demanded an exhibition of virtuosity— but by whom we do not know (by Mrs. Lucas?). One of the notable musical features of *The Lying Lover* was the contribution made by Leveridge, singer and composer, during many decades acclaimed for his occasional songs and operatic roles, at this time a singing member of the Company. According to Steele's statement in the printed text he sang in the first run, 'Venus

has left' and the solo cantata, 'The rolling years'; and the song-
sheet version provides evidence that he both set and sang 'Since
the day'. This convivial song, suited to his powerful, deep bass
voice, was long a favourite with him as with the public; and
possibly because of his famous singing it eventually suffered a
transformation. A ballad-writer took liberties with the text and
by adding numerous stanzas (to fill up a broadside sheet?)
changed Steele's brief, sweetly melancholy 'bubble song' into a
drawn-out, cynical love-ditty.

One of the songs in *The Tender Husband* fell stillborn from his
pen. Though elevated in theme and tone, the long Blenheim
dirge, 'See Britons see', with its pompous phrases and cadences
failed to attract a composer. Lewis Ramondon, a French
musician, who at this time was singing in pre-Handelian opera
and who later turned his talents entirely to composition, furnished a graceful setting for 'With studied airs' and, we know
from the song-sheet, sang it himself. On 30 May 1706 bills for
the play announced 'Songs by Mr. Hughes, Mr. Ramondon,
and the Boy', and there is no reason to doubt that their singing
was within the play; Ramondon would perform his song as
Mrs. Clerimont's spinet-master. 'Why, lovely charmer' had two
settings of its own and two borrowed. Daniel Purcell's score,
with its airy lift and play, is a match for the lyric. But the
musical fretwork called for a skilled executant—and had at
least one in Francis (?) Hughes, 'counter-tenor', like Ramondon
a playhouse musician and an opera singer, whose name is on
the song-sheet. It is the serenading song, to be performed,
Steele's direction implies, by an attendant, a vocal part at
times undoubtedly assigned to Hughes. As early as the 1720's
admirers of 'Lovely charmer' liked to sing the words to tunes
by Dr. Greene and Geminiani, not intended for it but suitable
and less difficult than the playhouse music. Then at mid-
century an anonymous composer gave it a new lease of life, but
without any mention of Steele or the play, in a second setting of
its own.

'Gentle Parthenissa' in *The Tender Husband*, apparently the
most celebrated of them all, was sung for many decades to the
music of at least four composers. Daniel Purcell's setting was
put aside at the middle of the century for two new tunes, if less
brilliant, fresh and easier to play and sing. The setting and
singing of the song by Mr. Sullivan, a musician at the theatre,

gave it a very happy vogue; and it received a left-handed
compliment from one Bagley, who, without acknowledgements,
altered the first line to 'Whilst in the grove Timandra walks'
(and three words elsewhere) and called it 'a new song'. For
his generation, Dr. Arne, like Purcell, made playhouse music
of it with a score of style and finish designed for the voice of the
incomparable Mrs. Clive, who must surely have sung it with
archness and gaiety. For a certainty she was cast as Biddy
Tipkin on 10 December 1745 and 24 November 1750. Steele's
words were sung to the notes of violin, flute, and harpsichord
in the London theatres; on summer evenings at Vauxhall,
Marylebone, and Ranelagh; and, without doubt, by amateurs
in private gatherings of friends. The Arne setting was appreciated across the Atlantic, for we know that in Philadelphia the
music-loving patriot Francis Hopkinson played it on his harpsichord. The Parthenissa of this song is no relation to the swarm
of conventional Celias, Chloes, and Flavias. This was the name
of the foolish little romance-reading heroine, christened Bridget,
who demanded of her lover to be courted as Parthenissa. His
compliance is expressed in the half-tender, half-mocking verses:

I

While gentle Parthenissa walks,
And sweetly smiles, and gaily talks,
A thousand shafts around her fly,
A thousand swains unheeded die.

II

If then she labours to be seen,
With all her killing air and mien;
From so much beauty, so much art
What mortal can secure his heart?

Only one song was written for *The Conscious Lovers*, and that
was ready together with its setting by John Ernest Galliard, so
Steele tells us, two years before it was needed for the production
in 1722. 'From place to place forlorn I go' is not exactly an
essential part of the play: as he explains in the preface, where
it was printed, it was designed to serve in Act II as entertainment for Indiana, but for 'want of a performer' had to be
omitted and instead 'Signor Carbonelli played admirably well
on the fiddle'. As the music-master summoned by Bevil Junior,
he performed a sonata (the text reads), probably one of his own

compositions.[1] But the original intention must have been realized many times in succeeding performances. Playbills for the comedy, often revived, usually announce 'Singing in the Second Act by ——', whoever at the moment was a favourite of the town: Thomas Lowe, John Beard, Master Mattocks, Miss Isabella Young. And sometimes the choice of music would fall on *Indiana's Song* or, as Steele called it, *The Love-Sick Maid*, a melodious little wail that almost sings itself. The eighteenth century, in general, liked Indiana and liked her song also. All three of its known settings were issued anonymously. Two of them, that presumed to be Galliard's and another of the same period—both suited to the lyric in mood and musical phrasing—are simple, plaintive tunes, in a minor key, trailing off at the end in a few bars of flute music. The third, which evidently belongs to the middle years of the century, has a more pretentious score for voice and instruments. Galliard was a versatile musician—composer, critic, and concert oboist—who had come to England from Germany early in the century to direct chamber music for Anne's Prince of Denmark and who at the time of his interest in Steele's play was producing music for songs, cantatas, masques, and opera.

Whether or not Steele liked music aesthetically, whether or not he wholeheartedly supported the vogue for musical entertainment, it is undeniable that the fourteen songs (and Croft's act-tunes) gave a distinctly musical atmosphere to his comedies. Possibly he was a demurrer. Possibly he thought he was throwing his weight on the side of 'rational' entertainment by insisting that, whenever possible, his songs be a part of the dramatic action, that they have lyrical value as poems, and that the verbal have equal prominence with the musical phrases. But as time passed these bits of verse were usually printed anonymously, detached from their dramatic context, and hence owed nothing to the famous name of 'The Censor of Great Britain' or Sir Richard, the political pamphleteer, and little even to that of Captain Dick Steele for their modest popularity as poems and songs. They were able to make their way alone. True, the revival, decade after decade, of the comedies (*The Lying Lover* excepted) kept them before the theatre audience.

---

[1] Giovanni Stephano Carbonell came to London from Rome in 1720. His twelve sonatas were published with a dedication to the Duke of Rutland in 1722—*Carbonell's Solos: Sonate de Camera a Violino e Violone o Cembalo* (Library of Congress).

Attractive musical settings and celebrated singing were also important factors in their survival. But generous credit must be given to their own stamina: as songs they have individuality—and wit and charm. They are lacking in the heartiness of Tom D'Urfey's and in the sparkle of Congreve's. They do not have the polished beauty of Dryden's at his best; but on the other hand they are not marred, as are many of his, by cynicism or sensuality. While it never could be maintained that Steele was a poet, it is true that he turned a deft hand to light verse. A good word might even be said for the end-tag rhymes of his acts and scenes. But of the lack-lustre blank verse passages, all too numerous in the early comedies, perhaps the least said the better.

The concluding thought is this: even a small excursion into theatrical history reminds one that the printed pages of an early eighteenth-century English play may be more enjoyably read within the sound of the music rippling through them.

The Funeral

'Let not love on me bestow
Soft distress and tender woe'   ii. iii.

A Collection of the Choicest Songs and Dialogues Composed by the Most Eminent Masters of the Age, folio, J. Walsh, [*c.* 1704], p. 112. 'Set by Daniel Purcell and Sung by Mrs. Harris.' Key of C major with figured bass [for harpsichord, spinet, or bass-viol]. A short concluding passage for the flute. (Folger Library.)

Thomas D'Urfey, *Wit and Mirth: or Pills to Purge Melancholy*, 1706, 1707, 1709, iv. 184–5; and in his *Songs Compleat, Pleasant, and Divertive*, 12mo, 1719–20, vi. 22–3. Purcell's setting, melody only. (Library of Congress.)

John Stafford Smith, *A Collection of Songs of Various Kinds and for Different Voices*, [177–], p. 6. 'A Chearful Glee,' set for three voices, two trebles and a bass. (Library of Congress.)

G. A. Aitken, *Life of Richard Steele*, 1889, ii. 372–4. Purcell's setting.

The words without music are found in *The Hive*, 1724, i. 201, as 'The Painful Part of Love Renounc'd'; *The Choice*, 1733, ii. 179; *The Lark*, 1740, p. 59; *The Thrush*, 1749, p. 213; *The Aviary*, [1744], p. 312; *The Warbling Muses*, 1749, p. 280; *The Charmer*, 1751, ii. 194; *The Vocal Magazine or Compleat British Songster*, 1784, no. 123; Joseph Ritson, *A Select Collection of English Songs with their Original Airs*, 1783, 1813, i. 136: with the note that 'it was set in a most labored, mechanical manner by Daniel Purcell, but his music was not thought worthy of insertion'; John Aikin, *Essays on Song-Writing with a Collection of Such English Songs as are Most Eminent for Poetical Merit*, [1772], 1810, p. 199, classified as 'a witty song'; Aikin, *Vocal Poetry*, 1810, p. 209.

'Ye minutes bring the happy hour
And Chloe blushing to the bower'   iv. ii.

A Collection of the Choicest Songs and Dialogues, [*c.* 1704], p. 213 (listed but missing from the Folger copy); [*c.* 1710], p. 192. 'Set by Daniel Purcell and Sung by Mrs. Campion.' With figured bass.

Aitken, op. cit. ii. 374–5.

The words without music are found in *The Choice*, 1733, ii. 179; *Vocal Miscellany*, 1734, i. 306; *The Syren*, 1735, p. 252; *The Cupid*, 1736, p. 55; *The Aviary*, [1744], p. 645; *The Charmer*, 1751, ii. 194. In several of these miscellanies Chloe's name becomes Phillis, and Corinna becomes Ardelia.

> 'On yonder bed supinely laid
> Behold thy loved expecting maid'   v. iv.

A Collection of the Choicest Songs and Dialogues, [*c.* 1704], p. 130. (Folger Library); [*c.* 1710], p. 124. 'Set by Daniel Purcell.' With figured bass.

The words alone are given in *The Hive*, 1725, iii. 70; *The Choice*, 1733, ii. 180; *The Thrush*, 1749, p. 398; *The Warbling Muses*, 1749, p. 281.

> 'Arise, arise, great dead, for arms renowned
> Rise from your urns and save your dying story'   v. iv.

In the printed play Steele labels the song, 'Set by Daniel Purcell'; but the music has not been found.

The words are given in *The Hive*, 1725, iii. 33; *A Complete Collection of Old and New Songs*, 1736, iv. 58; *Vocal Miscellany*, 1734, i. 310; *The Syren*, 1735, p. 234; *The Aviary*, [1744], p. 47; *The London Songster or Polite Musical Companion*, 1773, pp. 394–5; *The Vocal Magazine*, 1784, no. 1083; *The Masque*, [*c.* 178–], p. 80; F. S. Boas, *Songs and Lyrics from the English Playbook*, [1945], p. 196.

> 'Cynderaxa, kind and good,
> Has all my heart and stomach too'   iv. ii.

I have found no trace of the music, but Mr. Harding has a note written some years ago, the authority now forgotten, to the effect that the composer was William Croft.

The words are given in *The Hive*, 1724, ii. 118; *The Choice*, 1733, ii. 180; *The Linnet*, 1749, p. 284; *The Warbling Muses*, 1749, p. 280; *The Charmer*, 1751, ii. 195; *Songs and Lyrics from the English Playbook*, [1945], p. 196, as 'The Fair Kitchen-maid'.

The Lying Lover

> 'Venus has left her Grecian isles
> With all her gaudy train'   iii. ii.

'A Song by Mr Leveridge. Sett by Mr Dan: Purcell', folio, double sheet, 2 pp., [n.d.]. Key of A major with figured bass [for harpsichord, spinet, or bass-viol]. Symphony at the end 'For the flute'. (Library of Congress.)

The Monthly Masks of Vocal Musick, Containing all the Choicest Songs by the Best Masters Made for the Playhouses, Public Consorts, and Other Occasions, folio, J. Walsh, July, 1704. The score is that described above. (Houghton Library, Harvard University.)

The words without music are given in *The Choice*, 1733, iii. 25; *The Warbling Muses*, 1749, p. 283, the first line changed to 'blissful isles' and the heroine to Florella.

To Celia's Spinet: 'Thou soft machine that dost her hand obey'   ii. i.

The Monthly Masks of Vocal Musick, 2 pp., April 1704. 'A Song to Celia's Spinnett. Sett by Mr William Crofts.' With figured bass. Symphony at the end 'For the flute'. (Houghton Library.)

The words are given in *The Hive*, 1725, iii. 12.

'The rolling years the joys restore
Which happy, happy Britain knew'   v. iii.

In the printed play Steele labelled it 'Song by Mr. Leveridge', but no information concerning the setting or the composer has been found.

The words are given in *The Choice*, 1733, iii. 26; *The Syren*, 1735, p. 272; *The Aviary*, [1744], p. 491; *The Robin*, 1749, p. 119.

'Since the day of poor man
That little, little span'   iv. iii.

The Monthly Masks of Vocal Musick, July 1707. 'A Song Set and Sung by Mr. Leveridge.' In the key of E minor, with figured bass. With an instrumental passage between stanzas for the bass and a concluding symphony 'For the flute'. (Houghton Library and Library of Congress.)

A Collection of Songs by Mr. Richard Leveridge, folio, J. Walsh, [c. 1723], p. 32. (In Mr. Harding's Collection.)

A Collection of Songs with the Musick by Mr. Leveridge, Engraved and Printed for the Author. With a Frontispiece Designed and Engraved by Hogarth, octavo, 1727, two vols. in one, ii. 3. 'Life a Bubble.' Treble and bass. The score differs slightly from the *Monthly Mask* music. (Boston Public Library.)

The Merry Musician or a Cure for the Spleen, J. Walsh, [c. 1729], p. 159. 'Life a Bubble by Mr. Leveridge.' Melody only. (Boston Public Library.)

Aitken, op. cit. ii. 377–8. The score as given in the edition of 1727.

The words are given in *The Hive*, 1732, iv. 39 as 'Life Improved' and in *The Warbling Muses*, 1749, p. 283. With five additional six-line stanzas the poem is found in *Collection of Bacchanalian Songs*, 1729, p. 14; *The Choice*, 1733, iii. 13; *The Syren*, 1735, p. 268; *The Aviary*, [1744], p. 439; *The Robin*, 1749, p. 46.

The Tender Husband

'See, Britons, see with awful eyes
Britannia from her seas arise'

This song follows the Prologue in the printed play and has the heading, 'A Song Designed for the Fourth Act, but not Set.' The only song-book reference found is in *The Choice*, 1733, iii. 23.

'With studied airs and practised smiles
Flavia my ravished heart beguiles'   iii. i.

The Monthly Masks of Vocal Musick, 2 pp., May 1706. 'A Song in the Tender Husband. Sett and Sung by Mr Ramondon at the Theatre Royal.' With instrumental passages at the beginning and between stanzas for the bass; symphony at the end 'For the flute'. (Houghton Library.)

A song-sheet edition of the item described above, folio, double sheet, 2 pp., [n.d.]. (Houghton Library: Mus. 505.7 F*, sheet music.)

The words are given in *The Hive*, 1724, i. 24 under the title 'The Artful Mistress'; *The Choice*, 1733, iii. 21; *The Warbling Muses*, 1749, p. 281, where the heroine becomes Celia.

'Why, lovely charmer, tell me why
So very kind and yet so shy'   iv. i.

The Monthly Masks of Vocal Musick, May 1705. 'A Song in the Tender Husband, Sung by Mr Hughes. Set by Mr. Dan: Purcell. Within the Compass of the Flute.'

Opening line: 'Why, Belvidera, tell me why'. With figured bass [for the harpsichord, spinet, or bass-viol]. (Houghton Library.)

The Musical Miscellany. A Collection of Choice Songs Set to the Violin and Flute, small octavo, J. Watts, 1729–31, i. 170. Words only with the statement that the song can be sung to Mr. Green's [Maurice Greene] setting of 'Did ever swain a nymph adore' or *Robin's Complaint*, the melody given on p. 168. (Boston Public Library.)

The Vocal Miscellany, 1734, p. 316. Words only with the statement that the song can be sung to the tune of 'Gently touch the warbling lyre'. These words are by Arthur Bradley and the music is Geminiani's *Minuet*, given in *Musical Miscellany*, I. 49.

A Collection of English Songs, folio, [175–], i. 55. 'A New Song.' This is a different setting from that in the *Monthly Masks*. Composer's name not given. With figured bass and a symphony 'For the flute'. (Boston Public Library.)

'A New Song', folio, single sheet, [n.d.]. Like the preceding item. (Julian Marshall Collection of Sheet Music: Houghton Library.)

The words without the music are found in *The Hive*, 1724, i. 249 as 'The Nonplus' and in ii. 131 as 'To His Various Mistress'; *The Syren*, 1735, p. 271; *The Cupid*, 1739, p. 60; *The Choice*, 1733, iii. 22; *The Musical Companion*, 1741, p. 218; *The Aviary*, [1744], p. 622; *The Warbling Muses*, 1749, p. 282, where 'lovely charmer' becomes 'Sweet Inchantress'; Aikin, *Vocal Poetry*, 1810, p. 176; *The Book of English Songs*, 1851, p. 56; E. B. Reed, *Songs from British Drama*, 1925, p. 225; F. S. Boas, *Songs and Lyrics from the English Playbook*, [1945], p. 197, as 'So very kind, and yet so shy?'

'While gentle Parthenissa walks
And sweetly smiles and gaily talks'   IV. ii.

The Monthly Masks of Vocal Musick, April 1705. 'A Song by the Boy in the Tender Husband. Set by Mr Daniel Purcell. Within the compass of the Flute.' Treble and bass. Key of B flat major. (Houghton Library.)

The Musical Miscellany, 1731, vi. 163. Words only with the statement that they can be sung to 'Fame of Dorinda's conquests brought', a song by John Hughes, music by Dr. Pepusch, given on p. 161.

London Magazine, 1745, p. 302. 'A Song Set by Mr. Sullivan.' The first line reads: 'When gentle Parthenissa . . . .'

Universal Harmony, octavo size, J. Newberry, 1745, p. 92. Ornamental head-piece. 'Sung by Mr. Sullivan.' With figured bass; introductory and concluding instrumental passages. (Library of Congress.)

Amaryllis, octavo size, 1746, p. 60. 'Sung and Set by Mr. Sullivan.' (Boston Public Library.)

A Collection of English Songs, folio, [175–], i. 117. 'Gentle Parthenissa. Set by Mr. Sullivan.' With figured bass. Symphony at the end 'For the German flute'. (Boston Public Library.)

Apollo's Cabinet or the Muses Delight, octavo size, Liverpool, 1756, i. 112. 'Sung by Mr. Sullivan.' (Boston Public Library.)

Thomas Augustine Arne, *The Songs in the Comedies Called As You Like It and Twelfth Night . . . with Another in the Tender Husband*, folio, W. Smith, [1745–50], p. 2. 'When gentle . . . Sung by Mrs. Clive.' Scored in three clefs: violin (?), voice, and figured bass. Transposed for the German flute, p. 21. (Folger Library.)

The Delightful Pocket Companion for the German Flute, J. Simpson, [1745], ii, no. 20. Arne's music without the words. (Library of Congress.)

Songs. Francis Hopkinson His Book, oblong folio, manuscript, Philadelphia, 1759, p. 124. Arne's music with harpsichord accompaniment. (Library of Congress.)

Benjamin Martin, *Miscellaneous Correspondence*, octavo, 1759, ii. 739 (for Feb. 1758). 'Whilst in the Grove Timandra Walks. A New Song by Mr. Bagley.' Treble and bass. (Houghton Library.)

Aitken, op. cit. ii. 378–81, Purcell setting; ii. 382–4, Arne setting.

The words without music in *The Hive*, 1724, ii. 113, as 'The Irresistable Charmer'; *The Choice*, 1733, iii. 22; *The Syren*, 1735, p. 271; *The Robin*, 1749, p. 293; *The Aviary*, [1744], p. 608; *The Warbling Muses*, 1749, p. 282, where the first line becomes 'Whilst in the grove Timandra walks'.

The Conscious Lovers

'From place to place forlorn I go
With downcast eyes a silent shade'   Designed for ii. ii.

The Musical Miscellany, 1729, i. 104–5. 'Sung in the Conscious Lovers.' Composer's name not given; but as it is in company with ten other songs set by Galliard and is written in a similar style, this is conjectured to be the Galliard setting. Melody only, with short concluding passage 'For the flute'.

Calliope or English Harmony, octavo, J. Simpson, [*c*. 1737–9], i. 10. 'A Song in the Conscious Lovers.' Composer's name not given. Treble and bass, in Key of G minor. Concluding passage for the flute. Headed by engraved vignette. This is a different setting from that in *Musical Miscellany*. (Boston Public Library.)

'A Song with Symphony for the Entertainment of Indiana in the Conscious Lovers', folio, double sheet, 2 pp., [n.d.]. Composer's name not given. Treble and bass. With instrumental introduction, interlude passages, and symphony at the end 'For the flute'. This is a third setting. (Julian Marshall Collection of Sheet Music: Houghton Library.)

Joseph Ritson, *A Select Collection of English Songs*, 2nd ed., 1813, words in i. 179; melody in iii. 91. Same air as in *Musical Miscellany*.

Aitken, op. cit. ii. 384–5. 'Indiana's Song, Composer not known.' Same score as in *Calliope*, and presumably that listed in *The Catalogue of Printed Music in the British Museum*, single sheet folio.

Ursula Greville, *Charming Sounds: a Volume of Early Eighteenth-Century Songs. Arranged with Pianoforte Accompaniment by Owen Mase*, folio size, 1926, p. 9. 'Words and melody anonymous.' Same air as that in *Musical Miscellany*. (Boston Public Library.)

The words are given in *The Theatre*, no. 18, 1 March 1720, by Steele: 'The Love-Sick Maid / A Song. Set by Mr. Galliard.' The text printed here differs slightly from that in the Preface of the play, printed in 1722. *The Hive*, 1724, i. 112, as 'The Bashful Virgin'; *The Cupid*, 1736, p. 21 and 1739, p. 18, where it is stated that the song can be sung to 'My goddess Celia heav'nly fair,' setting by Mr. Monro (to be seen in *Musical Miscellany*, 1730, iv. 124–5); *The Choice*, 1733, ii. 178; *The Nightingale*, 1738, p. 293; *The Musical Companion*, 1741, p. 213; *The Aviary*, [1744], p. 175; *The Linnet*, 1749, p. 378; *The Buck's Bottle Companion*, 1775, p. 13; *The Vocal Magazine*, 1784, no. 1148; Aikin, *Essays on Song-Writing*, 1810, p. 143, and *Vocal Poetry*, 1810, p. 134.

JOHN GAY

JAMES SUTHERLAND

THE serious temper of the present age, the contemporary
tendency to think of literature as a discipline rather than
a delight, and to value the literature of the past in proportion as it is relevant to our present distresses and has power
to 'interpret life for us, to console us, to sustain us', all this
creates a rather astringent atmosphere which is unfriendly to
the reputation of such a writer as John Gay. If Gay is not
actually a forgotten poet, he is not very actively remembered
to-day except as the friend of Swift and Pope; he remains, like
so many literary and other monuments in England, not so
much because he has an important function to perform as
because he is already there. He is not doing any harm, and no
one is particularly interested in removing him. His surest hold
upon immortality is *The Beggar's Opera*, and any dividends that
may come to him from a revival of that charming piece he must
share with the modern producer, the costumier, the adaptor
of the music, and the contemporary impersonators of Polly
Peachum and Macheath. Certainly, if he is still among the
English poets, he hardly owes that position to the literary
critics. He has suffered, in fact, from that most damaging kind
of criticism that gives with one hand and takes away with the
other: everyone rather likes Gay, and no one is prepared to
make any serious claims for him as a poet. 'It would be idle
to pretend . . .', the critics say in unison, 'it would be foolish to
suggest . . .'; and Gay, waiting anxiously in the wings for the
verdict of posterity, hears only a little tepid applause falling like
coppers into a charity-box.

The critical attitude to Gay (as to most other eighteenth-
century poets) is probably still influenced, if no longer determined, by the judgement of Dr. Johnson. In his account of the
poet he decided that Gay could not be rated high; he was, as
Johnson had once heard a female critic remark, 'of a lower
order'. That is bad enough for a start, but worse is to follow.
Johnson proceeds to consider Gay's works one by one, and by
nicely balancing the blame with the praise he casts up his
poetical account and finds him not much more than solvent.

The *Rural Sports* are 'never contemptible, nor ever excellent'; *Trivia* may be allowed 'all that it claims'; the minor poems are 'neither much esteemed, nor totally despised'.[1] In the end Johnson leaves his readers with the impression that if they skip Gay altogether they will not be missing much. Two years later Joseph Warton dismisses him in much the same style: 'He wrote with neatness and terseness, *aequali quadam mediocritate*, but certainly without any elevation.'[2]

It must be added that Gay's own friends rarely asserted his claims as a poet. They thought of him, and when he was dead they remembered him, as a man—gentle, good-natured, indolent, lovable in the extreme, shiftless, impracticable, innocent, volatile, a sort of Augustan Peter Pan riding in the coaches of his noble friends, dining at their tables, shooting their pheasants, but quite incapable of attending to his worldly affairs. They all loved him, and they all looked after him; he was a sort of joint responsibility, and he repaid them by his wit and geniality and by his unselfish interest in their own concerns. Swift in particular tried to instil into Gay some of his own sense of husbandry and responsibility. He urged his friend to take more exercise, and to plan some big work that would take several years to write; he should think of laying up something for his old age. And Gay really tried—as an undergraduate will try to please his tutor. 'I remember your prescription,' he tells Swift, 'and I do ride upon the Downs, and at present I have no asthma.' Or again: 'I find myself dispirited for want of having some pursuit. . . . If you would advise the Duchess to confine me four hours a day to my own room, while I am in the country, I will write; for I cannot confine myself as I ought.'[3] No wonder Swift complained on one occasion to Pope:

> I suppose Mr. Gay will return from the Bath with twenty pounds more flesh, and two hundred less in money. Providence never designed him to be above two-and-twenty, by his thoughtlessness and cullibility. He has as little foresight of age, sickness, poverty, or loss of admirers, as a girl at fifteen.[4]

Spiritually, indeed, Gay did remain about two-and-twenty all his life, and in the rather too-adult eighteenth century that is

[1] Samuel Johnson, *Lives of the English Poets*, ed. G. B. Hill (1905), ii. 282–4.
[2] Joseph Warton, *An Essay on the Writings and Genius of Pope* (1782), ii. 314.
[3] *The Correspondence of Jonathan Swift, D.D.*, ed. F. E. Ball (1913), iv. 134, 173, 272, 286, 294.　　　　　　　　　　　　　　　　　　　　[4] Ibid. 39.

one of his most endearing qualities. When he died in 1731 and was buried in Westminster Abbey (as if, Arbuthnot remarked to Swift, he had been a peer of the realm), his friends in their various ways all felt that they had lost a part of themselves. None of them, perhaps, expressed so completely what Gay had meant to those who knew him best as the Duchess of Queensberry, with whom the last years of his life had been spent in such debonair and unaffected friendship. Writing almost three years after his death, she mentions the successful purchase of some property which 'for this four or five years last past we had set our hearts on'. And yet, she reflects:

I have not felt delighted, only mighty well satisfied: is not this astonishing? I often want poor Mr. Gay, and on this occasion extremely. Nothing evaporates sooner than joy untold, or even told, unless to one so entirely in your interest as he was, who bore at least an equal share in every satisfaction or dissatisfaction which attended us.[1]

To live on so in the memory of one's friends is indeed something. To those friends, so various in temperament and character, he was a sort of extension of their own personalities; he entered into their schemes, he gave them his time and his affection, he was never too busy or too preoccupied with his own affairs to break off and attend to theirs. He was therefore the perfect companion, equally welcome at the tea-table or in the coffee-house or over a bottle of claret, the right man for a walking tour (if he had ever been willing to walk), the amiable and adaptable guest, the delightful correspondent. It was so that they all tended to think of him and to value him, and only secondarily as the author of *The Shepherd's Week*, or *Trivia*, or even *The Beggar's Opera*. This affectionate and faintly protective attitude of his friends has descended to those who never knew him. Not, it is true, to Johnson, for whom Gay's unassertive and accommodating nature had little appeal. But few later critics have written of him without betraying a slightly patronizing affection, and without referring (even Johnson does this once) to 'poor Gay'. No one ever thinks of saying 'poor Swift', and only, perhaps, Miss Sitwell of saying 'poor Pope'.

What men *are* lives after them, and often gets between us and what they wrote. The world's verdict on an author is based,

---

[1] *Letters to and from Henrietta, Countess of Suffolk* . . . (1824), ii. 109.

more often than we are apt to believe, on the impression made
by his personality, and not solely on what he wrote. It is
notorious that Matthew Arnold, who warned us against this
very error, went on to commit it himself in his estimates of
Byron, of Shelley, of Keats; and with reputations less secure than
those, some weakness or ineffectiveness of character may lead
to the partial or total neglect of a reputable author.[1] Of Gay it
may perhaps be said that while his attractive and unassertive
character has to some slight extent helped to keep his memory
alive, it has tended at the same time to blur his achievement as a
poet. The habit among critics of patronizing Gay, of not taking
him quite seriously *as a man*, has spread to his poetry. When
Johnson wrote of him that he had not in any degree 'the *mens
divinior*, the dignity of genius',[2] we may perhaps suspect that the
judgement is partly due to the impression made by Gay the man,
who had not, in Johnson's opinion, 'the character of a hero'.[3]
It is true enough ('it would be idle to pretend') that Gay is the
wrong man to go to if you are looking for the *mens divinior* in its
most pronounced degree. But how much of it would you find in
Horace, in Herrick, in Cowper, in Lamartine? Does the '*mens
divinior*, the dignity of genius' turn out to be something, like
Arnold's 'grand style', that helps us to a qualitative rather than
a quantitative distinction?

The only way to do Gay justice is to accept his poetry on its
own terms. If we look to him for 'a criticism of life', or expect
to find in his poetry a substitute for religion, we shall look for
what he is hardly ever concerned to give. His poetry bears
about as much relation to contemporary eighteenth-century
life as a Victorian sampler bears to the flowers and trees and
cottages that it reproduces in bright needlework. Gay did not
run away from life; he accepted it as his point of departure. In
the medium of poetry he did what had long been familiar in the
medium of pottery—he produced *objets d'art*, delicate, formalized, artificial, glazed and polished by his poetic diction, and
removed from actuality by a process of refining and idealizing

---

[1] Who would guess from the histories of literature that *The Duke of Lerma* is
almost the finest English tragedy written in the second half of the seventeenth
century? But the author, Sir Robert Howard, appears to have been a pompous ass,
and was generally recognized and satirized as such by his contemporaries. The
character of the man prejudiced the reputation of his tragedy, and though his
character is now as little known as his play the harm had been done.

[2] *Lives*, ed. cit. ii. 282.   [3] Ibid. 272.

that was his own peculiar secret. What Gay had in a high
degree, and what he has rarely been given sufficient credit for,
was a delicate and sophisticated craftsmanship. The thing
perfectly said, the tone perfectly caught and maintained: are
these so common that we can take them for granted?

If we want the actual movement and stench and uproar of the
London streets (as in certain moods we may) we can go to, say,
Ned Ward; if we want to get the feeling—coarse, vulgar,
palpitating—of a London crowd on holiday in the eighteenth
century, we may find what we are looking for in the contemporary newspapers:

The Holidays coming on, the Alewives of Islington, Kentish
Town, and several other adjacent Villages, are in great Expectation
of a considerable Trade from the Citizens, as Harlots are from their
Apprentices. If the Weather proves favourable, whole Shoals of the
former, with all their Living Utensils, viz. Their Wives and Children,
will be flocking thither, to the utter Destruction of Stuff'd Beef,
Gammon of Bacon, Cheese-cakes, Bottle-Ale, and Cyder, which will
be devour'd like Custard on a Lord-Mayor's Day, or Flummery by
a Club of Welsh Attorneys. . . . The Fields will swarm with
Butchers Wives, and Oyster-Women, known by wadling Gates, and
Gold Chains; with a Medley of other frail Matrons and Damsels
diverting themselves with their snotty Offspring, whilst their
Spouses and Sweethearts are sweating at Ninepins, some at Cricket,
others at Stool-Ball, besides an amorous couple in every corner; so
that the poor Town will be left as empty as a long Vacation, or a
Pawnbroker's Conscience; only Stock-Jobbers will stick close to
Business, to find the Way to the Devil, at Jonathan's. Much Noise
and Guttling in the Morning; much Tippling all Day; and much
Reeling and Kissing at Night.[1]

How remote from Gay is this guzzling, sweating, jostling
crowd! He knows, of course, how the citizens eat and drink
and amuse themselves, and how they smell; but before they are
fit for his verse they must be devitalized, deodorized, and gently
formalized. They must, in fact, be transformed into Chelsea
shepherds and shepherdesses:

> When the sweet-breathing Spring unfolds the buds,
> Love flys the dusty town for shady woods.
> Then Totenham fields with roving beauty swarm,
> And Hampstead Balls the city virgin warm;

[1] *The Weekly Journal; Or, British Gazetteer*, 4 June 1720. If this is not by Ned
Ward it is by one of his imitators.

Then Chelsea's meads o'erhear perfidious vows,
And the prest grass defrauds the grazing cows.[1]

The two last lines are pure Gay; they have his own special note
of delicate absurdity and sophisticated mockery. But the whole
passage is characteristic of his habit of refining the raw materials
of life. In *Rural Sports* he explains to the angler in georgic
fashion how to clean the worms he is going to use as bait:

> Cleanse them from filth, to give a tempting gloss,
> Cherish the sully'd reptile race with moss;
> Amid the verdant bed they twine, they toil,
> And from their bodies wipe their native soil.[2]

Gay submits contemporary life to this same self-cleaning process
until it shines with a delicate and not quite earthly lustre. The
actual, the real, are of interest to this poet mainly because they
enable him, as in *The Shepherd's Week* and *Trivia*, to obtain a kind
of contrapuntal effect with the artificiality of his glossy diction
and the orderliness of his balanced rhythm. The gently
deliberate contrast comes out in *Trivia*:

> When all the Mall in leafy ruin lies,
> And damsels first renew their oyster cries . . .[3]

or in *The Shepherd's Week*:

> Lost in the musick of the whirling flail,
> To gaze on thee I left the smoaking pail . . .[4]

or, again in *Trivia*:

> When on his box the nodding coachman snores,
> And dreams of fancy'd fares . . .[5]

or finally, in a winter scene in the streets of London:

> On silent wheel the passing coaches roll;
> Oft' look behind, and ward the threatning pole.
> In harden'd orbs the school-boy moulds the snow,
> To mark the coachman with a dext'rous throw.
> Why do ye, boys, the kennel's surface spread,
> To tempt with faithless pass the matron's tread?
> How can ye laugh to see the damsel spurn,
> Sink in your frauds, and her green stockings mourn?

---

[1] 'An Epistle to the Right Honourable William Pulteney, Esq.', 101 ff.
[2] Op. cit. i. 167 ff.   [3] Op. cit. i. 27 f.
[4] Op. cit. 'Tuesday', 57 f.   [5] Op. cit. i. 153 f.

At *White*'s the harness'd chairman idly stands,
And swings around his waste his tingling hands:
The sempstress speeds to '*Change* with red-tipt nose;
The Belgian stove beneath her footstool glows;
In half-whipt muslin needles useless lie,
And shuttle-cocks across the counter fly.
These sports warm harmless; why then will ye prove,
Deluded maids, the dang'rous flames of love?[1]

In the picture of the frozen Thames that follows, Nature has come half-way to meet the poet by herself appearing in an artificial dress; it is just this natural artificiality that Gay seeks habitually to create. On this occasion Nature has saved him the trouble by effecting the delicate transformation herself. To get the precise effect of Gay's habitual softening of the actual it is sometimes necessary to substitute the England of the twentieth century for the London of Queen Anne—to replace the water-man, the hackney coachman, the sempstress by the taxi-driver, the bus-conductor, the typist. How is the typist, for instance, to become a piece of Chelsea china? By the same delicate process of formalizing her, emptying her of all seriousness, and glazing her with poetic diction. There she sits at her machine (Gay would have done it better, but we may at least make the attempt)

> And dreams of Damon still with melting eye,
> While rattling stops beneath her digits fly.

Life was indeed a jest to Gay. Cheerful, sociable, kind-hearted, he nevertheless remained slightly aloof from human concerns. Confronted by life he had the detachment of the artist, just as at a death-bed his friend Arbuthnot had the detachment of the physician. His special kind of perception was for the ironical, the delicately absurd, the piquant contrast between the growing artificialities of town life and the natural man or the natural background. When Spring comes to the Town,

> The ladies gayly dress'd the *Mall* adorn
> With various dyes, and paint the sunny morn;
> The wanton fawns with frisking pleasure range,
> And chirping sparrows greet the welcome change.[2]

The ladies, the fawns, the sparrows: it is characteristic of Gay

[1] *Trivia*, ii. 327 ff.
[2] Ibid. i. 145 ff.

to bring them together in this way, the sophisticated and the natural. When a rainstorm threatens,

> The bookseller, whose shop's an open square,
> Foresees the tempest, and with early care
> Of learning strips the rails. . . .[1]

Again the delicate contrast: the books in the street, the rain on the books. An umbrella is perhaps the perfect symbol for the world of Gay's peculiar, half-mocking vision; an umbrella that 'guards from chilly show'rs the walking maid', faintly absurd in itself, an apparatus devised by civilized man and yet spread out in the face of a hostile nature.

This contrast between the natural and the artificial runs through all Gay's work. Sometimes it is emphasized, as when he notes how

> On doors the sallow milk-maid chalks her gains;
> Ah! how unlike the milkmaid of the plains![2]

Sometimes it is only implied, as when he goes on to remark upon the ass's milk which was prescribed by physicians for 'the love-sick maid' and 'dwindling beau' (even here the contrast is implicit), and which was brought to the invalid not in milk-pails but in the still-unmilked ass herself:

> Before proud gates attending asses bray,
> Or arrogate with solemn pace the way. . . .[3]

It was, we may be sure, the odd solemnity of those patient animals picking their way over the London cobblestones that caught and held Gay's attention. With Gay we have at last reached a genuinely urban civilization (a state of affairs so frequently and so superfluously deplored by critics of a romantic turn), and we can recognize in him the town-dweller's delighted interest in such manifestations of natural life as come his way— the cat caught in a tree and rescued by the fire brigade, the pigeons in Trafalgar Square (citizens of a smaller growth), the well-groomed greys at a royal wedding.

Aware of this contrast between the natural and the artificial, Gay is constantly modifying the one by the other: the natural becomes artificial, and the artificial natural. But Gay's tendency is always, if not actually to idealize, to soften and harmonize.

---

[1] *Trivia*, i. 161 ff.   [2] Ibid. ii. 11 f.   [3] Ibid. 13 f.

He presents his world not under fluorescent lighting but in the kindlier glow of candlelight. In *Trivia* (where the joke begins with the sedentary Gay writing a poem on walking at all) the disorderly human material of the London streets is quietly folded away in his orderly couplets, patted gently into place, and scented with lavender. His method of dealing with the poor and the humble was made possible by the wide gap between the educated and the uneducated in the early eighteenth century, but again Gay has his own special perception of their touching and amusing simplicity. His own peculiar note of kindly sophistication comes out in the charming ballad, 'Sweet William's Farewell to Black-ey'd Susan'. When William, high on the ship's mast, 'rock'd with the billow to and fro', heard the voice of his sweetheart,

> He sigh'd and cast his eyes below:
> The cord slides swiftly through his glowing hands
> And (quick as lightning) on the deck he stands.

It is a drawing-room piece, another perfect example of Gay's Chelsea china. So is the equally sophisticated "'Twas when the seas were roaring', and so are most of the earlier Fables, and many of the songs scattered through *The Beggar's Opera* (e.g. 'Before the barn door crowing', 'Were I laid on Greenland's coast').

In the *Fables*, once so popular and now hardly read at all, Gay is, as usual, taking his art seriously and wearing his morality lightly. Written for the edification of the young Prince William, Duke of Cumberland, they have sometimes the most unexpected application. 'The Tame Stag' (No. XIII) recounts pleasantly the progress of a young stag which has been captured by a country clown and kept in captivity. Timid at first, he soon begins to feel at home in his new surroundings, 'munches the linen on the lines', expects to be fed by the servants ('examines every fist for meat'), and ends at last by attacking his captors. The moral of all this?

> Such is the country maiden's fright,
> When first a red-coat is in sight,
> Behind the door she hides her face,
> Next time at distance eyes the lace,
> She now can all his terrors stand,
> Nor from his squeeze withdraws her hand;

> She plays familiar in his arms,
> And ev'ry soldier hath his charms;
> From tent to tent she spreads her flame:
> For custom conquers fear and shame.

So far as Gay's moral purpose is concerned, it could not have been much less if he had been illustrating the behaviour of stags by that of country wenches. What concerns him here, as always, is the polished and precise statement, the nice conduct of a critical intelligence, and the urbane cultivation of a literary 'kind'.

If Gay was not an earnest moralist, neither was he a determined satirist. We may suspect that his satirical tone was acquired mainly from living among satirists in a satirical age. We can see him occasionally in his letters working himself up to a fashionable indignation with the age in which he lives, but there is no conviction in his protests. When in his verse he attempts the mode of Juvenal, he is 'a little o'erparted'; his indignation is no more than what he thinks the occasion requires, not what he really feels or has ever had much occasion to feel. Of this kind are some lines on the Parisian dames:

> This next the spoils of fifty lovers wears,
> Rich Dandin's brilliant favours grace her ears;
> The necklace Florio's gen'rous flame bestow'd,
> Clitander's sparkling gems her finger load;
> But now, her charms grown cheap by constant use,
> She sins for scarfs, clock'd stockings, knots, and shoes.
> This next, with sober gait and serious leer,
> Wearies her knees with morn and ev'ning prayer;
> She scorns th'ignoble love of feeble pages,
> But with three Abbots in one night engages. . . .[1]

Gay knew about as much of such things as a precocious schoolboy; he is right out of his element here. He was happy enough bringing down the Duke of Queensberry's partridges; he had no experience of hunting the more dangerous creatures of the woods or of eighteenth-century society. There is one poem, however, 'The Birth of the Squire', in which his satire takes on a deeper tone. It begins quietly enough:

> Hark! the bells ring; along the distant grounds
> The driving gales convey the swelling sounds;

---

[1] *An Epistle to the Right Honourable William Pulteney, Esq.*, 167 ff.

Th'attentive swain, forgetful of his work,
With gaping wonder, leans upon his fork.
What sudden news alarms the waking morn?
To the glad Squire a hopeful heir is born.

The poet goes on to describe the duteous offerings of the tenants
on this joyful occasion and the beer-swilling that accompanies
it, the young Squire's early introduction to the glories of the
hunting field, his furtive amours with the milkmaid in dairy,
barn, and hayloft, his broken collar-bone at the five-bar gate,
his translation to Westminster 'to snore away debates in Parliament', his pompous activities as a Justice of the Peace whose
chief concern is the enforcement of the game laws, until finally
we reach the last scene of all:

Methinks I see him in his hall appear,
Where the long table floats in clammy beer,
'Midst mugs and glasses shatter'd o'er the floor,
Dead-drunk his servile crew supinely snore;
Triumphant, o'er the prostrate brutes he stands,
The mighty bumper trembles in his hands;
Boldly he drinks, and like his glorious Sires,
In copious gulps of potent ale expires.

We might have expected this Hogarthian poem to figure prominently in the anthologies, if anthologies were not so often compiled with an eye to the young and the timid. In 'The Birth of
the Squire' Gay had behind him a long satirical tradition; he
was the man of wit and taste mocking at the booby squire, as
Farquhar had mocked at Squire Sullen, and Congreve at Sir
Wilful Witwoud, and Ravenscroft at Sir Simon Softhead, and
Crowne at Sir Mannerly Shallow—and so back to their ancestors
in Caroline and Jacobean comedy. But Gay's tone is, for him,
oddly uncompromising; it comes near to disgust. We may
perhaps suspect that he had some particularly unfavourable
specimen of the squirearchy in mind, some arrogant lout
remembered from his boyhood years in Devon.

With Gay the tone is all important. Criticism is apt not to
talk at all about those matters which it finds difficult to discuss
on easily intelligible terms. The poet's rhythm (as distinct
from his metre) is one of those topics that most critics pass by
rather uneasily: on such matters criticism has not yet got much
farther than using words like 'magical' and 'hypnotic'. Similar
difficulties are felt in discussing the poet's tone, his attitude to

his readers. 'Tone' is something of which any sensitive reader of Pope or Gay or Johnson is subconsciously aware (it is an element in the poetical experience that is peculiarly relevant to eighteenth-century poetry) but which, for lack of a critical vocabulary or any accepted means of measuring it, is usually passed over in silence.[1] Gay's tone varies, of course, from poem to poem; but he is almost everywhere in polite touch with his reader, walking slightly ahead of him to point out this object or that, dwelling with his habitual mock-seriousness on some homely detail; adding a touch of humorous exaggeration or picturesque embellishment to some familiar appearance. In 'A Journey to Exeter', for instance, where he is addressing himself to the Earl of Burlington, he has nothing very remarkable to tell, but the poem is a minor triumph of the politely familiar mode. And once again Gay manages to transform the ordinary into that something more delicate and remote that is his most characteristic achievement. He contrives even to throw this 'unbought grace' of style over the very meals he ate on his journey. At Stockbridge—

> O'er our parch'd tongue the rich metheglin glides,
> And the red dainty trout our knife divides. . . .

and, at Bridport:

> On unadulterate wine we here regale,
> And strip the lobster of his scarlet mail.[2]

On both occasions the gross act of feeding has taken on something of the precision and formality of an anatomical dissection: the heroic couplet alone would have seen to that. Yet quite

---

[1] But not by Mr. I. A. Richards, who has some admirable remarks on Gray's attitude to the reader of the *Elegy*, and who concludes: 'Indeed, many of the secrets of "style" could, I believe, be shown to be matters of tone, of the perfect recognition of the writer's relation to the reader in view of what is being said and their joint feelings about it' (*Practical Criticism* (London, 1929), pp. 206–7). One might have expected Mr. Richards's preoccupation with theory to interfere with his response to the individual work of art; but he has remained the perfect reader, and his ability to draw from a poem all that is there, and no more, gives authority to his criticism, and should procure a willing suspension of disbelief for his theory.

[2] *Op. cit.* 49–50, 99–100. 'Unadulterate' is a good example of Gay's keeping in touch with his reader, and appealing to his past experience. At the time (1715) when Gay wrote this poem, complaints about the adulteration of wine by vintners were frequent. (See, for example, *Brooke and Hellier: a Satyr*, 1712.) Gay's reference to the adulteration of wines would arouse the same ready response as a reference to whalemeat or snoek in the England of 1949.

apart from the balanced metre, with its tendency, as Wordsworth noted, to 'divest language, in a certain degree, of its
reality, and thus to throw a sort of half-consciousness of unsub-
stantial existence over the whole composition', the effect is also
due to Gay's cool detachment, that delicate withdrawal from
the object contemplated which was, with him, the essential
preliminary to seeing it.

Gay raises in an acute form the problem of the right critical
attitude to minor poets. In the eighteenth century they were
accepted without question. Johnson had no illusions about the
importance of many of the poets whose lives he wrote, but (with
one or two possible exceptions) he obviously thought that they
were worth writing about, and that their poetry (judiciously
selected) was worth reading. The modern attitude is apt to
be far less tolerant. The sort of fluctuation in taste which is
represented by 'Who now reads Cowley?' is natural and
almost inevitable. But in the increasingly astringent atmosphere
of twentieth-century criticism the question is as likely to be:
'Who now would dream of reading Cowley?'—or Cotton, or
Matthew Prior, or Beddoes? This new tendency, not merely to
neglect the minor poet but to insist that he is not worth reading,
may derive from Matthew Arnold, a potent critic, but a very
busy man, who (as Saintsbury put it with a nice meiosis) had
no special bent towards literary history. Certainly, if a man's
time is limited, he would do well to restrict his reading to the
greatest writers. No doubt, too, the intelligent critic, particularly if he moves in academic circles, may be forgiven if he
reacts sharply against the modern tendency to encourage the
young scholar to spend several years in excavating the life and
literary remains of some irredeemably minor poet. But this will
hardly explain or excuse the uncompromising attitude of some
modern critics to writers of long-established reputation whose
work is not of the very first order of importance. Among the
literary achievements of the twentieth century may be reckoned
a much closer and more detailed investigation of the work of
art than was normally attempted in earlier periods; but as the
criticism of poetry becomes more and more intensive the law
of the conservation of energy seems to come into play, and it is
found that fewer and fewer poets are worth reading at all. This
exclusiveness, which is associated, not entirely to its credit, with

a school of criticism at Cambridge,[1] seems to arise from a disproportionate emphasis on values: the critic who is pre-occupied with the question of values is in danger of discounting any writer who has not got an impressive balance at the bank. With such a critic the best becomes too great an enemy to the good; but to neglect or denigrate the good because it is not the best is to leave the best in an unnatural and misleading isolation, and to make poor use of the great resources of English poetry. 'Shine, Poet! in thy place, and be content.' The attitude of Wordsworth to the minor poet is generous and reasonable:

> The stars pre-eminent in magnitude,
> And they that from the zenith dart their beams . . .
> Are yet of no diviner origin,
> No purer essence than the one that burns
> Like an untended watch-fire on the ridge
> Of some dark mountain; or than those which seem
> Humbly to hang, like twinkling winter lamps,
> Among the branches of the leafless trees.
> All are the undying offspring of one Sire:
> Then, to the measure of the light vouchsafed,
> Shine, Poet! in thy place, and be content.

Shine, Critic, too, in thy place, and be content. And one part of the critic's function, when he is not just pontificating, or effecting the dislodgement of Milton, or Shelley, or whoever else owing to some change in the intellectual climate may have gone temporarily out of fashion, is to act, more humbly and usefully, as a sort of caretaker for literary reputations. In this capacity he can at least open the front door for visitors, see that the rooms are kept dusted and ventilated, and, if need be, comment on the exhibits if any visitors arrive. Such employment is not spectacular, but it is honourable; it expresses the relative importance of the critic and the creative writer, and it keeps the critic in the place that heaven has assigned for him.

[1] Cambridge, Eng., not Mass.

ETHICS AND POLITICAL HISTORY IN THOMSON'S *LIBERTY*

ALAN DUGALD MCKILLOP

IN writing *Liberty* James Thomson was actuated by some of the motives that had led to success in *The Seasons*. Both poems centre on the enthusiast in private or public life—the virtuoso in congenial retirement, or the patriot on models at once British and Roman. Shaftesbury's influence, inclusive and eclectic, may be given first place here, specifically coloured in *Liberty* by the editorial patterns of the opposition to Walpole. The poem is, to be sure, 'Whig panegyric', but more precisely it is 'dissident Whig panegyric'.[1] Its high views and broad claims take a special form, one that is still appropriate to the Shaftesburian virtuoso. No writer had tried to enrich the concept of liberty with more significance than Shaftesbury. His liberal views had become the standard attitude for the young Briton taking the grand tour, and *Liberty* of course is the result of Thomson's travels with young Charles Richard Talbot in France and Italy. British observers of the continental scene had underscored the political moral so emphatically that the traveller knew in advance what he was going to see and think. Molesworth, in a famous and controversial Whig tract, had regarded foreign travel for the Englishman as a clinical examination of the effects of the loss of liberty. 'Thus 'tis a great, yet rare advantage to learn rightly how to prize *Health* without the expence of being sick, but one may easily and cheaply grow sensible of the true value of *Liberty* by travelling into such Countries for a season as do not enjoy it.'[2] Addison's *Letter from Italy* (published December 1703) combines enthusiasm for ancient culture and Renaissance art with Whig politics and insular pride: the paradox develops that Italy, with all her cultural riches, starves and pines, while Britain, poorer in arts

---

[1] See Cecil A. Moore, 'Whig Panegyric Verse', *P.M.L.A.* xli (1926), 368–9. There are brief but valuable comments on this point in the summary of Hubert Coleman Howard's thesis, 'The Poetical Opposition to Sir Robert Walpole', *Abstracts of Dissertations . . . Spring Quarter, 1939–40* (Columbus: Ohio State University, 1940), pp. 101–5.

[2] *An Account of Denmark* (London, 1694), sig. a3 recto. This book was in Thomson's library.

and climate, moves like another Rome towards imperial power. Addison's lines are closely imitated by the author of *Liberty. A Poem* (1705), who shows interest in Italian architecture, painting, and music, only to add austerely:

> We envy not such Arts, but boast our own,
> Our *Learning* and our *Law*.   (p. 8.)

As we come to Thomson's generation, we find George Lyttelton moved in France by 'the spirit of Whiggism', while he predicts that 'it will still encrease when I come into Italy, where the oppression is more sensible in its effects, and where the finest country in the world is quite depopulated by it'.[1] His *Epistle to Pope* written from Italy echoes Addison and urges the poet to sing of English liberty:

> sing the Land, which now alone can boast
> That Liberty unhappy Rome has lost.

In Thomson's own work, we find Whig liberty prominent in the early versions of *Winter* and *Summer*—the Plutarchan catalogue of Roman worthies in *Winter*, the retreat of Cato and the catalogue of British worthies in *Summer*—and also in *Sophonisba* (1730), echoing Addison's *Cato*. In *Britannia* (1729) we already have a transition from the general dogma of liberty to specific political comment, and the passages on the Jail Committee and the promotion of Scottish industries added to *Winter* in 1730 may also be described as timely editorials. The descriptive travel poem which his tour might be expected to inspire would inevitably embody political sentiments, though his earliest references to such a project emphasize description:

There are scarce any travellers to be met with, who have given a *landscape* of the countries through which they have travelled; that have seen (as you express it) with the *Muse*'s eye; though that is the first thing that strikes me, and what all readers and travellers in the first place demand. It seems to me, that such a *poetical* landscape of countries, mixed with moral observations on their governments and people, would not be an ill-judged undertaking. But then, the description of the different face of Nature, in different countries, must be particularly marked and characteristic, the *Portrait-painting of Nature*.[2]

---

[1] Letter of 16 Oct. 1729 (quoted by Rose Mary Davis, *The Good Lord Lyttelton* (Bethlehem, 1939)), pp. 24–5.

[2] William Seward, *Supplement to the Anecdotes of Some Distinguished Persons* (London, 1797), pp. 139–40. To George Dodington, Paris, 27 Dec. 1730.

When we consider the successful descriptions of foreign land-scapes in the later versions of *The Seasons*, this plan would seem to have promise. The same letter indicates the direction the 'moral observations' were to take: Thomson speaks of the incongruity of the praise of republican liberty in Voltaire's *Brutus*, and belittles the 'shewy magnificence' of France in comparison with the British alliance of industry and liberty. 'I shall return no worse Englishman than I came away.'

Thomson's studies in connexion with his tour included ancient history as found in Plutarch and the currently popular Rollin, and the standard guide-books for Italy and manuals of the fine arts. The stock reflections of the enlightened Briton appear in Part I, *Antient and Modern Italy Compared*, the readings of ancient history in Parts II and III, *Greece* and *Rome*, the history of Renaissance art in the first half of Part IV, called *Britain*. Thereafter the poet concentrates on England, with the 'Abstract of the English History' in the second half of IV, and the editorial *Prospect* of V. A full account of the background here would include the cult of Greek and Roman heroism, the doctrine of the connexion between high cultural attainment and political freedom, the classical antithesis of liberty versus luxury and corruption, the application of this antithesis to the 'Gothic' barbarians who overran the corrupted empire, and lastly the application to modern Britain. The poem assumes the tone of the Opposition, and the advertisements of the later parts would sound political to contemporaries:

The Design of this Poem, is to Trace the Rise, Progress, and Fall of Liberty, thro' the several States where she has flourished, to her Establishment in Britain, with the melancholy Prospect attending the Loss of it, and Advice to Britons how to preserve and compleat theirs.[1]

The purport of many lines in the last part may be found in passages from Thomson's letters of 1735 and 1736:

But this [the state of the drama], alas! is only one of the Pillars of that vast Temple of *Corruption*, under which this Generation, more than any other that ever boasted Freedom, worships the dirty, low-minded, insatiable Idol of Self-interest.

I may, however, very well live to see all Poetry reduced to Maga-zine-Miscellanies, all Plays to Mummery Entertainments, and, in

[1] *Fog's Weekly Journal*, 18 Sept. 1736.

short, all Learning absorb'd into the Sink of hireling scurrilous
News-Papers.

For whence is it, save the Want of Taste, that the continual Tides
of Riches, pour'd in upon this Nation by Commerce, have been lost
again in a Gulph of ungraceful, inelegant, inglorious Luxury? But
whence, you will say, this want of Taste? Whence this sordid Turn
to cautious Time-serving, Money-making, sneaking Prudence,
instead of regardless, unfetter'd Virtue? To private Jobs, instead of
public Works? To profitable, instead of fine Arts? To Gain, instead
of Glory? In a Word, to the whole venal System of modern
Administration? And to those gross perishing Luxuries, that reconcile, at once, Avarice and Profusion, centering all in Self, and even in
the meanest, the material Part of Self.[1]

The shift of emphasis in Thomson is clear. The Briton on the
grand tour viewed the monuments of history and art with
frequent reference to British freedom. But such themes might
be used to point a contrast not only between continental tyranny
and British freedom, but between true constitutional government in Britain and the political degeneration that came from
jobbery and corruption. This pattern of ideas was taken up by
the opponents of Walpole. Thus Thomas Gordon and John
Trenchard, in the series called 'Cato's Letters' published in the
London Journal in 1721-2, had directed against Walpole the
familiar thesis that 'all Civil Virtue and Happiness, every moral
Excellency, all Politeness, all good Arts and Sciences, are
produced by Liberty; and all Wickedness, Baseness, and Misery,
are immediately and necessarily produced by Tyranny'. In the
following number the writer says he has shown that 'Population,
Riches, true Religion, Virtue, Magnanimity, Arts, Sciences and
Learning, are the necessary Effects, and Productions of Liberty;
and shall spend this Paper, in proving that an extensive Trade,
Navigation, and Naval Power, entirely flow from the same
Source'.[2] Frequent historical allusions claim all Greek and
Roman culture as the effect of liberty, and belittle the age of
Louis XIV. The distinction between Whig and Tory is irrele-
vant; all that counts is devotion to liberty. Walpole soon took
over the *London Journal* and Gordon withdrew from active
controversy, though he still expounded such doctrines in the
discourses prefixed to his translation of Tacitus (1728-31). But

[1] *A Collection of Letters Written to the Late Aaron Hill* (London, 1751), pp. 72-5.
To Hill, 23 Aug. 1735, 11 May 1736.
[2] Repr. 1733, ii. 257, 266.

this vein of political journalism leads us directly to the famous *Craftsman*.

We need consider the editorial policy of the *Craftsman* only as it bears on Thomson, without passing judgement on Bolingbroke's wisdom or morals or on the authorship of individual papers. Bolingbroke's general responsibility may be assumed. He professed to set a truly national policy, with King, Parliament, and people in harmony, over against the selfish faction that was Walpole's. Such a national consensus would transcend the distinction between Whig and Tory, which had become merely 'an idle Distinction of Names'.

> If any nobler Passion yet remain,
> Let all my Sons all Parties fling aside,
> Despise their Nonsense, and together join.
>
> (*Liberty*, v. 353-5.)[1]

At the same time, Bolingbroke would cut the ground from under Walpole by asserting that his is the true Whig gospel. As the *Old Whig* remarked, 8 May 1735:

> There has been one good Effect of [Bolingbroke's] Writing, that the Tories, who were his former Friends, are come much into the Popular Notions of Liberty; and the old Doctrines, of the Divine Authority of Princes, and of absolute Submission to them, which they consider'd as Sacred, seem now totally discarded by them.

To gain his ends Bolingbroke invoked the teachings of history and the lofty abstractions of ethics. Political action was conceived of as taking place simultaneously on two levels: below there was the conflict of interest in a competitive society and the tension of balanced powers in a 'mixed' state; on a higher plane were the spontaneous and generous acts of the patriot. The familiar formula of the classical historian appears: the poverty and austerity of the virtuous freeman lead to power, power breeds corruption, and corruption in turn undermines liberty. This was accepted as the normal cycle of history, but also as a warning that social virtue and disinterested patriotism can alone preserve the state. Benevolist ethics blended with Plutarchan ideals.

In these ethical presuppositions Thomson would find himself

---

[1] References to *Liberty* are to the line-numbers of the first edition. Thomson's italics and small capitals are not reproduced.

on familiar ground. The contrast between social love and self-love lay ready to hand:

The Excellent ones of the Earth, in the Exercise of Social Love, feel it as much to be an original Impulse, as the low World that blind Affection, they bear themselves; nor are they, in the least, conscious of that forc'd, cold Reasoning by which it is deduc'd from so mean an Original.

How many deathless Heroes, Patriots, and Martyrs, have been so gloriously concern'd for the Good of Mankind, and so strongly actuated by Social Love, as frequently to act in direct Contradiction to that of Self?

A great many more Arguments might be adduced to prove, that Social Love is a nobler, independent Principle, by itself, were not the secret Sense, that every good Man has of the Matter, instead of a thousand.[1]

Transposed to a political and historical context, 'social love' becomes 'public zeal', and blends with the strain of Whig liberty in Thomson's early work.

> Historic truth
> Should next conduct us thro' the deeps of time:
> Point us how empire grew, revolv'd, and fell,
> In scatter'd states; what makes the nations smile,
> Improves their soil, and gives them double suns;
> And why they pine beneath the brightest skies,
> In nature's richest lap. As thus we talk'd,
> Our hearts would burn within us, would inhale
> That portion of divinity, that ray
> Of purest heaven, which lights the glorious flame
> Of patriots, and of heroes.
>
> (*Winter*, octavo edition, 1730, ll. 489–99.)

In *Britannia* the exaltation of liberty—'The light of life! the sun of human kind!'—already has as its inevitable correlative the warning against luxury, corruption, and selfishness. *Liberty* is an unsuccessful attempt to develop this theme still further by Thomson's eclectic method, by an elaborate synthesis of religion, ethics, cultural history, and politics.

The appeal to the example of the Roman patriot had been commonplace since the Renaissance.[2] One need only think of

---

[1] *A Collection of Letters Written to the Late Aaron Hill*, pp. 56–7. To Hill, 18 April 1726.

[2] See G. Chinard, 'Héritage de la Liberté', *Renaissance*, i (1943), 60–80; Zera S. Fink, *The Classical Republicans* (Evanston, 1945).

Cato. It was natural for Thomson to call Algernon Sidney the 'British Brutus', later the 'British Cassius'—

> Of high determin'd Spirit, roughly brave,
> By antient Learning to th'enlighten'd Love
> Of antient Freedom warm'd.   (*Summer*, 1744, ll. 1516-19.)

The classical theme was an important part of the Whig formula which Bolingbroke was adopting as the idiom of the Opposition. But the principal point is that Rome *lost* her liberty. Bolingbroke here works in the republican tradition of which Machiavelli was a principal exponent.

> We must not imagine that the Freedom of the Romans was lost, because one Party fought for the Maintenance of Liberty; another for the Establishment of Tyranny; and that the latter prevail'd. No. The Spirit of Liberty was dead, and the Spirit of Faction had taken its Place on both Sides. As long as the Former prevailed, a Roman sacrificed his own, and therefore no Doubt every other personal Interest, to the Interest of the Commonwealth. When the Latter succeeded, the Interest of the Commonwealth was considered no otherwise than in Subordination to that particular Interest, which each Person had espous'd. . . .
>
> It is plain that the Liberty of Rome would not have been irretrievably lost, though Caesar had finished the Civil War with absolute Success, and was settled in Power, if the Spirit of Liberty had not been then lost in the whole Body of the People; if the Romans had not been ripe for Slavery, as the Cappadocians were fond of it; for I think They were the Cappadocians, who desired that a Prince might be set over Them, and refused to be a free People.[1]

> The Steel of Brutus burst the grosser Bonds
> By Cesar cast o'er Rome; but still remain'd
> The soft enchanting Fetters of the Mind,
> And other Cesars rose.   (*Liberty*, v. 202-5.)

Thomson uses the Cappadocians in his Preface to the 1738 edition of *Areopagitica*: 'We are told in History, of a People that after they had been inured to Slavery, were in a panick Fear, when their Liberty was offered to them.' Lacking a third

---

[1] 27 June 1730; vii. 19-20, 12 Sept. The essays in the *Craftsman* as reprinted in the collected edition of 1731-7 often differ from the original issues in numbering, date, and text. References are given when possible to the date of the original issue, followed by volume and page of the collected edition and also by the date given in this edition when it differs from the original. When the original issue has been inaccessible, the reference is only to the collected edition. Quotations from the *Craftsman* do not reproduce the frequent italics.

estate, republican liberty was constantly threatened by the
contentions of patrician and plebeian, and the eternal vigilance
of the patriot was required to prevent an almost inevitable loss
of balance:

> The Roman Commonwealth would have been dissolved much
> sooner than it was, by the Defects I have mentioned; which many
> Circumstances concurred to aggravate, if such a Spirit of Wisdom,
> as well as Courage, and such an Enthusiasm for the Grandeur, the
> Majesty, and the Duration of their Empire had not possessed this
> People, as never possess'd any other.[1]

> Their Virtue such, that an unballanc'd State,
> Still between Noble and Plebeian tost,
> As flow'd the Wave of fluctuating Power,
> By that kept firm, and with triumphant Prow
> Rode out the Storms. Oft tho' the Native Feuds,
> That from the first their Constitution shook,
> (A latent Ruin, growing as it grew)
> Stood on the threatening Point of Civil War
> Ready to rush: yet could the lenient Voice
> Of Wisdom, soothing the tumultuous Soul,
> These Sons of Virtue calm.   (*Liberty*, iii. 197–207.)

If the Opposition exalts the self-sacrificing patriot, it assumes
also that power will be abused, especially by Walpole, and
encourages endless ingeminations about corruption and faction.
It is an old story, and the *Craftsman* had no monopoly of
such ideas. Thomson used Rollin and Plutarch, and a special
source for his version of Roman history was Vertot's *History
of the Revolutions that Happened in the Government of the Roman
Republic*, to use the title of the English translation (1720).
What brings the *Craftsman* closest to *Liberty* is the political and
moral animus of the application of the classical precedents to
modern Britain.

The famous series of papers on English history in the *Craftsman* (nos. 213–55, 1 August 1730–22 May 1731) proceeds on
the basic parallel: the spirit of liberty waxes and wanes alike
in Rome and Britain; but though every opportunity for a parallel
is improved, the emphasis now falls less on the Plutarchan hero
than on the citizen's primordial rights and their embodiment in
the British constitution. Both journalist and poet use the idea

[1] xiii. 80, 16 Nov. 1734.

of the 'Gothic' origin of modern liberty, a vein of thought which has been brilliantly traced by Dr. Samuel Kliger.[1] The doctrine lay ready to hand in Temple's essay *Of Heroic Virtue*, Molesworth's *Account of Denmark*, and Rapin's *History of England*, all works well known to Thomson. The basis of British freedom, according to this view, is a fierce love of liberty characteristic of the hardy barbarians of the north—Scythians, Goths, Celts, Scandinavians, or Saxons. These people were spontaneously warlike rather than austerely altruistic like the idealized early Romans, and their martial virtues were identified with 'that natural Love of Liberty, which resided formerly in the Northern Nations more eminently than in other Parts of the World'.[2] This love of liberty plays a dual role: in its original form it is the fierce individualism of the hard fighter, but as it finds political realization it makes the Goths, in the words of Temple, 'civil, orderly, and virtuous'. Thomson follows a famous passage in Lucan in connecting the northern 'contempt of death' with the Druids and so with the Britons, who thus represent man 'erect from Nature's Hand'.[3] It is among the invading Saxons that constitutional liberty first appears:

> Nor were the surly Gifts of War their All.
> Wisdom was likewise theirs, indulgent Laws,
> The calm Gradations of Art-nursing Peace,
> And matchless Orders, the deep Basis still
> On which ascends my British Reign. Untam'd
> To the refining Subtilties of Slaves,
> They brought an happy Government along;
> Form'd by that Freedom, which, with secret Voice,
> Impartial Nature teaches all her Sons,
> And which of old thro' the whole Scythian Mass
> I strong inspir'd. Monarchical their State,
> But prudently confin'd, and mingled wise

[1] 'The "Goths" in England', *M.P.*, xliii (1945), 107–17. See also, for a further introduction to the literature of the subject, Erwin Hölzle, *Die Idee einer altgermanischen Freiheit vor Montesquieu* (Munich, 1925).

[2] Molesworth, op. cit., p. 264. Farley's standard monograph, *Scandinavian Influences in the English Romantic Movement* (Boston, 1903), neglects the political aspects of this familiar theme.

[3] *Liberty*, iv. 626–40. The *locus classicus* in Lucan (*Pharsalia*, i. 447–62) was translated in part by Temple in the essay *Of Heroic Virtue*, and Rowe's version of the same passage is in Tindal's translation of Rapin (2nd ed., London, 1732, i. v note). This edition was in Thomson's library. Thomson's lines show verbal borrowings from both Temple and Rowe.

Of each harmonious Power: only, too much,
Imperious War into their Rule infus'd,
Prevail'd the General-King, and Chieftain-Thanes.
(*Liberty*, iv. 685–99.)

Thus the Saxon was a freeman from remotest time, yet attained
freedom more and more fully in the course of British political
history—a striking example of the coexistence of the ideas of
primitivism and progress. While the writers of the *Craftsman*
are less interested than Thomson in the primitive stage, they
show his pride in the early British resistance to Roman invasion,
and they assert more emphatically than he does the actual
realization of political freedom in Anglo-Saxon times: 'the Principles of the Saxon Commonwealth were very Democratical;
and these Principles prevailed through all subsequent Changes.'
Though the Saxon *Heretoges*, originally leaders in war, became
kings, 'the supreme Power center'd in the *Micklemote*, or *Witta-
genmote* [*sic*], composed of the King, the Lords, and the Saxon
Freemen, that original Sketch of a British Parliament'.

The original State of Monarchy is justly described very different
from what it is now in all arbitrary Governments. Kings were then
no more than Chiefs, or principal Magistrates, in States Republican
and free.

It ought to give every Englishman the greatest Satisfaction to find
the Constitution we now live under, since its last Renewal, bearing so
near a Resemblance to primitive Liberty.

Let us then 'continue to ourselves the peculiar Honour of maintaining the Freedom of our Gothick Institution of Government,
when so many other Nations, who enjoy'd the same, have lost
theirs'.[1]

The question of the origins of popular representation in
Parliament, a complex problem for the impartial historian, was
a stock theme of political journalism in the 1730's. The *Craftsman* dwelt on the ancient tradition of British liberty in order to
throw into sharper relief the alleged violations of the Constitution
by Walpole's régime. Both the series of papers on British
history and the second series called 'A Dissertation on Parties'
appropriated the originally Whig doctrine of ancient Gothic
liberty and forced the other side to minimize the early liberties
of England in order to exalt the Revolution settlement. The

---

[1] vii. 50–1, 2 Oct. 1730; xi. 117–18, 11 Aug. 1733; xii. 94–5, 19 Jan. 1734.

British government, argued the *London Journal*, has evolved from tyranny to freedom (1 September 1733). Walpole's new organ, the *Daily Gazetteer*, professed to hold with Shaftesbury that 'late England' was better than 'old England' (5 July 1735). 'As to the Constitution in former Ages, how fair soever it may appear when adorned and deck'd out by the Pens of learned and eloquent Men, yet it was certainly far inferior to ours, or at least absolutely unfit for us in the State we are now in' (2 February 1740). Among the ancient Britons, said another Walpole organ, the *Free Briton*, we find only 'the meer Shadow of that Structure which the Wisdom of many succeeding Ages raised and improved, till it became the Glory and Strength of the People' (18 July 1734). Hervey's widely known pamphlet, *Ancient and Modern Liberty Stated and Compared* (1734), formulates the current Whig position in exaggerated style by asserting that there was no English liberty until the Restoration, no full liberty until the Revolution. This pamphlet was of course denounced by the *Craftsman*, whose writer summed up triumphantly:

this Point, concerning the Antiquity of Parliaments, hath been vigorously maintain'd by many of the ablest Writers, in the Cause of Liberty, ever since the contrary Doctrine was first broach'd; such as Selden, Sidney, Petit, Hody, Tyrrel, West, St. Amand and Others. It looks therefore a little odd to see a Set of Men, who call themselves the Advocates of a Whig Ministry, defending these Prerogative Principles, and licking up the Spittle of such Slavish Writers as Brady and his Followers.[1]

Both sides appealed to the great authority of the historian Rapin de Thoyras, a best-seller in the England of the 1730's. Rapin expounded the classic Whig view of the ancient Gothic constitution and its full realization in the course of English history, and yet he was, as Hervey says, 'the Craftsman's own political Evangelist'. The *Craftsman* taunts the *London Journal* for praising Rapin and yet asserting that ancient tyranny evolved only in modern times into full liberty.[2] It is hardly necessary to say that Thomson was a follower of Rapin. The Dissertation appended to Rapin gives what was taken to be an authoritative account of the 'mixed government' of the Anglo-Saxons, and from this point Thomson follows Rapin down to the Revolution. His notes to *Liberty* indicate as much, but his

[1] xiv. 21, 14 June 1735.
[2] *Gentleman's Magazine*, ii (1732), 1023; iii (1733), 464–5; vi (1736), 249–50.

indebtedness goes far beyond his acknowledgements, and could be illustrated at length. It is the progress of liberty, and yet liberty had to be there already to produce and maintain itself. The head accepted progress; the heart preferred to dwell on origins. Thomson as a child of the Enlightenment could not fail to see some merit in the contention of the Whig journalists that England had struggled up from darkness and slavery, but the thought of old glorious Rome or the unsubmitting Goths imparted more fervour to his rhetoric, and the *Craftsman* encouraged this emphasis.

The *Craftsman*'s papers on English history run parallel with Rapin in Thomson's background, and to them he frequently turned, making more concessions, however, to the contemporary Whig view that early royal power had been excessive, that the Middle Ages were bad times, and that later reforms were essential. On the question of when popular representation actually began, Thomson follows Rapin; he is inclined to make the Anglo-Saxon king more of a military dictator, less of a constitutional magistrate, than the *Craftsman*.[1] Rapin is sceptical about the existence of a popular Anglo-Saxon legislature, and is inclined to date the true beginning of popular representation from Henry III's famous orders of 1264. Thomson's note on this point, appended to *Liberty*, iv. 796, is made up of extracts from Rapin:

The Commons are generally thought to have been first represented in Parliament towards the end of Henry the third's Reign. To a Parliament called in the Year 1264, each County was ordered to send four Knights, as Representatives of their respective Shires: And to a Parliament called in the Year following, each County was ordered to send, as their Representatives, two Knights, and each City and Burrough as many Citizens and Burgesses. Till then, History makes no Mention of them; whence a very strong Argument may be drawn, to fix the Original of the House of Commons to that Era.[2]

[1] If the view of monarchy in the *Craftsman* is Bolingbroke's, its difference from the famous doctrine of the *Patriot King* should be noted. See Paul Baratier, *Lord Bolingbroke: ses écrits politiques* (Paris, 1939), pp. 255-7.

[2] See Rapin, trans. Tindal, 2nd ed. (1732), i. 155, 340. Tindal's note, protesting against Rapin's scepticism about early popular representation, and appealing to the Whig authorities Petit, Tyrrell, and Hody, is taken without acknowledgement from Echard's *History of England*, 3rd ed. (London, 1720), p. 124. It is quoted approvingly by the *Craftsman* (xii. 186, 6 April 1734). In this instance Thomson follows the text of Rapin without heeding Tindal's protest.

On this point he is somewhat closer to the pro-Walpole journalists than to the *Craftsman*. But in the ensuing survey there is evidence of his direct use of 'Oldcastle', to use the pen-name of the writer of the series on English history. Here he got the elaborate contrast between weak and tyrannous kings like Richard II and great national leaders like Edward III, 'Favourers of Liberty'.[1] The contrast was of course pointed at George II. Elizabeth is for Oldcastle and Thomson a supreme example of the incarnation of public spirit in the monarch, but both dwell on her extreme use of the prerogative, Thomson more emphatically than Oldcastle. Thomson's unfavourable account of James I is primarily Rapin. But a clear example of borrowing from the *Craftsman* rather than from Rapin is found in the account of Henry VII. 'His Jealousy, his Pride, and his insatiable, sordid Avarice had their full Swing', says Oldcastle.[2] In Thomson it runs:

> Proud, dark, suspicious, brooding o'er his Gold,
> As how to fix his Throne he jealous cast
> His crafty Views around.   (*Liberty*, iv. 874–6.)

The importance of the law of Henry VII 'opening a Way to the Lords to alienate their Lands' (*Craftsman*)—'permitting the Barons to alienate their Lands' (Thomson)—is stressed by both, but not mentioned by Rapin. The parallel could be elaborated by showing the emphasis placed by both on the importance of the growing power of the Commons for the development of constitutional balance in the state. Such specific instances confirm our impression of the general relationship.

Another example takes us beyond the publication of *Liberty* into the years when Thomson was openly and prominently identified with the Opposition. In the course of the argument on the antiquity of Parliament, the *Craftsman* noted with satisfaction that 'his Royal Highness the Prince of Wales had order'd a fine Statue of King Alfred to be made for his Gardens in Pall-mall, with a Latin Inscription; in which it is particularly said, that this Prince was the Founder of the Liberties and Commonwealth of England'.[3] (There was also a statue of the

---

[1] *Liberty*, iv. 822–67. For Edward III, see *Craftsman*, 15 Aug. 1730, vii. 59–65, 9 Oct.; for Richard II, 29 Aug. 1730, vii. 70–6, 16 Oct. 'Mr. Francklin was taken up for printing this Paper and the preceding one, on the Reign of Edward the third' (vii. 70).

[2] 17 Oct. 1730, vii. 117–18, 21 Nov.   [3] xiv. 104, 6 Sept. 1735.

Black Prince.) *Liberty* is dedicated to Prince Frederick, and the poem has a perfunctory line or two about Alfred, but it is evident that the theme of the liberty-loving Saxon king, elaborated as an anti-type to George II, found later expression in the masque of *Alfred*, by Thomson and Mallet, produced before the Prince and Princess at Cliefden, 1 August 1740.

Five months after *Liberty* iii had appeared, the *Craftsman* devoted a leading essay to the poem under the caption, 'Of a Passion for Liberty'. The essay begins with a long quotation, i. 346–63, the address to the Goddess of Liberty, and comments, after a bitter reference to the 'abandoned Crew of Scribblers' who write 'in Defence of ministerial Authority':

As the great and virtuous Sentiments, convey'd in the Motto to this Letter, are equally of Use to strengthen the Foundation of Liberty, and to elevate any System of publick Good, that can be rais'd upon it, every servile Pen hath been employ'd, either absurdly to question the Truth, or infamously to weaken the Force, by endeavouring to divert the Influence of them.[1]

The *Craftsman*, always alert for acts of political censorship, is surprised that *Liberty* has not already incurred official disapproval:

The Poem itself, indeed, from whence these Lines are taken, hath pass'd uncensur'd, and the Author unblemish'd; but it seems to be the only Exception to that unlicens'd Abuse, which has been thrown upon every Man, who has express'd his Fear for the Publick, or his Concern for the Welfare of it. So little Decency has been observ'd in This, that the sincerest Friends of the Government have been treated as the Enemies of it, and the warmest as the Destroyers of the Constitution. The Hands prostituted in this detestable Service have not discovered less Readiness to engage, than Incapacity to succeed in it; and therefore They are too low to draw any farther Remarks from me. But the destructive Views of Him, who prompts and supports them, creates [sic] in a good Mind an honest Indignation, accompanied with such Reflections as ought not to be stifled.

Another quotation from *Liberty*, iii. 103–52, on public spirit among the Romans, is the basis for a long discussion of public spirit in general, which must be derived, says the writer, not

---

[1] 16 Aug. 1735, reprinted in part in *Gentleman's Magazine* (1735), v. 475–6, dated 23 Aug. *London Magazine*, iv (1735), 433, also prints this number in part, but omits the long passages on Thomson's *Liberty*. These passages are also omitted from the collected edition of the *Craftsman*.

from the cold guidance of reason but from overmastering passion. It follows, the editorial application continues, that he who is moved by such a passion will prefer 'Independency' and a 'private Fortune' to 'publick Plunder'. The writer thus sums up the doctrine of the earlier parts of the poem, anticipates Thomson's apostrophe to Independence in *Liberty* v, and in general helps us to place *Liberty* in the political context of the 1730's.

THE FIRST HISTORY OF ENGLISH POETRY

JAMES M. OSBORN

PARADOXICALLY, the earliest History of English Poetry was written in French, and has not hitherto been printed. The author was the Reverend Joseph Spence, whose *Anecdotes, Observations and Characters of Books and Men* are familiar to all students of the eighteenth century, particularly to specialists in the Age of Pope.

The manuscript containing this History is preserved among Spence's literary and personal papers, now in my library. A small octavo volume, handsomely bound by the fifth Duke of Newcastle,[1] the spine carries the misleading title, 'J. Spence. Lessons in Learning French & Italian'. The first leaf serves as a table of contents in Spence's hand, and is also headed 'Lessons, in learning French; and Italian'. The first item in this table is described as 'History of English Poetry. p: 1–40'. The right-hand pages carry the text, and the left-hand pages were left for notes, about half of them being blank. The title at the beginning of the text reads, 'Quelques Remarques Hist: sur les Poëts Anglois'.

When did Spence write this History? Why did he do so, and why in French? These questions cannot be answered with certainty. The most challenging problem is *when*, because the answer bears so heavily on *why* Spence wrote this essay. Even *where* enters into the discussion, since Spence's travels on the Continent affect the case. The first of Spence's three extended absences from England began in December 1730 and continued until July of 1733, when he accompanied the youthful Charles Sackville, Earl of Middlesex (later second Duke of Dorset), to France and Italy. In May 1737 Spence made a tour through Holland, Flanders, and France with a Mr. Trevor, returning to England in February 1738. In 1739 he again set out to make the Grand Tour with Henry Clinton, Earl of Lincoln, afterwards second Duke of Newcastle. Two and a half years were spent in Italy and France before their return in November 1742.

The evidence suggests that Spence's 'History of English

---

[1] From whose heirs I purchased the Spence MSS. at Sotheby's on 16 Feb. 1938. His great-grandfather, the second Duke, had been a pupil of Spence, of which more hereafter.

Poetry' was written on the first tour, perhaps late in 1732, or early in 1733. The volume contains so many notes and quotations from French and Italian books that most of the writing in it probably was done on the Continent. These numerous source-books, combined with the character of the manuscript as an exercise-book for 'Lessons in Learning French and Italian', support this conclusion. Only one British publication quoted in the manuscript requires explanation; it is given as 'Chambers', and refers to Ephraim Chambers's *Cyclopaedia or Universal Dictionary of the Arts and Sciences*, 1728.[1] Chambers's two folio volumes would have been heavy baggage to cart around Europe, but they may have been available in one or more of the continental libraries. It is more likely that this one English publication would be found on the Continent than that all the Italian and French volumes quoted by Spence would be readily available to him in England. Other explanations are possible, such as that Spence made notes from Chambers before leaving England.

Three other jottings make 1732 the earliest possible date that Spence could have been working at some of the other articles in this manuscript. The third essay in the volume is headed 'Quelques Remarques Historiques sur la Renaissance de la Literature'. In this essay (p. 67) Spence wrote the note, 'Q in Bayle, Chambers, and ye Hist: of Printing lately publisht in England.' This jotting unquestionably alludes to Samuel Palmer's *General History of Printing*, of which two volumes had already appeared before Palmer's death on 9 May 1732.[2] Advertisements for this publication may have appeared months earlier. The words 'lately printed' argue in favour of the first tour, and against 1738 or later.

On p. 185 of the manuscript Spence refers to 'ye 2 Ed: 1732' of the Abbé du Bos's *Réflexions sur la Poësie et sur la Peinture*.[3] If

---

[1] Spence's note occurs in the second section of his manuscript, entitled 'Quelques Remarques Historiques sur la Renaissance de la Poësie.' Opposite p. 45 he referred to 'Chambers (frō Bouche's Hist: of Provence) Art: Troubadours', a valid reference.

[2] See *D.N.B.* article on Palmer, and obituary notice in *Gentleman's Magazine* for 1732, p. 775.

[3] This is in a section headed 'R[emark]s Toward the Literary History'. But the pages are not on this subject; except for the last four pages they consist of notes on the invasion of the Roman Empire by successive waves of Goths. The reference to du Bos is in the pages that were written some time later; how much later cannot be determined.

we accept the premiss that Spence wrote these notes in France
or Italy, the edition of 1732 could have been available soon
after publication. Similarly, on p. 237 Spence has jotted a
comment from the lips of his Florentine friend, the learned
Dr. Cocchi. Since copious quotations from the same source
appear in the published *Anecdotes* under 'Section III, 1732–33',
it is reasonable to attribute this note to the same period.

The possibility that this manuscript was written not in 1732–3
but on one of Spence's later tours seems unlikely. None of his
comments, notes, or allusions argue in favour of the later dates.
In the absence of evidence to the contrary, there is reason to
believe that he wrote these pages in 1732–3, while in an early
flush of enthusiasm during his first visit to France and Italy
when acquiring fluency in the tongues of those countries.

To revert to the question, '*Why* did Spence write this history
of English Poetry', two leading alternatives are present. The
first is that he prepared this essay for the benefit of Lord
Middlesex as a double-barrelled assignment—to teach his pupil
a valued subject-matter while drilling him in the French
language. Formerly I considered this the most likely explanation.[1] But continued familiarity with the text prompts the
conclusion that Spence wrote this History for himself, and not
for a pupil. The tone and nature of the notes indicate that he
was writing for a mature audience, rather than his young
companion. Spence's erudition is not great, but his attitude is
adult, especially considering the status of literary history in the
decade 1730–40.

Another factor to be remembered is that in 1728, while still
less than thirty years of age, Spence had been elected Professor
of Poetry at Oxford, succeeding the elder Thomas Warton
(father of the great historian of English poetry, who later
occupied the same professorship). How many lectures on
poetry Spence delivered at Oxford is not known, since none are
extant.[2] Yet he says in the preface to *Polymetis* that the professor-

---

[1] This suggestion appears as note 98 on p. 228 of *The Rise of English Literary
History* (1941) by my friend René Wellek. I supplied information for this note
when reading his invaluable book in typescript. In the interval I have revised my
opinion. Throughout the following pages I am repeatedly under obligation to
Wellek's published writings, and for suggestions and criticisms made orally.

[2] Among the Spence papers sold by S. W. Singer at Sotheby's on 3 Aug.
1858 was item 197, 'Mr. Spence's Lectures on the Iliad'. Where are they
now?

ship 'obliged me to deal in Poetical Criticism', and states that he prepared the groundwork for *Polymetis* during the same period. It is not unlikely that the three dialogues on the history of Roman poetry (II, III, and IV of *Polymetis*) were based on studies made during this time.

Similarly Spence may have utilized lectures prepared at Oxford when he wrote Dialogue XIX, 'The Defects of our Modern Poets, in their Allegories: instanced from Spenser's Fairy Queen', and Dialogue XX, 'The Defects of our Translators of the Antient Poets; in relation to these Allegorical Subjects: instanced from Mr. Dryden's Translation of Virgil'. Before being appointed Professor of Poetry, he had given much thought to poetic problems, as is evident from his *Essay on Pope's Odyssey in which some particular Beauties and Blemishes of that work are Considered* (1726). Indeed, Spence's little 'History of English Poetry' could not have sprung into existence without a good deal of reflection and ordering of ideas. The more one examines the inchoate strivings of his contemporaries towards a history of English poetry, the more likely it seems that Spence had formulated his ideas in consequence of his appointment as Professor of Poetry at Oxford.

Surprisingly enough, synthetic thinking on the history of English poetry developed tardily in a nation that derived an almost narcissistic pleasure from contemplating its political and economic growth.[1] Materials for such a history continued to accumulate under the hands of antiquarian and linguistic giants like Wanley, Hickes, Hearne, Langbaine, Oldys, and dozens of lesser lights. But the achievements of these researchers into biographical and textual problems had left synthetic writing far behind. The concept of literary historiography was a late arrival.

Perhaps one reason for this slow development arose from the high state of biographical compilation in England. The 'Lives of the Poets' were in popular demand, either by themselves, or as colourful passages in more general compilations. It will suffice to mention the following: Phillips's *Theatrum Poetarum* (1675), Winstanley's *Lives of the Most Famous English Poets* (1687), Langbaine's *Account of the English Dramatic Poets* (1691), Jacobs's *Poetical Register* (1719), Cibber's *Lives of the Poets*

---

[1] 'No systematic attempt to write the History of English Literature was made before Warton [1774].' Wellek, op. cit., p. 133.

(1753), Birch's augmented edition of Bayle's *General Dictionary, Biographical and Critical* (1734–41), and the *Biographia Britannica* (1747–66).

Concurrent with these purely biographical compilations, anthologies developed: books of specimens from the writings of selected poets, preceded by introductory remarks, biographical and critical. Mrs. Elizabeth Cooper's *Muses Library* (1737) was a landmark in this field. Percy's *Reliques of Ancient English Poetry* (1765) applied the plan to anonymous poems and ballads. Dr. Johnson's *Lives of the Poets*, though nowadays printed separately from the poetic selections, were the eighteenth-century culmination of this tradition—biographical and critical introductions to pages of poetical specimens.

In the 'progress of poetry' genre the historical approach made its first toddling steps. Addison's *Account of the Greatest English Poets* (1694) opened with the age when 'Chaucer first, the merry bard, arose' and hurried through Spenser, Cowley, Milton, Waller, Roscommon, Denham, Dryden, Montague and Congreve. (Observe that *only* four of these 'greatest poets' were dead before Addison's own lifetime.) Samuel Cobb's *Of Poetry; Its Progress* (1700) began with Moses and Orpheus, and worked its way through the mention of over two dozen English poets, all but six of them living after the Restoration. Similarly with Mrs. Judith Madan's 'flower piece' entitled *The Progress of Poetry* (1721); her primary attention was devoted to the poets of Greece and Rome, followed by a succession of English worthies culminating in Nicholas Rowe. Thomas Gray's *Progress of Poesy* (1757) concerned itself primarily with 'the higher and truer', though Gray admitted Shakespeare, Milton, and Dryden into the main stream of poetry flowing from Mount Olympus. The genre of 'progress poems' never emerged from its self-imposed restrictions; they shuffled in the well-worn path of chronology instead of bounding with strength derived from an organic concept.

Other authors of the eighteenth century, in striving to create an art of literary history, became involved in a number of confusing ideas. Wellek has examined these misconceptions in detail, and has shown their evolution; some of them were soon discovered to be nonsense, and others are still flourishing. A favourite topic, for example, was the influence of climate on poetry. Though the idea derives originally from Plato and

Vitruvius, Bodin and the French critics of the seventeenth century elaborated it so that the 'climate' idea appears in Barclay, Cowley, Dennis, Dryden, Congreve, and especially in Sir William Temple's valuable essay *Of Poetry*. To cite another example, the Longinian idea that liberty is a prime cause of literary excellence became popular, especially in the wake of the Whig revolution. Similarly, ideas of the primitive origin of poetry in the folk preoccupied the eighteenth century. The fallacy of 'biological fatalism'—the youth, maturity, and decline of poetical excellence—attracted many minds, from Shaftesbury to Goldsmith and Blair. Another favourite test of critical ingenuity involved the construction of parallels between English and other literatures; for example, by matching together Chaucer and Villon, Davenant and Ronsard, Waller and Malherbe. Baggage of this sort is happily absent from Spence's little narrative.

Another analogy that appeared in the pages of nearly every critic or historian who contemplated writing the history of poetry was the idea of 'schools'. This analogy derived from the histories of painting, where lists of 'masters—disciples—imitators' were commonplace. Dryden had given this idea a slight modification in the *Preface to the Fables*, when he wrote, 'we have our lineal descents and clans', and traced the poetical inheritance from the Provençal poets through Chaucer and Spenser to Milton. Alexander Pope carried the idea to a Procrustean conclusion in the outline he drew for an intended 'Discourse on the Rise and Progress of English Poetry, as it came from the Provencial Poets'. In Pope's sketch there were six schools in modern poetry, those of Provence, Chaucer, Petrarch, Dante, Spenser, and Donne.

Thomas Gray also contemplated writing a History of English Poetry, and sent the summary of his design to Thomas Warton. Admittedly based on the 'scribbled paper of Pope', Gray's project far surpassed Pope's in scale and conception. It shows further refinement on the idea of schools, and denominated four of them: the Sicilian School (Dante, Petrarch, Boccaccio, &c., to Chaucer), the Second Italian School (Ariosto, Tasso, &c., down through Spenser, Fairfax, and Milton), the Third Italian School (Donne, Crashaw, and Cowley), and the School of France (Waller, Dryden, Prior, Pope, &c., 'continued to our own times'). Gray had done a great deal of reading and thinking on this subject, but his project never got beyond the drafting board.[1]

Spence's brief history is innocent of this analogy, and says nothing at all about 'schools'. This raises a very interesting point, for in the epistle dedicatory to the 1736 edition of *Gorboduc*, undertaken at the request of Pope, Spence states, '. . . there are Schools in Poetry, as distinguishable as those in Painting'. If Spence had been aware of this idea when he wrote the 'History of English Poetry' it is highly probable that he would have employed it there. Here we have another bit of evidence that the 'History of English Poetry' was written on the first Grand Tour. This incident also suggests that Spence may have acquired the 'schools' concept from Alexander Pope between 1733 and the publication of *Gordobuc* in 1736.

Several features of Spence's History deserve attention. First is the fact that Spence organized it according to the centuries in which the poets lived and wrote. Most historians in England were still thinking in terms of the reigns of kings, instead of by centuries. Spence shows an awareness of the age in which his subject authors existed.[2] Another feature is Spence's concept of his own time as '. . . nôtre Age Augustaine: qui commence avec la Restauration de Charles 2'. This term was beginning to be used in Spence's day, but instances are rare.[3] It is especially interesting to observe Spence's awareness that the Augustan age in England began at the Restoration in 1660.

Some of Spence's critical judgements are worth noting. He shows a close familiarity with the writings of Sackville, whose merits he felt were inadequately appreciated. The explanation of this familiarity is found in the epistle dedicatory to the 1736 *Gorboduc*, cited above on this page. Addressed to his pupil on the Tour of 1730–3, the Earl of Middlesex, the epistle began, 'I have often had the pleasure of talking with Your Lordship of

[1] Gray's letter to Warton was first published in the *Gentleman's Magazine* for Feb. 1783, pp. 100–1. Pope's sketch first appeared in Ruffhead's *Life of Pope* (1769), p. 425. When Pope wrote it is unknown.

[2] William Cave anticipated Spence in using historical centuries to show the respective times when his authors lived, in the *Scriptorum Ecclesiasticorum Historia Literaria* (1688). See Wellek, op. cit., p. 19. Bale had used the word 'centuries' in a different sense; he included one hundred authors in each chapter, and designated them as a 'century'.

[3] See Bateson, F. W., *English Poetry and the English Language* (1934), p. 49; Isaacs, J., *Times Literary Supplement*, 9 May 1935, p. 301; Wellek, René, in the *English Institute Annual* (1940), p. 78.

your noble Ancestor the Lord *Buckhurst*. When I came to town this winter, Mr. *Pope* told me, he had given his Tragedy [*Gorboduc*] to be printed; and ask'd me for some Collections I had made, relating to that great Man.'[1] The *Induction* to the *Mirroir for Magistrates* attracted Spence's particular attention, and he was the first to point out that the *Induction* pre-dated Spenser's *Fairy Queen*: 'Il me semble que *Spenser* a etudié la maniere de Milord Buckhurste. . . .'[2] Spence also demonstrated a very high opinion of *Gorboduc*: '. . . la meilleure Tragedie, de toutes celles qui furent écrites avant Shakespear: et surpasse les premieres piéces de Shakespear même.'

The passage on the Metaphysical poets is a good example of neo-classical taste. Donne suffered particularly from Spence's disfavour: '. . . ces sentimens sont toûjours embarassés d'une puerile affectation de dire quelque chose de beau.' In contrast, he singled out Suckling for special praise: '. . . le seul Genie tout pur; & qui par sa pureté ne se laissa pas infecter de la contagion generale.' Dr. Johnson would not have been surprised at these judgements had he seen this History when forty years later he borrowed other manuscripts of Spence's while writing *The Lives of the Poets*.

Spence's 'Quelques Remarques', modest in size and attitude, represents a great advance over his contemporaries. Though brief and unpretentious, and written in wretched anglicized French, it is cast in narrative form, and was conceived and written as a 'History of English Poetry'. In fact, Spence infused a surprising amount of narrative flow and justness of evaluation into this brief essay. With very few exceptions (some early writers of Latin verse whose names he took from Leland and

---

[1] P. i of the 1736 *Gorboduc*. Note the historical awareness in the following passage from p. iv: 'The Dawn of our *English* Poetry was in *Chaucer*'s time: but it shone out in him too bright, all at once, to last long. The succeeding Age was dark and over-cast. There was indeed some Glimmerings of Genius again in *Henry* the 8th's time: but our Poetry had never what cou'd be call'd a fair settled Daylight, till toward the End of Queen *Elizabeth*'s Reign. It was between these two Periods that Lord *Buckhurst* wrote: after the Earl of *Surrey*, and before *Spenser*.'

[2] Spence made this point even more strongly on p. vi of the 1736 *Gorboduc*: 'The first time I read it, these two Authors seem'd so evidently of the same School . . . that I immediately concluded Lord *Buckhurst* might be set down as a Scholar of *Spenser*'s: but when I came to compare Dates, it appear'd that (if one form'd himself by the other) it must have been *Spenser* that was a Scholar of Lord *Buckhurst*'s.' In *Two Centuries of Spenserian Scholarship* (1936, p. 70) Miss Jewel Wurtsbaugh speaks of Thomas Birch's biography of Spenser (1751, p. xxx) as being the first to suggest this influence.

Bale) Spence based his comments on first-hand knowledge of the poems themselves. He individualized each poet from Chaucer onward, and attempted a brief evaluation of the achievements of each in the main stream of English poetry. He even showed a passing concern for the genres—satire, drama, occasional poetry, translations, wit, among others. In comparison with Spence's predecessors and contemporaries his pages are far ahead of their time. Spence recognized this situation when he wrote in 1736, 'Literary History has not to this day got much ground in our Island'.[1] His little French essay, though it has lain unrecognized for over two hundred years, marks the first foothold of literary history in England.

Of significance equal to the 'History of English Poetry' is a larger project that took form in Spence's mind apparently as an offshoot of this volume of 'Lessons in Learning French and Italian'. From notes on the title-leaf to this manuscript it is clear that Spence contemplated compiling a large 'Poetical Dictionary; in 12 Sections'. That he made a beginning is evident from jottings in the manuscript with references to his 'Mss Dict'.[2] Whether this compilation is still extant is a question; it is not among the Spence Papers, and Spence's biographer, Professor Austin Wright, has never encountered it.[3]

The notes on the title-leaf occupy the lower half of the page, and read as follows:

> For Preface to Poetical Dictionary; in 12 ? Sections
> (Hist^y of Poetry for above 2000 yrs.)

> 1. Druidical Poetry.
>   Roman Poetry? Contr[acte]d from Pol[ymeti]s

> 2. How far in this Island
>   Revival of Poetry: in Provence
>   Italian shoot from it.

> 3. Chaucer, Piers Plowman, Mir[roi]r &c.
>   Revival of Classical Learning in Italy
>   Improvement of the Italian Poetry.

---

[1] Preface to *Gorboduc*, p. iv.

[2] pp. 53, 69, 71, 89, 223, 225, 229, 231, 239, 243, 247, 249, 251.

[3] Perhaps these were lot 200 among the Spence MSS. sold at Sotheby's, 3 August 1858, by S. W. Singer: 'Collections relating to the Lives of the Poets; catalogue of curious books and papers relating to poetical history by Mr. Spence'.

In the lower corner of the page are two afterthoughts. The first says 'Short of yᵉ Gr[ee]k Poetry', an obvious deficiency in the plan. The second reflects an idea for reorganizing the project, 'Our Six ages rather all together? then, in two parts. Progress of Poetry, in Europe; Progress of Poetry in Great Britain'.

As far as can be determined, Spence never wrote the preface for this projected volume. Perhaps, if the 'Poetical Dictionary' ever is found, it will have such a preface, either sketched in outline or written in a complete draft. In its absence the notes just quoted are our only evidence of Spence's planning for the preface. After comparing them with Pope's 'scribbled paper' and Gray's sketch as sent to Warton, it is clear that Spence's outline possesses an historical interest equal to theirs. All are mere outlines, but all are different.

Several points in Spence's plan deserve comment. First of all, despite his intimacy with Pope and his espousal of the 'schools' concept in 1736, there is little indication that Spence knew of Pope's sketch based on six schools. The differences between the two outlines are more noticeable than the similarities. Secondly, Spence's plan possibly was written much later than the 'History of English Poetry' that occupies the first forty pages of the manuscript. The reference to *Polymetis* (published 1747) suggests that this outline might be as much as twenty years later than the rest of the manuscript volume. On the other hand, Spence was working on *Polymetis* for fifteen years before it reached publication, and undoubtedly had settled upon the name early in the task. Indeed, the three dialogues on the history of Roman poetry may have been formulated at Oxford in connexion with his Professorship of Poetry, a year or two before leaving England in December 1730.

The outline itself has every appearance of having been written after the body of the manuscript volume. In fact, the space first contained pencilled notes on the same subject (some words can still be read) before ink was employed to make the outline permanently legible. It seems likely that Spence perused this manuscript at some date after he had filled its pages with French and Italian 'lessons'. This perusal started him thinking about the preface to the poetical dictionary, and he used the blank lower half of the title-leaf to record the outline of the preface as it became formulated in his mind.

What is the significance of this outline? Historically it is a link in the development of the organic concept of the history of English Poetry, growing from the past to the present. Judging from the other contents of the manuscript, especially the 'History of English poetry', and from the dialogues in *Polymetis* tracing the history of Roman poetry, Spence's finished preface would have been a landmark in the history of histories of English poetry. The essay reproduced on the following pages deserves that value on its own merits, though being heretofore unpublished, it did not, to the best of our knowledge, influence any of Spence's own generation or those following. The preface to the 'Poetical Dictionary', had it been written as effectively as the *Polymetis*, could have had an importance beyond mere historical position.

Spence did not possess one of the most powerful minds of his generation, but within its limitations it was one of the clearest. Our profession is more indebted to him than to any other Professor of Poetry at Oxford before Thomas Warton.

QUELQUES REMARQUES HIST: sur les Poëtes Anglois.[1]

Gyralde, fameux Auteur Italien, et surtout très sçavant dans l'Histoire de la Poësie, remarque que les Anglois ont toûjours aimé la Poësie, & qu'ils ont toûjours eu des Poëtes celebres.[2] Cet eloge semblera d'abord manquer un peu de verité, à la plûpart des

[1] Because of space limitations it seemed best to print all of Spence's own notes, but to keep other annotation to a minimum.

Spence's notes show that he made extensive use of the following:

> *Histoire d'Angleterre* by Paul de Rapin Thoyras (10 vols., The Hague, 1724).
> *Commentarie de Scriptoribus Britannicis* by John Leland (2 vols., Oxford, 1709).
> *Réflexions Critiques Sur la Poësie et Sur La Peinture* by Jean Baptiste Du Bos (3 vols., Utrecht, 1732).
> *Traité de l'Origine des Romans* by Pierre Daniel Huet (1671).

Other single references are specific enough, so that the trained student can locate them should he have occasion to do so. Nearly all of the early poets are described by Leland, and can be easily found, thanks to Anthony Hall's helpful indexes. Similarly, it is often interesting to compare Spence's remarks in the *Anecdotes*, on various poets, with the comments in this history; this is easily accomplished by using the index in Singer's edition.

[2] Quoted by Leland, op. cit., p. 17.

Anglois mêmes: mais peutêtre on le trouvera mieux fondé qu'il ne semble l'être à la premiere vuë. Voici ce que je vais un peu éclaircir ci-desous.

Les commencemens de nôtre Histoire sont tout obscurcis de nuages. Nous avons, comme les Grecs, nôtre siécle Fabuleux. Je me servirai donc seulement de ce que je puis me souvenir des Auteurs les plus dignes de foi.

Avant l'Epoque Chrétienne, lors que Julius Caesar arriva en Bretagne, il y eût un grand nombre de ce qu'on appelle Druïdes.[1] C'est ce que Caesar nous a dit lui-même, dans ses Commentaires. Ces Druïdes étoient distribués en trois parties. L'une de ces parties fût instituée uniquement pour instruire les jeunes gens dans la vertù. Leur methode de les instruire fût par les vers, comme la plus convenable à la memoire. Il y en avoit parmi leurs ecoliers, qui pouvoient reciter plus de vingt mille vers de leur façon. Voilà une bonne preuve d'un assez grand nombre de Poëtes dans ces com-mencemens. S'ils étoient, ou mauvais, ou bons, c'est ce que je ne sçai pas.[2]

Cent: VI. Pendant que les Empereurs Romains ont tenus la Bretagne comme une Province, les Anglois ont acquis quelque chose des moeurs & de la langue Romaine.[3] Gyralde parle d'un *Plem-mïdie*, d'un *Oronie*, & d'un *Gildas*, qui ont reüssi de ces tems-là dans la Poësie. En Angleterre ces Plemmidies & ces Oronies sont des Inconnus: mais quant à Gildas, il y a encore un nom assez célébre.[4] J'ai veu des vers Latins, qui passent pour être des siens. Ils sont assez nets et elegans. Geoffroy de Monmouth est le premier qui les

[1] 'Rapin calls 'em *Druides, Bardes* & *Eubages*. Of yᵉ Bards he says; Ils s'occu-poient à composer des Vers & des Chansons qu'ils accompagnoient de la Harpe, pour célébrer les loüanges de leurs Heros. He gives you some of yᵉ maxims of yᵉ Druids in yᵉ same place. V: 1, p: 9. 4ᵗᵒ,' [Spence].

[2] 'L'esprit des Bretons, disoit Agricola, étoit de meilleure trempe que celui des Gaulois; & il ne temoit qu'à eux, s'ils vouloient s'appliquer, de réussir mieux que ces voisins. He usd ys argument particularly to raise our emulation in studying Rhetoric: Only study it says he, & I'me sure you'll soon exceed yᵉ French in it. (This may be meant by Juvˡ in yᵉ line below.) Refl: sur la Poesie &c V2. § 15.' [Spence.]

[3] 'Ils se fussent assez polis par leur commerce avec les Romains, depuis que ceux-ci se furent rendus maîtres de l'Isle. Rapin; (V; 1. p, 7. 4ᵗᵒ).
See ib: pp. 42 & 47. insignis: by Agricola under Titus.
Dicitur et nostros cantare Britannia versus. Mart:
Nunc totus Graias, nostras que habet orbis Athenas. (Philosophers?) Gallia causidicos docuit facunda Britannos: De conducendo loquitur jam rhetore Thule. Juv: Sat: 15.' [Spence.]

[4] 'Gildas *de Badon*, B: the Year in which Arthur fought yᵉ famous Battle of *Badon*, which Rapin places to 511. We have still his piece de excidio Britanniae. There's another History, or Romance, of a *Gildas* whom some affect to call *Albanien*. Stillingfleet says that both belong to Gildas de Badon, & yt yᵉ other is an imaginary name. Rapin. T: 1, p: 123. 4ᵗᵒ.—Huet speaking of Hunibaldus Francus.' [Spence.]

rapporte: & comme cet auteur avoit un grand penchant à faire des contes, je croirois facilement que ces vers sont supposés, s'ils étoient plus mauvais, qu'ils ne sont pas. Mais en verité ils surpassent le gout de Geoffroy lui-même, et peutêtre de tous ses contemporains.

Aquila & *Perdix* sont apparemment des noms imaginés; & leurs noms reéls sont à present inconnus. Quels qu'ils soient, leurs poëmes étoient tout prophetiques; comme ceux aussi du fameux *Merlin*. Nos Ecrivains vulgaires parlent de trois Merlins: mais les Savans les reduisent à un seul, qu'ils mettent au milieu du sixiéme siécle. Dans ces tems-là personne n'a acquis une plus haute reputation en son païs que *Thaliessin*.¹ Il étoit de la Province des Galles. Les Gallois conservent encore de ses poëmes; & les chantent quelque fois, avec beaucoup de loüanges.²

VII. *Cedmon* vecût dans le septiéme siécle.³ Brute, & ignorant, qu'il étoit; il fut inspiré tout d'un coup de l'amour de la Poësie, comme on dit, dans un songe. Ce conte est de même trempe avec celui-ci d'Hesiode parmi les Grecs. Ce qui est certain c'est, qu'au lieu d'un bon marmiton, il se fit un poëte celebre. Il quitte la broche tres subitement, pour faire des vers; & composa des piéces surprenantes.

VIII. Dans le siécle suivant, *Aldhelme*,⁴ neveu du roi Ina,⁵ rapporta de Rome l'usage des vers Latins en Angleterre. Ce même siécle a donné au monde *Bede*, qu'on appelle le Venerable, et *Albine*, de qui Charles le Grand s'est servi particulierement pour le premier etablissement d'une Université à Paris.

---

¹ '*Thelesin*, que quelques uns mettent au nombre de Bardes, à cause des Propheties en vers qu'il a composées, & qui l'on dit avoir vescu vers le milieu du 6 Siécle; & *Melkin*, qui fut un peu plus jeune, écriverent l'Histoire de la grand' Bretagne, leur patrie; du Roi Artus; & de la Table Ronde; & la défigurerent de mille fables: comme Balaeus le reconnoit dans son Catalogue, ou il leur a donné place. Huet; (d l'orig: de Romans, p: 154. Ed: 8.) Shakespeare speaks of yᵉ Welch Poets Henry, 4 (P. 1.) A, 3. Sc: 1. Wᵗ Glendower says & Hotspur's answer.' [Spence.]

² '(Some of our History taken from old Songs, Rap: T, 1. p: 280. 4ᵗᵒ Fr. Q?)' [Spence.]

³ '*Theodore*, a Greek, Native of Tharsus & ArchBᴾ of Canterbury: He was consecrated & sent from Rome to yᵗ See; & Adrian, a Roman, with him. He founded a School at Greecklade; where he & Adrian taught Theology, Music, Arithmetic, & yᵉ Greek & Lat: tongues. Bede knew some of his scholars; who, he says, cᵈ talk those two Languages, as well as their mother tongue. He brought several books into England, & wrote too [*sic*] himself. Fragments of his works were publᵈ at Paris 1677, with notes by Petit. He died in 690. Rap: T: 1, p: 199. 4ᵗᵒ. See Du Pin?' [Spence.]

⁴ 'The first of yᵉ Saxons yᵗ wrote in Latin. Rap: T: 1, p: 216. 4ᵗᵒ.' [Spence.]

⁵ 'Ina founded the English College at Rome in 727. Rap: T, 1. p, 177.

Ethelwolph, rebuilded yᵉ English College at Rome (which was founded by Ina, & enlargd by Ossa) more more magnificently than ever, in 855. It had been destroyed by Fire. Rap: T. 1. p. 246. 4ᵗᵒ Fr.' [Spence.]

IX. Le siécle neuviéme a produit *Alfrede le Grand;*[1] qui favorisa beaucoup les gens de lettres, & qui institua l'Université d'Oxford. Il étoit lui-même fort assidu à traduire & à composer des livres. Monsr. Rapin dit dans son Histoire, Que ce Roi fût le meilleur de tous les Poëtes Saxons de son tems.

Les Pirateries & les Invasions presque perpetuelles des Danois, grands ennemis de la litterature, font ici un Vuide des plus considerables.[2] C'est la principale raison, pour laquelle nous ne trouvons point de poëte de quelque poid, d'ici jusqu'au milieu du douziéme siécle.

XII. Ce siécle commença sous les auspices d'un Roi, qui merita par son erudition le surnom de Beauclerc.[3] Il restitua l'Université de Cambridge; & fit batir un Palais à l'autre Universitè, pour jouïr de la conversation des Savans. Les Lettres allerent revivre, & surtout la Poësie. *Briton*[4] etoit un des premiers parmi les poëtes de ce tems-là. J'ai veu de ses vers, qui étoient ecrits avec assez d'esprit et qui n'avoient qu'un peu du Stile Monachal. *Jean de Salisburie* fut un grand Savant, & passablement bon Poëte, mais l'homme de la reputation la plus haute, & de merite le plus grand fût *Joseph d'Exeter.* Il nous reste encore une partie de son Antiocheïde; & son poeme entier, sur la Guerre de Troye. Ce dernier a été imprimé deux fois au moins en Allemagne, sous le nom de Cornelius Nepos. Leland & Camden ont rendus justice à notre *Iscane:* et en verité le Stile, quoique tres bon pour le siécle ou il vecut, seroit peu digne d'un ancien Romain. *Annaevillane* écrivit un peu apres ce poëte. Dans son Architrenius il fait l'eloge de Brute & des vieux Brétons.[5]

---

[1] Alfred, livd several days in ye Camp of ye Danes to discover their weakness, under ye disguise of an *Harper*. ib: 262. an: 877. [Spence.]

His Care for ye Increase of Learning, ib. 270. 273. [Spence.]

[2] 'Q of the Military Songs, usd by Willm ye Conqueror's Army? Rap:' [Spence.]

[3] Beauclerk was a name given to Henry I.

[4] 'Ger: John Vossius (De Hist: Lat: L, 3. P: 2) places Brito among y[e] Writers temps incerti: but Christof: Sandys (Notes in Vol: p, 251) says he publish'd his Philippeid in 1224. In y[e] tenth B[k] Brito speaks of Otho y[e] 4th invading y[e] Patrimony of S: Peter w[ch] was in 1209. Fontanini, Elog: Ital: p. 47.

Q? W[r] Brito (Auth[r] of y[e] Phillippeid?) s[d] be recon'd among our Poets. Fabricius in his Biblioth: Lat: calls him Brito Armoricus; & says du Chesne gives an account of him among the other French writers. Art: Brito. His Poem (Draco Normanicus) on y[e] Acts of y[e] Normans in France & England was found at Rome by Baron Stoche. 'Tis in Long & short verse, without Rhime; in 3 Books, beside ye Proaemium & Epilogus, B: St:' [Spence.]

[5] 'Polycarpi Leyseri (Poes. Prof. Ord. In Acad: Helmstadiensi) Historia Poetarum & Poematum Medii aevi. Decem, post annum à Nato Christo 400, Saeculorum. Halae Magdel: 1721. A book that may be very useful for this part. Baron St: knew the Author at Rome, in 1716 or 17. He took the petit collet at Rome for convenience: & was a Protestant again, as soon as he set a foot on German Ground. He was in mean circumstances; but had such a desire to inquire

Pendant tout ce tems, la langue Angloise n'existoit pas encore. Le dernier siécle fut un siécle de Poëtes Latins: et tous les precedens n'avoient produit que des Poëtes ou Latins ou Saxons. La Conquête a introduit des alterations dans le Langage, aussi grandes que dans l'Etât. Après tant de confusions, & tant de mêlanges, il falloit un grand espace de tems pour lui donner quelque forme assez reguliere. XIV. Le Chevalier *Chaucier* est le premier qui a travaillé avec succés. Chaucier étoit d'un naturel heureux, et bien cultivé. Il avoit beaucoup d'esprit, & de discernement. C'étoit un homme de Cour: & le Roi s'est servi de lui en trois Ambassades. Il joüissoit de très grands biens. Enfin il ne lui manquoit rien pour devinir poli. Ses Ouvrages sentent de sa politesse. Ils sont pleins de Descriptions & de Caractéres: & il est peutêtre le premier qui ait fait des Contes Poëtiques, du stile qu'on appelle à present le stile Naif. *Gower* fût son Contemporain: mais il lui manque cette vivacité d'esprit, et cette force à dépeindre, que nous voyons avec tant d'admiration dans tous les traits de ce pere de notre Poësie Angloise.[1]

XV. Dans le siécle quinziéme, à peine trouveroit on quelqu'un qui ait réussi en poësie Angloise: si on excepte l'auteur de *Pierce le Laboureur*. Il y avoit alors une Partie des hommes qui voyagoient ensemble; & qui profitoient beaucoup en Italie des Lecons publiques d'un Guarini qui etoit bien fameux dans ce tems.[2] Mais ils ont ecrit tous en Latin. *Flemyng* et *Phreas* semblent etre les plus celebres de tous ceux-ci. Leland donne des loüanges, extraordinaires à un certain de ses Contemperains nomme Widdois ou *Viduus*, a cause de son poëme sur le fameux Edoüard, Prince de Galles.[3] Ce poëme est aussi écrit en Latin.

XVI. Dans le commencement du siécle suivant, Milord *Vaux*, et les Chevaliers *Brian* & *Vyate*, ont acquis quelque reputation: mais le Comte de *Surrey* étoit le premier Genie de ce tems. Il est encore regardé comme un homme d'Esprit. Ils etoient tous Poëtes Lyriques,

into things, that he walk'd most of the way frō his own home to the Vatican: he was perpetually transcribing out of Manuscripts &c, there. A good clever man.' [Spence.]

[1] 'Rem: A. Our first Poetry was chiefly either of the Lyric or yᵉ Satirical kind: both of wᶜʰ Fashions were probably deriv'd from yᵉ Italians, as they receiv'd them frō the Provençals.—Gugl: Figuiera (Cresc: or Notr: Art: 45:) was call'd il Poeta Satirico. He wrote always against ill Princes; & there's a Poem of his in particular entitled, Lo Flagel mortal des Tirans. This was the general Practice of the Provençal Poets in his time, from 1200 to 1300; & so on, all yᵉ while? the Popes were settled at Avignon. Hence many things in Chaucer; Piers Plowman; yᵉ Mirrour for Magistrates, &c.' [Spence.]

[2] 'Yᵉ famous Guarini was not born till 1538. Was not this yᵗ Guarini of Verona (p: 72 posth:) that publish'd Strabo, & dedicated it to Nic: V? His Papacy was frō 1447 to 1455.' [Spence.]

[3] 'Widdows, Canon of Wells.' [Spence.] See Leland, op. cit., pp. 484–6. Phreas is John Free, described by Leland, pp. 466–8.

et tous imitateurs des Italiens.[1] *Skelton* dans le même tems a écrit si fortement contre les Ecclesiastiques, qu'il se trouva obligé de se jetter dans un Azile; où il finit ses jours assez tristement: prisonnier pour la Satire, qu'il n'a sçu que trop aiguiser.

Sur la fin de ce siécle il parût un nombre de trés bons traducteurs. *Phaër* commença la version de l'Aenéide de Virgile: *Golding* acheva les Metamorphoses d'Ovide; et *Fairefax*, la Ierusalem Delivrée de Tasse. Le Chevalier *Sidney* a travaillé avant eux à une traduction de toutes les Pseaummes.[2] Mais il n'a mis au jour que quelques piéces Lyriques, de son invention; et un Roman mêlé de prose & de vers, selon la facon de l'Arcadie de Sannazar. Sidney étoit un beau genie. Il avoit beaucoup de Science, et de grandes Vertus. Mais nos auteurs semblent se piquer de le faire paroître en toutes choses plus grand qu'il n'étoit. Le nom de Milord *Buckhurste* ne fait pas tant d'eclat à present, quoi que ses ouvrages poëtiques en meritent beaucoup plus. Les meilleurs traits dans le celebre recüeil des Histoires Tragiques, qui s'appelle le Miroir,[3] viennent de sa main. Son Gorboduc est la meilleure Tragedie, de toutes celles qui furent écrites avant Shakespear: et surpasse les premieres piéces de Shakespear même. Il me semble que *Spenser* a etudié la maniere de Milord Buckhurste parce que l'Introduction de celui-ci, et le Poëme Epique de celui-là, sont apparemment du même gout en plusieurs endroits. Spenser a réussi si bien dans ce poëme, qu'il devint le Premier Poëte de ce Siécle. Il s'y trouve beaucoup de grandeur; des descriptions fort vives; et toute la force d'une imagination heureuse sans regles & sans bornes. On voit aussi dans ses Pastorales, qu'il a pouvoit se rendre maître de la plus grande simplicité qu'on peut desirer. *Ferrers* est la meilleure, après Milord Buckhurste dans le Miroir: & *Norton* étoit associé avec lui dans la composition de son Gorboduc.

---

[1] 'His Ear (Ric: II[ds]) is stopt wth other flatt'ring charms,
    As Praises of his State—There are beside
    Lascivious* Meeters, to whose venom'd sound
    The open ear of youth doth always listen,
    Report of fashions in proud Italy,
    Whose manners still our tardy apish nation
    Limps after in base awkward imitation.
                Shakespeare's, Ric: 2. A, 2. Sc: 1.
(Q? of Hall, S.ˢ great authority.)
    * (ys explained partly, Hen: 4. Part: 1. Act: 3, Sc: 1.)
       (He had been in Italy,
       And learn'd the manners prettily;
       Sing High ho! Harry Neville.)
[2] 'The Mss of this in yᵉ Pembroke Family. Mr. N: Herbert.' [Spence.]
[3] 'See p: 11 anteh: Rem: A. Q? of Scipio & Hannibal a Trag: Mr Crow.' [Spence.]

XVII. Le Siécle dix-septiéme fournit d'abord beaucoup de beaux Esprits, qui étoient preparés sous le siécle precedent. Les meilleurs d'entre eux, étoient des auteurs Dramatiques. Shakespear commençoit donc d'étre dans le plus haut point de sa gloire. Il avoit un Genie tout particulier; & presque inimitable. Sans le secours d'aucunes regles, il devint plus agreable que les artistes les plus reguliers. L'excellence de ce grand homme éclate le plus, dans l'Expression, dans la Varieté, dans la Sublime, dans l'Entousiasme, & même dans l'Extravagance de ses caractéres. Il depeint les hommes, de quelque profession & de quelque Humeur qu'ils soient, comme ils doivent étre. Il donne des Rois, qui parlent tous en Rois; et chacun en particulier selon son charactére Historique. Il reüssit parfaitement à peindre des Ecervelés & des Fous de toute sorte: et quand il passe les bornes de la nature, le langage & les manieres d'agir qu'il donne a ses personnages surnaturelles, sont si bien imaginés; que, tout le monde, ignorant si ces charactéres sont vrays croit cependant d'abord qu'ils sont vraysemblables. *Johnson* étoit plus docte.[1] Il est en plusiers endroits, un Copiste des Anciens. Sa maniére est souvent dure, & trop étudiée. Mais il excelle dans ce que nous appellons en Anglois, *Humour*; c'est à dire, en conservant partout les traits particuliers de quelques caracteres bizarres toujours bien remarquables, & quelquefois mêmes en outres.

Fletcher au meme tems releva beaucoup le Théatre. Il s'associa avec *Beaumont* dans une partie de ses ouvrages. Ils étoient, l'un et l'autre, d'une naissance assez noble; et écrivoient plus en Gentils-hommes que les precedens. Fletcher donnoit des vers avec rapidité; mais Beaumont le surpassoit en traçant des desseins. L'un avoit le jugement plus solide; l'autre avoit beaucoup plus de vivacité &

---

[1] 'The different manners of three of our best Poets in expressing the very same thought; i.e. their opinion of Johnson & Shakespear.

Y^e easy enlivened style

> The sweat of Learned Johnson's brain,
> And gentle Shakespear's easier strain,
> A Hackney coach conveys us to,
> In spite of all that Rain can do.
>
> > Suckling.

Y^e simple

> What frō Johnson's oil & sweat did flow,
> Or what more easy nature did bestow
> On Shakespear's gentler Muse.
>
> > Denham.

Y^e metaphoric or exalted

> Then to ye well trod Stage anon,
> If Johnson's learned Sock be on;
> Or sweetest Shakespear, fancy's child,
> Warble his native Wood-notes wild.
>
> > Milton.' [Spence.]

d'esprit. Tous les deux ensemble joüissent encore du nom des auteurs du premier rang.

Les autres parties de la Poësie n'étoient pas si bien cultivées. La Lyrique par exemple, qui étoit la plus usitée, étoit aussi la plus corrompuë. La plûpart des Poëtes alors, comme dans le siécle précedent, imitoient des Italiens: mais les Italiens mêmes commencoient à tomber: & nos poëtes Lyriques suivoient principalement ceux qui étoient les plus corrompus en Italie. On affectoit beaucoup d'ornemens, et on detestoit la simplicité de la nature. Un goût très mauvais dominoit dans leurs ouvrages. Tout étoit plein de jeux de mots, de pensées brillantes, d'étranges Comparaisons & de Metaphores outrées.   *Donne* étoit universellement declaré le Prince de l'Esprit, dans cet Interregne de bon Sens. En verité, il s'y trouve beaucoup de sentimens judicieux dans ses Satyres, & dans quelqu'unes de ses Epîtres: mais ces sentimens sont toûjours embarassés d'une puerile affectation de dire quelque chose de beau. De là il vient que la plûpart de ses Piéces ne sont qu'un Tissu d'Epigrammes. Sa versification, comme celle des autres Poëtes de son tems, est très mauvaise. *Drayton* a mieux réüssi à ce côté, dans son poëme allegorique; & *Sandys* dans ses traductions alloit encore plus loin en relevant nôtre versification. Mais le Chevalier *Suckling* fut le seul Genie tout pur; & qui par sa pureté ne se laissa pas infecter de la contagion generale. Son Stile est net et elegant: ses pensées libres & naturelles. Il y a une gayeté de coeur, & une naïveté, repanduës dans tous ses ouvrages, qui marquent son caractére particulier. Sa vie fut très courte; & ses perfections tres grandes. *Mennis* participe un peu de la gayeté de Suckling; mais il est plus porté pour le Burlesque. *D'avenant* écrivoit dans le gout mauvais: cependant il e plein de sentimens, et de bon sens. *Randolphe* est plus net; surtout dans ses Pastorales:

J'ai omis ici quelques hommes d'une reputation plus haute, que ceux que j'ai nommés. J'ai differé leurs noms, parce qu'ils ont vecu jusqu'à nôtre Age Augustaine: qui commence avec la Restauration de Charles 2. Tels étoient *Waller*, le plus doux de nos Poëtes Lyriques: *Cowley*, leger dans ses Anacreontiques; hardi dans ses Pindariques; mais toujours trop plein d'affectation de briller, particuliérement dans son livre intitulé La Maitresse. *Milton*, le Prince de tous nos poëtes, étoit un de ces-ci.[1] Pour ne parler point de ses autres

---

[1] 'The Sweedish Embassador complain'd, That wⁿ he had desired to have yᵉ Articles of yᵉ Treaty put into Latin, it was fourteen days that they made him stay for that Translation; & *sent it to one Mr. Milton, a blind man, to put them into Latin*: who, he said, must make use of an Amanuensis to read it to him, &, that Amanuensis might publish the matter of the Articles as he pleasd: & *that it seemed strange to him, there shou'd be no* [other] *but a blind man capable of putting a few Articles into Latin.*—The Employment of Mr Milton was excused to him, because several other servants of yᵉ Council, fit for that employment, were then absent. Whitelocke's Memorials. May 6, 1656.' [Spence.]

ouvrages, son Epique surpasse par la grandeur de la matiére, les chef-d'oeuvres et d'Homere & de Virgile. Son sujet est presque tout surnaturel. Ses personnages humains mêmes sont hors de la nature, comme nous la voyons à present. Tout cela ressent trop le mauvais goût des Italiens. Mais il y a tant de magnificence, & tant de simplicité ou il en faut, dans son poëme, qu'il est admirable, même dans ses erreurs.

Dryden, acquit toute sa reputation dans ce tems, que j'appelle nôtre siécle Augustain. Il a travaillé presque de toutes sortes de Poësie. Ses Satyres sont les plus fortes de ses pieces; comme ses Contes sont les plus agreables. De trente ou quarante Piéces de Theatre, qu'il a écrites, il n'y en a que trois ou quatre qu'on approuve à present. Ses traductions ont beaucoup de feu Poëtique: mais elles manquent quelquefois de justesse. Tout le monde sçait son indigence & que sa plume fut contrainte d'obeir à la tyrannie d'un impertinent Libraire. En particulier dans sa traduction de Virgile, il se trouva obligé de remplir la plûpart de ses feuilles au coup d'oeil de ces gens-là. Malgré tout cela, ses traductions sont des plus spirituelles que nous avons dans nôtre langage. Enfin, il surpassa tous ses rivaux dans la perfection de la Versification; il releva beaucoup nôtre poësie, et nôtre langage: & devint apparemment le premier poëte de son tems.

Cette Periode fut trés feconde en Satire.[1] Outre le grand Dryden, elle produisit Dorset, Rochester, Oldham, Buckingam, et Butler. *Butler*, fut inimitable dans une épece de Burlesque Satyrique, trés particulier, & trés ingenieux. *Buckingham*, est encore regardé comme l'auteur d'une fameuse Piéce de Théatre, qui s'appelle le *Rehearsal*, toute pleine de Satyre & d'Esprit. *Oldham*, écrivit d'une maniere trés forte & trés severe. *Rochester*, fut plus clairvoyant sur les caractéres des hommes; il eût une force plus penetrante & plus polië.[2]

---

[1] 'W[t] Machiavel says in dispraise of his countrymen, was one of y[e] Chief Recom[m]endations in Charles II Court. That Tornarono i cittadini al loro consuelo modo di vivere pensando di godersi senza alcun rispetto quello Stato che s'havevano stabilito e fermo. Di che ne nacquero alla città quelli mali che sogliono nelle paci il più delle volte generarsi; perche i giovani piu sciolti che l'usitato, in vestire, in conviti, in altri simili lascivie sopra modo spendevano: e essendo otiosi, in giuochi e in femine il tempo e le sustanze consumavano. E gli studii loro erano apparire col vestire splendidi, e col parlare sagaci e astuti; e quello, che più destramente mordeva gli altri, era più savio e da più stimato. Flor: Hist: lib: 7, p: 407.

K[g] Charles, Reign was an Age of Wit. A great aim of the Men in Fashion was to shine in conversation. Nothing takes so easily or passes so soon for Wit as what is severe: this might make Satirical Strokes y[e] most com[m]on topic then: as that may account for so many of the Poets of y[t] Age being Satirists.' [Spence.]

[2] 'Jamais aucun Tragique Grec ne tâcha de rendre les Souverains odieux autant que My lord Comte de Rochester l'a voulu faire dans sa Tragedie de Valentinien. de Boze (Poet: & Pg) V: 1. § 20.' [Spence.]

Et *Dorset*, fut & le plus aimable dans sa maniere de vivre; le plus
redoutable des hom[m]es dans sa maniere d'écrire:[1]

Sur la fin de ce siécle, les Poëtes pour le Theatre suivirent une
maniere, bien differente de ceux qui ecrivirent dans ses commencemens. Ils abolirent quelques de fauts, qui dominoient auparavant:
et en introduisirent d'autres, qui dominent encore.

Dryden fut un des premiers qui a affoibli la diction Dramatique:
surtout, dans ses Tragedies rimées. *Lee* retint plus de la force
ancienne. Il eût peûtetre l'esprit le mieux tourné pour le Théatre,
de tous les Poëtes de son tems: mais il eut aussi un ardeur, qui
l'Emporta souvent aux dernieres extravagances. Cet ardeur de son
ame fut indomtable: il parut, comme des eclairs subits & violens,
dans ses ecrits: & le mit enfin du Théatre aux Petites maisons. *Otway*
est plus tempere.[2] Il surpasse tous dans les mouvemens de l'ame:
ses pieces sont très interessantes, & pleines de Passions fortes & bien
ménagées. *Shadwell* eût quelque genie pour la Comedie; et *Etheridge*
réüssit dans le peu qu'il en a écrit: mais *Wycherley* et *Congreve*
acquirent la plus haute reputation de tous dans ce genre. L'un est
assez heureux en diversifiant ses caractéres; L'autre est sententieux
& plein de bon sens: celui-ci coulant, mais trop addonne aux
comparaisons, & aux traits d'esprit: celui-là sage, mais avec un stile
trop dur, & un peu dégoutant.

Quant aux Traducteurs, il y en avoit plusieurs entre les gens du
Commun & de la Noblesse. Ceux qui faisoient le plus d'éclat, après
Dryden, étoient Milord *Roscommon*, le Duc de Lauderdale & Monsr.
Creech. Je passe sous silence les noms des plusieurs, qui étoient
associés dans les traductions de Juvenal & d'Ovide. L'Art de la
Poësie d'Horace par Roscommon est encore bien celebré; peutêtre
un peu plus qu'il ne merite. L'Aneide de Lauderdale aidoit beaucoup
à Dryden même dans sa traduction de Virgile. Creech avoit un
esprit fort: & ses traductions sont si vives, qu'elles ne semblent pas
être des traductions. Sa maniere est tout originalle. Heureux, s'il
n'eut jamais suivi que son propre gout! et n'eut porté tant de
dommage, au moins à sa reputation, par la facheuse ambition
d'éclater dans la Gayeté d'Horace, comme dans le Serieux de
Lucrece.

Il y avoit aussi dans ce tems des Poëtes occasionels, qui ont écrits

---

[1]   'Je veux Dorset sur tous pour la piquante Satire;
       Dans ses manieres si doux, dans ses traits si severe.
             Rochester. Trad: 10 Sat: d'Hor. l: 1.' [Spence.]

[2] 'Otway takes? his subject of ye Plot Discoverd, & his Don Carlos, from ye Abbe
de Saint Real. The French Play of Andronie by Monsr Campisbron is ye story of
Don Carlos, under borrowd names; & transplanted as far as to Constantinople.'
[Spence.] This fact about Campistron's *Andronic* (1685) is mentioned by Langbaine.

sur diverses sujets; & qu'on ne peut mettre dans aucune classe
reguliére: comme *Sidley*, bien touchant dans ses piéces amoreuses;
Scrope, pas mal tourné pour la satire; & un grand nombre d'autres.
XVIII. Le Siécle present a plusieurs noms dont la Posterité lui
sera redevable. *Addison* est un des premiers de ceux-ci: quoi qu'il
faille avouer, qu'il a beaucoup mieux réüssi à la prose qu'à la
poësie. Milord *Lansdown* a suivi la maniere de Waller, & est à
present le premier de nos Lyriques. Pour les vers Latins, *Dibben* &
Bourne surpassent tous les autres: & celui-ci peutêtre ne cede pas à
quelqu'un parmi les Italiens mêmes, dans la facilité & la netteté de
la Poësie Latine.

Pour le Théatre, nous n'avons personne qui peut en meriter le
nom d'un auteur general: mais il y en a plusieurs qui ont écrits une
ou deux pieces avec quelque succés. Tels sont Addison, *Steele*,
Vanbrugh, et *Cibber* pour la Comedie; le même Addison, *Trap, Smith,
Heughs*, & le jeune *Philips* pour la Tragedie. *Rowe*, l'excellent
Traducteur de Lucain, fut aussi le Premier poëte Tragique de son
tems; & il y a bien de l'apparence que *Heughes* lui auroit succedé,
si sa vie n'eût pas été si courte.

Dans les ouvrages d'Esprit *Pryor* étoit très naif & très charmant.
Il est le De-la-Fontaine d'Angleterre. *Garth*, dans sa Dispensarie, a
bien imité le Lutrin de Boileau: mais il est trop addonné aux jeux
d'esprit & aux antitheses perpetuelles. *Gay* aime presque toûjours
a se joüer des autres Poëtes. Ses Comedies sont de Satires sur les
Comedies: & ses Pastorales sont faites pour rendre ridicules celles
du Jeune Philips. Il a ecrit des Contes, comme a fait aussie le feu
Parnelle; mais celui-ci est toûjours trop dur; & celui-là, dans
quelques unes de ses pieces, est trop bas. *King* se sert tres heureusa-
ment d'un ridicule particulier: mais D^r. *Swift* est l'homme du monde
le mieux porté pour le Ridicule, & le plus propre à faire un Trium-
virat avec Cervantes & Rablais. Le vieux *Philips* étoit le meilleur
imitateur du Stile du grand Milton comme *Thomson* l'est à present.
Young est plus heureux dans ses Satires, que dans ses autres ecrits;
& *Pitt*, outre plusieurs beaux poëmes, a fait une traduction de Vida
qui est très bonne. Le Premier Poëte de ce siécle, ou en Angleterre,
ou ailleurs, est Monsr. *Pope*: qui a écrit presque en toutes ces sortes
de Poësie; & qui a surpassé presque tous ces particuliers, dans leur
propre maniere d'écrire.

POPE AND OUR CONTEMPORARIES

JOSEPH WOOD KRUTCH

WHEN Austin Dobson tossed his cap 'for polish and for Pope' he was indulging in an act of humorous perversity. Since that time several revolutions in taste have occurred and it is no longer eccentric to express an admiration for Augustan verse. The mere fact that T. S. Eliot gave a nod of approval to Dryden—and even Johnson—as well as to Pope, was sufficient to guarantee at least lip-service on the part of those who follow the fashions. Yet it is perfectly obvious that whereas contemporary admiration for seventeenth-century literature is warm and fructifying, the professed admiration for eighteenth-century literature is not. However abundantly eighteenth-century scholarship may flourish and however unfashionable it would now be to deny that Pope is a poet, contemporary poets do not write like Pope and one may legitimately doubt that they actually read him very often. Everyone can now quote—as few Victorians could—half a dozen poems of Donne and at least 'To His Coy Mistress' and perhaps a few lines from 'Upon Appleton House'. But probably even the Victorians, living in the afterglow of Pope's reputation, were more familiar with at least a few tag ends of his verse than most of our contemporaries.

Moreover, it has been my experience, at least, that undergraduates to whom one introduces the poetry written between the death of Shakespeare and the romantic revival react to it in much the manner one would be led to expect from what has just been said about the taste of their immediate elders. Most students who have any literary susceptibility are at least intrigued by the ingenuities and obscurities of Donne and most of them respond with enthusiasm to the best-known of Marvell's lyrics. How much this is due to some genuine kinship of mind and temper, how much to the knowledge that admiring these poets is very much the fashion, I do not know; but the attitude of receptivity is obvious enough. Even Dryden, though he comes as something of a shock, ultimately awakens some considerable degree of admiration, but it is relatively rare to find a student who will 'toss his cap' for Pope.

These two last facts mean, I take it, not that Dryden is a better poet than Pope but partly at least that Dryden belongs to the seventeenth century as well as to the eighteenth; that his poetic style and temper are strongly tinged by qualities which suggest those of some of his predecessors but have been purged away in Pope. After 'Annus Mirabilis' he never again (except in the Heroic plays) permitted the pursuit of conceits to lead him into howling absurdity; but to the very end some of his best and most characteristic effects depend upon either ambiguities or *concordia discordia*, both of which suggest his predecessors rather than his descendants. Pope neither could nor would have written the tantalizing obscure line 'Your chase had a beast in view' which, significantly, opens the stanza Mr. Eliot chose for especial admiration. The last section of the Ode to Mistress Anne Killigrew, with its elaboration of a fantasy suggested by the dogma of the resurrection of the body, is certainly very far from being Augustan, and in the same poem so characteristic a phrase as 'the last promotions of the blessed' represents precisely the kind of deliberate incongruity which many seventeenth-century poets sought, but which Pope would have avoided as a violation of propriety. Even in the satires the thing which most clearly distinguishes Dryden's manner from that of Pope is the choice of words and images which are grotesque rather than decorous. Dryden, in other words, often strives to surprise and shock; Pope, most characteristically, to assume that perfect aptness alone is the ideal.

The conclusion I wish to draw is simply that some appreciation of Dryden does not necessarily mean a real liking for the unique excellences of Augustan poetry. and that the tendency to prefer him to Pope can be, probably often is, no more than another indication of the fact that Pope's poetry has not 'come back' as completely as we sometimes like to assume. Those of us who are convinced that it is great and unique in an important way have not entirely succeeded in persuading any very large public of the fact; certainly have not succeeded—as the admirers of Metaphysical poetry did, when they revived a poetic taste—in making Pope's poetry an important influence on contemporary writing. Either the temper of our times is such that the fundamental aims and methods of Augustan poetry cannot make a very strong appeal, or those of us who have undertaken to recommend it have to some extent failed—perhaps merely

because we have not been sufficiently persuasive, perhaps
because we have not found the best approach.

Certainly, however, there is much in the theory, explicit and
implicit, of Augustan poetry which is rather curiously consonant
with the professed ideals of contemporary poetry and its critics.
Many of the latter have scornfully rejected the common romantic
idea of the poet as 'dreamer' and of poetry as an escape into
'fairyland'. Poetry, they are likely to insist, is 'cognitive'; a
method of dealing with reality, rather than an escape from it.
The poet is not a man who escapes from the world but one who
grapples with it; and his subject-matter ought to be, not
eccentric and private concerns, but the whole world, including
the political world, in which he lives. Translated into seven-
teenth- and eighteenth-century terms this should mean that
knowledge and judgement are more important than fancy; that
good sense is superior to mere originality; and that the poet
differs from the ordinary man chiefly in being better informed
as well as wiser than he. Imlac's description of the poet ought,
and as an abstract description perhaps does, satisfy the modern
critic better than it would, for example, have satisfied Keats.
Even the assumption that the best poet is the one who, in the
long run, wins the largest audience can hardly be escaped by
those moderns who profess to believe both that a poet's first
duty is to society and that society ought to be democratic. Yet
many of those who reject obscurity, inaccessibility, and esoteric
concerns as an ideal, nevertheless write for a fantastically
restricted audience in styles so intricate and so highly personal
as to be almost secret codes.

The usual explanation of this paradox is, if I understand it
aright, that the peculiar complexity of our times, together with
the ambiguities and doubts which that complexity generates,
makes plain statement inadequate and forces the poet who
would grapple with modern life, thought, and sensibility, into
a style which does not seek obscurity or eccentricity for its own
sake, but must accept them if it is to say anything not obviously
false or inadequate. Though I do not remember ever to have
seen the following stated in just this way, the contention seems
to be something like this: The theory that poetry should be a
wise and well-informed man's impersonal expression of his
deepest and maturest convictions about the real world is a
theory to which both the Metaphysicals and the Augustans could

subscribe. But for reasons political, sociological, psychological, and philosophical, we can imitate, or at least learn from, the former but not the latter. Donne and Herbert are, but Pope is not—at least to anything like the same extent—part of our 'usable past'.

Now I have no intention of undertaking the alarming task of attempting to examine the extent to which all this is necessarily true or need remain so. That modern poets have used the Metaphysicals much and the Augustans very little is an obvious fact. But it is obvious also that if they could use the latter more, the effect would certainly be to make them accessible to a far wider audience than at present they have, and I am raising the question whether the case for Pope and, therefore, the possibility that he might be more 'usable' than is commonly assumed, has been presented as effectively as it might be, either on the high level of the best criticism, or on the lower level of class-room presentation to the undergraduates who are, after all, to-morrow's poets and readers of poetry.

When Dryden decided to become a professional poet he had immediately at hand neither an audience, a subject-matter, nor a style, and in this respect his situation was not unlike that of the earliest Post-Georgians. In Dryden's youth the Metaphysical school was moribund and the Elizabethan already so remote that its themes and its vocabulary were as unusable for him as those of the Victorian age were for the Post-Georgians. If Dryden was to make a living either directly or indirectly as a poet, he had to have an audience which would buy new verses in numbers at least sufficient to encourage a printer to print them. Unlike the Post-Georgians he proceeded to supply himself with a subject-matter, a style, and an audience in the most prosaically practical manner. Whereas they sought esoteric subjects, imitated the most difficult contemporary French as well as the most difficult of the earlier English writers, and sought the suffrage of a small cult, he chose journalistic subjects for which there was a ready-made public, and evolved a style so clear, so direct, and so accessible to the ordinary reader that to some it seems mere prose. That it is not actually mere prose is due partly to the fact that he continued to use sparingly and temperately certain characteristic devices of the Metaphysicals, but more importantly to the further fact that he succeeded in demonstrating how 'the best words in the best order' can be poetry even though it refuses to respond positively to Arnold's touchstone, or to any other test based upon the assumption that poetry is necessarily something over and above the seventeenth- and eighteenth-century definitions of it.

John Masefield, it may be noted in passing, approached the problem very much as Dryden did and achieved success, though he won no important disciples. Dryden, on the other hand, became not only successful himself but created a style which helped Pope to become more widely admired and more widely read in his own time than perhaps any other English poet ever was before or ever has been since. The result of the Post-Georgian approach was, on the contrary, to win only the most minute of audiences and to develop a style which confessedly appeals to those who are prepared for very arduous efforts and are willing to read the most esoteric exegeses. Yet many at least of those who have chosen this thorny path deprive themselves of the easiest explanation by admitting in theory that the Romantics were wrong when they protested that Augustan verse simply was not poetry. Moreover, and in one respect at least, they stand condemned by their own major prophet. Did not Mr. Eliot himself say that poetry should exhibit the minimal qualities of good prose, and are not these qualities those which their verse most conspicuously lacks? Would not a real effort to learn *something* from Pope rather than everything from the Metaphysicals be the surest way of restoring these minimal virtues to contemporary poetry?

I have already confessed that I am not prepared to deny *in toto* the contention that purely Augustan verse is possible only in a society surer than ours is of what it thinks, and means, and wants. Moreover, and though I am aware that this will not save me in certain quarters from the charge of philistinism, I am ready to assert my positive conviction that Pope has his limitations, considered even in relation to his own time. For instance: however sound the doctrine that Nature, or the universally human, is the only proper subject for poetry, may be, it becomes, in effect, unsound when Pope and his successors fail, as they often did, to recognize that this universally human includes a good deal more than they supposed it did. In so far as the Romantics actually enlarged the field of poetry, they did so not by introducing personal eccentricities into it but simply by demonstrating that what they sometimes believed unique in themselves was actually a part of universal human nature—as Rousseau did in the most famous of all instances when he proclaimed his absolute uniqueness only to discover that half the population of Europe believed itself just like him. That does not, however, change the fact that Pope remains more usable than any use which has recently been made of him would indicate, and it does not dispel the suspicion that the failure to use him is due in part to the operation of motives not wholly creditable to contemporary poets.

The very clearness with which a couplet says what it has to say is notoriously merciless in exposing either emptiness or absurdity—as Dryden often (at least in the Heroic plays) and even Pope, sometimes, demonstrates. Any poet not quite sure whether or not he is saying anything or whether or not what he is saying makes any sense at all is wisely reluctant to expose himself. Even though it be granted that some things can be suggested which can never be said, it still remains true that nonsense half-revealed is less demonstrably nonsense than it would be if plainly stated, and that a bad conceit in the manner of Donne can be argued about in a way that a bad couplet in the manner of Pope cannot.

Ingenuity and obscurity have, moreover, other and more hidden charms. Even the poet who professes without conscious hypocrisy to believe that a wide audience is in itself a desirable thing may, nevertheless, feel the romantic appeal of being rejected and alone. Even the most passionate admirer of the common man may not want to be too common himself, and the desire to be one of an esoteric band may struggle against the desire to speak for one's contemporaries at large. More important still is the fact that modern poetry having become more and more the concern of a special group—Robert Graves announced a year or two ago that he wrote poetry only for other poets—the tendency is more and more to produce poems which will provide that group with opportunities for exegesis and debate.

A very recent book on contemporary criticism[1] seriously proposed that since no single person, not even a single professional critic, could be expected to know enough adequately to interpret or evaluate a poem, criticism should in the future operate principally through panels of critics who will attack poems from

---

[1] *The Armed Vision*, by Stanley Hyman (Alfred A. Knopf, New York, 1948).

various angles and by such joint efforts render them under-
standable. In some such quarters it seems to be assumed, not
only that a poem exists chiefly for the purpose of providing a
problem for interpreters, but also that its merit is to a considerable extent measured by the difficulties which it presents.

Undoubtedly one of the reasons why the moderns' professed
admiration for the Augustans has produced so little writing
about them while their professed admiration for the Metaphysicals has produced so much is simply that the former afford
the critic comparatively few obvious opportunities to expatiate.
Many of these critics are very much in the position of Dryden's
religious sectaries, of whom it will be remembered that he said:

> Plain truths enough for needful use they found;
> But men would still be itching to expound—

and of them it might be said further, as Dryden did of these
sectaries, that 'Each was ambitious of th'obscurest place'.

Without attempting to deny that not everything worth saying
can be said as clearly as Pope generally says what he has it in
him to say, the fact remains that the desire to be as plain as
possible has a good deal more to recommend it than the desire,
by contemporary critics who like to explain, to be as cryptic as
possible. Several, if not all, of the Seven Types of Ambiguity may
be present in some of the finest poems in the English language
but they did not get there as the result of the poet's conscious
intention to work them in, and contemporary critics did not
encourage their authors deliberately to construct puzzles for the
critic to work upon.

Those of us who admire Pope and would like to teach others
to admire him sometimes, it seems to me, tend to be too much
apologists in the popular sense of that term. Some of us, I know,
have even undertaken to prove that Pope is 'as good as Keats'
and can do whatever Keats can. Not all of us take that line,
but few of us, I think, insist as firmly as we might, not only that
Pope should be taken on his own terms, but also that those terms
are themselves defensible against all comers. Few of us seem to
realize sufficiently that the Romantic and Victorian theories do
not need to be combated because they have already been pretty
thoroughly rejected by the proponents of modern poetry.

The best approach for the layman, including the undergraduate, is that which scholars commonly adopt when writing

for one another, namely, the approach via the later seventeenth
and eighteenth centuries' own theories, ideals, and critical terms.
If, for instance, a transcendental definition of the imagination is admitted, explicitly or by implication, then all is lost;
but it need not be admitted because the modern reader is not
usually a transcendentalist in regard to anything else, and
because modern theories of poetry have prepared him, as the
Victorian reader certainly had not been prepared, for a consideration of the problem in terms of memory, fancy, and
judgement—in connexion with which terms, incidentally,
Freudian concepts can be introduced far more easily than they
can as addenda to transcendental theories.

It has been my experience in the classroom that the most
effective interpreters of Pope are his contemporaries—for the
simple reason that they necessarily operate within the framework of the thought of the age. Johnson's essay on Pope makes
the case better than any other single essay does, and the student
who resists the contention that the 'Hills peep o'er Hills' passage
is one of the greatest in English poetry is more likely to be persuaded by Johnson's simple, rationalistic discussion of it in
connexion with the virtues possible to a metaphor than by
anything else. If the moderns are called in it had best be their
theory rather than their practice which is cited. *The Waste Land*
may not be a very good preparation for reading the *Essay on
Criticism*, but the student who is familiar with Mr. Eliot's
attitude toward tradition may be helped by it to appreciate
'Hail, Bards triumphant'.

I would, in conclusion, go just this one step farther. To the
charge that Pope is deficient in 'sensibility' and that he sticks
too close to the normal, waking, daylight world to appeal very
strongly to a generation proudly neurotic, dissociated, and
doubtful, I should be inclined to reply neither with denial nor
with apology, but with the forthright assertion that we need,
at this moment at least, his qualities rather more than a turning of the face against them. Even sensibility, however good
it may be, is good only in so far as it can be disciplined and
used, and it seems obvious enough that modern literature has
cultivated it to a point where it now has more sensibility than it
knows what to do with. No doubt Augustan poetry finally died
because it lacked fresh feelings and fresh thoughts. Perhaps
romanticism revived poetry by supplying both. But to call now

for still more of mere naked sensibility is to put oneself in the position of the enthusiast—described by the elder Samuel Butler and recalled by Samuel Johnson—who would go crying 'Fire! Fire! in Noah's flood'. It is generally agreed that the ideal of the eighteenth century was best summed up in 'Let us cultivate our garden'. One might, I suppose, say that the ideal of romanticism (and I mean in science as well as in art) could be summed up in some such exhortation as 'Let us explore our wilderness'. More than a century has been devoted to the attempt to do just that. Could a redeemable section of the long-neglected garden be found again?

A LIST OF THE WRITINGS OF
GEORGE SHERBURN

BOOKS

The Early Popularity of Milton's Minor Poems, privately printed, University of Chicago Libraries, 1920 (reprinted with corrections from *Modern Philology*, xvii [Sept. 1919], 259–78; [Jan. 1920], 515–40).

The Early Career of Alexander Pope, Oxford, Clarendon Press, 1934.

'The Restoration and Eighteenth Century (1660–1789)' in *A Literary History of England*, edited by Albert C. Baugh, New York, Appleton-Century-Crofts, 1948, pp. 699–1108.

Editor of *Selections from Alexander Pope*, New York, Thos. Nelson & Sons, 1929 (later called *The Best of Pope*, revised edition 1940, reprinted 1941, 1945; now published by Ronald Press).

Editor, together with Louis I. Bredvold and Robert K. Root, of *Eighteenth Century Prose*, New York, Thos. Nelson & Sons, 1932 (reprinted, Ronald Press, 1943).

ARTICLES

'The Thing about Wycherley', *Times Literary Supplement* [London], 11 May 1922, p. 308.

'Notes on the Canon of Pope's Works, 1714–20', *Manly Anniversary Studies in Language and Literature*, University of Chicago, 1923, pp. 170–9.

'A Note on Addison's *Drummer*', *Modern Philology*, xxiii (Feb. 1926), 361.

'The Fortunes and Misfortunes of *Three Hours after Marriage*', *Modern Philology*, xxiv (Aug. 1926), 91–109.

'Edward Young and Book Advertising', *Review of English Studies*, iv (Oct. 1928), 414–17.

'Songes and Sonnettes', *Times Literary Supplement* [London], 24 July 1930, p. 611.

'Huntington Library Collections', *Huntington Library Bulletin*, no. 1 (May 1931), 36–106.

'Two Notes on the *Essay on Man*', *Philological Quarterly*, xii (Oct. 1933), 402–3.

'The Shakespeare Industry: a Reply to President Rainey', *University of Chicago Magazine* (Jan. 1934), pp. 96–8.

'The Relation of the Humanities to General Education', *Proceedings of the Institute for Administrative Officers of Higher Institutions*, vii (1934), 55–8.

' "Timon's Villa" and Cannons', *Huntington Library Bulletin*, no. 8 (Oct. 1935), 131–52.

'Fielding's *Amelia*: an Interpretation', *ELH: A Journal of English Literary History*, iii (March 1936), 1–14.

'Walpole's Marginalia in *Additions to Pope* (1776)', *Huntington Library Quarterly*, i (July 1938), 473–87.

'Methods in Books about Swift', *Studies in Philology*, xxxv (Oct. 1938), 635–56.

'Pope's Letters and the Harleian Library', *ELH: A Journal of English Literary History*, vii (Sept. 1940), 177–87.

'The Dunciad, Book IV', *Studies in English, Department of English, The University of Texas, 1944*, University of Texas, 1945, pp. 174–90.

'Pope at Work', *Essays on the Eighteenth Century Presented to David Nichol Smith*, Oxford, Clarendon Press, 1945, pp. 49–64.

'An Accident in 1726', *Harvard Library Bulletin*, ii (Winter 1948), 121–3.

REVIEWS

(A SELECTIVE LIST)

Du Transcendantalisme considéré essentiellement dans sa définition et ses origines françaises, par William Girard, in *Modern Philology*, xv (Sept. 1917), 317–20.

The Poems of Edgar Allen Poe, edited by Killis Campbell, ibid., xvi (May 1918), 56.

Lewis Theobald, by R. F. Jones, ibid., xviii (May 1920), 57–63.

The Influence of Milton on English Poetry, by R. D. Havens, ibid., xxii (Aug. 1924), 107–8.

Alexander Pope: a Bibliography, by R. H. Griffith, ibid., xxii (Feb. 1925), 327–36.

Stephen Duck, the Thresher Poet, by Rose Mary Davis, in *Philological Quarterly*, vi (April 1927), 178–9.

The Grub-street Journal, by James T. Hillhouse, in *Modern Philology*, xxvi (Feb. 1929), 361–7.

The Poetical Works of Sir John Denham, edited by T. H. Banks, Jun., and *Evidences of a Growing Taste for Nature in the Age of Pope*, by P. K. Das, in *Modern Language Notes*, xliv (March 1929), 194–6.

The Dunciad Variorum, introduction by R. K. Root, in *Modern Language Notes*, xlv (Nov. 1930), 472–4.

Henry Fielding: Playwright, Journalist and Master of the Art of Fiction, by H. K. Banerji, in *Philological Quarterly*, x (April 1931), 200–1.

'Pope's Lost Sermon on Glass Bottles', by Norman Ault, in *Times Literary Supplement* [London], 20 June 1935, p. 399; 11 July, p. 448.

Boswell's Life of Johnson, edited by G. B. Hill and L. F. Powell (1st 4 vols.), in *Philological Quarterly*, xiv (Oct. 1935), 374–5.

L'Influence française dans l'œuvre de Pope, by E. Audra, in *Modern Language Notes*, l (Nov. 1935), 475–7.

On the Poetry of Pope, by Geoffrey Tillotson, ibid., liv (Jan. 1939), 69–70.

The Poetical Career of Alexander Pope, by R. K. Root, ibid., liv (Nov. 1939), 541–3.

Caroline of England, by Peter Quennell, in *Boston Evening Transcript*, 27 Jan. 1940, Part 6, p. 2.

A Bibliography of British History (1700–1715), vol. iii, by William T. Morgan and Chloe S. Morgan, in *Modern Philology*, xxxix (Feb. 1942), 324–5.

'Pope and Addison', by Norman Ault, in *Philological Quarterly*, xxi (April 1942), 215–16.

Literary Scholarship: Its Aims and Methods, by Norman Foerster and others, in *American Literature*, xiv (May 1942), 171–7.

The Twickenham Edition of the Poems of Alexander Pope, John Butt, General Editor, vols. ii and iv, in *Modern Language Notes*, lvii (May 1942), 385–6.

Four Essays on Gulliver's Travels, by Arthur Case, in *Yale Review*, xxxv (June 1946), 760–1.

INDEX